Firewalk

BOOKS FROM BERKSHIRE HOUSE

PSYCHOLOGY

Song of the Phoenix: The Hidden Rewards of Failure by John Lord

TRAVEL

Great Destinations Series

The Berkshire Book by Jonathan Sternfield
The Santa Fe & Taos Book by Brandt Morgan
The Napa & Sonoma Book by Tim Fish
The Coast of Maine Book by Rick Ackermann and Kathryn Buxton
The Chesapeake Bay Book by Allison Blake
The Adirondack Book by Elizabeth Folwell
The Aspen Book by Diane Tegmeyer

Berkshire Outdoors Series

Hikes & Walks in the Berkshire Hills by Lauren Stevens
Bike Rides in the Berkshire Hills by Lewis Cuyler
Skiing in the Berkshire Hills by Lauren Stevens and Lewis Cuyler
A Guide to Natural Places in the Berkshire Hills by Rene Laubach

Other travel titles

Travel Games for Kids by Andrew Langley
Music Festivals in America by Carol Rabin
Yukon Wild by Beth Johnson

Firewalk

THE PSYCHOLOGY OF PHYSICAL IMMUNITY

Jonathan Sternfield

BERKSHIRE HOUSE, Publishers
Stockbridge, Massachusetts

Publisher's Note: Although many people have walked on fire without suffering injury, firewalking is a potentially dangerous activity. Neither the publisher nor the author make any recommendation in this book that anyone should try firewalking; nor will the publisher or the author be responsible for any injury to readers who experiment with the ideas in this book.

ON THE COVER
A modern American firewalker walks steadily across the glowing coals at a seminar led by Tolly Burkan, the father of the American firewalking movement.
Photograph by Brian Garland

Firewalk: the psychology of physical immunity

Editors: Brandt Morgan, David Emblidge
Cover design: Jane McWhorter
Book design and composition: Jane McWhorter

Library of Congress Cataloging-in-Publication Data
Sternfield, Jonathan

Firewalk: the psychology of physical immunity / Jonathan Sternfield.
Berkshire House, 1992.

ISBN: 0-936399-04-X 90-81448

ISBN: 0-936399-04-X (paper); $12.95

Berkshire House, Publishers
Box 297, Stockbridge, MA 01262

Manufactured in the United States of America
First Printing 1992
10 9 8 7 6 5 4 3 2

Contents

Acknowledgments

People sparked my interest in the firewalk, and people made this book come to life. First, there were the firewalkers. If you've ever met, seen or heard Tony Robbins, you'll appreciate how many different kinds of events he might spark, and to him and his outrageous wisdom, I owe initial thanks. To Tolly Burkan, too, I owe a great deal — for rekindling the ancient rite in America, and for helping me keep at the forefront of this fast-breaking story. After an initial burst of open-minded curiosity, the mass media dropped the firewalk-in-America saga five years ago, but history doesn't stop because historians are unable to package it neatly. So the real story continues to unfold, and besides Tolly Burkan, I must thank other firewalking newsmakers, Michael Sky, Steve and Laura Bisyak, and Joe Nuzum.

Essentially this book is a study in the possibilities for human voluntary control, and no one is more qualified to comment on this significant subject than Dutch-American Jack Schwarz. Jack has repeatedly demonstrated and described a whole range of psychologically-induced immunity — to infection, to injury, and to burning from fire. Jack has written many popular books on voluntary controls, lectures all over America on the subject, and runs a school in Oregon that teaches ordinary humans how extraordinary we really are. My conversations with Jack Schwarz have been no less than illuminating, and to him in his brilliant, radiant state, we are all indebted.

I spoke with many men of science, too, men with great depth in their education and practice, and most of these men too were on the cutting edge of their professions, making serious inquiries into apparently unexplainable mysteries. Among the most significant of those for this report were physicist Dr. Bernard Leikind and psychologist Dr. William McCarthy. These two scientists have studied the firewalk, and been out on the fire themselves. Their conclusions will reassure many, and seem short-sighted and naive to just as many. Two reputable psychiatrists contributed greatly to this report, both having done significant field research in the psychology of physical immunity to fire. Beyond their landmark research, both Dr. Berthold Schwarz and Dr. Steven Kane gave generously of their time to me, entertaining questions and asking them, stretching my understanding of the possibilities of this miraculous creature, human being. Their field reports — not from faraway India or Tibet, but from the south of the

United States — make for hair-raising reading, and answer as many questions as they raise. Sociologist Dr. James McClenon, who has written about the firewalk and walked across many red-hot firebeds, was also a great wellspring of cool, reasonable observations and conclusions in an otherwise impassioned field.

They say a picture is worth 10,000 words, and we got our every word's worth, thanks to the fine photography of Brian Garland, David Goodman and Sara Raintree.

Finally, this book might never have seen the light of day had it not been for the support of editor and publisher, David Emblidge. David kept the faith, even in trying times, even when his belief in this book was as challenging as a walk across red-hot coals. Thanks too for the trials and tribulations of editor Brandt Morgan, who slimmed and massaged a researcher's tome into a reader's book. And for Mary Osak and Marguerite Maude Bryt, who typed and retyped, then tidied up.

To all these, and many unnamed others — firewalkers, researchers, librarians, word processors, book designers and manufacturers — I give my wholehearted thanks. What was once only a dream, now rests in your hands. Perhaps some of the mysteries of the firewalk are unshrouded now, because of you. Quite possibly the way has been opened by you, down a path of fire, through the psychology of physical immunity and into a realm of vast unimaginable empowerment.

Jonathan Sternfield

Foreword

Given our fascination and preoccupation in recent years with what the human potential movement likes to call "Personal Growth," it was predictable that *firewalking* would capture the public's attention. Made up, apparently, of equal parts self-discipline and hucksterism, with a dash of mysticism and theatrics, this ancient ritual has all the prerequisites to change our attitudes about ourselves — and, if you believe some analysts, about the physical world itself. Thousands of ordinary (and extraordinary) people have met the challenge of walking barefoot on hot coals; evidently, few were burned. Rather, many viewed their experience as a psychic awakening that ignited unrecognized inner energy. They say their lives changed.

When I first read reports of firewalking, I — like many observers of human nature — was amused, titillated and intrigued. I believe now (as I believed then) that the act of a successful firewalk has, as its basis, sound principles of physics. Unfortunately, not all these principles have been elucidated. In the early 1980's, I wrote in my medical column that this phenomenon ought to be studied by reputable investigators.

I wanted to know how a person could walk across burning coals and not be barbequed. I thought that if firewalking were merely a profitable scam and people were "psyching" themselves up over nothing, such phoniness should be revealed to the public.

On the other hand, if the ability to firewalk is an ability permitting us to transcend the physical world (as we perceive it) and if it reflects a new way to channel spiritual energy, protect ourselves from injury and assist healing, then the whole damn world ought to know about it. Forget the military implications and the obvious benefits to professional firefighters: the medical establishment would be turned on its ear. It was clear to me that firewalking could be the biggest revolution in the healing arts since Dr. Koch discovered bacteria and altered the course of human disease.

To date, there have been few, if any, disinterested investigations of firewalking. Questions remain. The spectacle of the firewalk is still elusive, challenging, scientifically undefined.

Therefore, it is appropriate that Jonathan Sternfield, an inquisitive reporter and skilled writer — and one who has walked on fire himself — has compiled a thorough analysis of firewalking. Unlike most previous writers on the subject, Jonathan Sternfield is neither a firewalk instructor, guru or promoter. His search for credible explanations is motivated by an honest curiosity about a puzzling truth. His text includes an historical perspective and an exhaustive review of the theories (scientific and otherwise) behind this remarkable business. Firewalk participants (successful and unsuccessful) are allowed to speak candidly here, and the voices of many authorities create a fascinating chorus of speculation. Well written and far ranging, this book answers many questions — and raises others. It is now the definitive work on firewalking, entertaining and informative.

I hope *FIREWALK* will spark the scientific and medical research that desperately needs to be performed. At the very least this book will make many readers re-think their assumptions about the limits of physical immunity and the possibility that the human species has powers it has not yet learned to use in everyday life. Meanwhile, I am forced to accept the inescapable: firewalking remains inexplicably unsolved, a mystery reminding us that despite astounding scientific achievements, we remain baffled by much of our world.

Dr. Peter Gott,
Medical Columnist,
United Features Syndicate

When you walk through fire,
you shall not be be burned;
and the flame shall not
consume you.

Isaiah 43:2

Introduction

"*Get stronger!*" Tony Robbins yelled at me, his eyes black with intensity.

In front of me lay a bed of glowing, red-hot coals, over 1,000 degrees Fahrenheit. The Dionysian scene quivered in the heat. Screams of ecstasy filled the cool night air. Onlookers pushed to get a better glimpse while policemen held them at bay.

There was no blaze now, so you could face the fire. Earlier, when the four little bonfires had been fanned by a gusty wind, they had raged so hot you couldn't look at them. But now there were only two beds of radiant coals, each about 12 feet long.

It was after two in the morning, on the first day in December, 1984. Though some 500 of us had gathered in front of Manhattan Center on W. 34th St., we could have been anywhere, anytime, so singleminded were we all, so attuned to our fear — and the fire.

Oddly dapper in sports jacket and tie, six-foot, six-inch master of ceremonies Tony Robbins burned almost as hot as the fires he had arranged. Sure, we had all signed formal releases. Sure, we were all here of our own questionable volition. But if I froze up while on the fire, or if I fell on my face, I would be badly burned. I didn't relish the thought of finishing my passage on "charred, bloody stumps," but Robbins had made it clear that this was a possibility if we were not properly focused.

Had I listened carefully enough, mentally practiced with enough intent? Most important, was my belief strong enough? Had I really internalized the "embedding commands" both Robbins and I had delivered to my subconscious? Why was I doing this, anyway? Wouldn't skydiving be a whole lot safer and more exhilarating?

I had entertained each of these questions at length. Now, at the moment of truth, none of them even entered my mind. As I faced the fiery bed, I was beyond questioning. My perspective shrank. I became one-pointed, completely focused. Hot embers flew up in the night wind, stuck to a nearby head of hair and singed before being brushed out. Yes, fire still burned, the evidence was everywhere.

I had been drawn to this firewalk by an itchy inkling that there is much more to life than meets the eye. My experience had proven that within my own body, at least, mind generally rules matter. But the creation of my own health or disease had historically been rather subtle. If I could bring about a body-mind harmony through walking on fire, I thought, I might gain a deeper acquaintance with the psychological controls of my physical health. Since I also view my life as an evolutionary experiment, playing with fire was not utterly irresponsible but rather aimed at further enlightenment.

Now, several years after that blazing experiment, I look back and realize that I have learned much from firewalking and its principal practitioners. I think of fire now as a hot foil in the drama of my life, a high-energy reflector of the psychic state I bring to it. My safe walk over glowing coals that night fused in me a new unity of body and mind. Momentary immunity from the damaging effects of fire gave me a whiff of the miraculous. One whiff led to another, and in a way I became hooked. The magic of firewalking and its deeper implications drew me into a lengthy investigation.

As a subject, firewalking has so many angles: religious, psychological, physiological, historical and cultural, to name a few. And now, with its hot, new profile on the American human-potential circuit, it has sociological impacts that are also worthy of attention. In fact, firewalking's principal American proponents claim that it can help people break through all the limiting factors in their lives. The subject then, is limitless — or limitlessness.

For centuries, firewalking has been practiced in cultures all over the world. Today, the ancient ceremony as it was passed on among tribal members may be fading. But now a new firewalking ritual has emerged, a distinctly Westernized version with conceptual framework to match. The dying embers of the ancient ceremony have been rekindled in America. By every indication, there are now more firewalkers in the United States than in the rest of the world's countries combined. Surely this is more than a fad.

"If it's a fad," said a local TV newsman, "it's the most bizarre fad in years. It has been compared to est and Yoga, but now *firewalking* has made its way into some parts of the country, including Connecticut."

That report focused on a firewalk in the tiny town of Tolland. And from the equally small community of Lakeville, a report came from my very own doctor, Peter Gott. Now, Dr. Gott is not your average M.D., and I had long since come to expect the unexpected from him. Nonetheless, I was surprised to meet him in the local deli one day in the spring of 1985 and to learn that he, too, had been writing about firewalking. In the latest of his nationally syndicated columns, this one entitled "Eerie, Fiery Feats," Gott urged research into this as-yet-unexplained phenomenon and wondered about the power that protects firewalkers: whether it might have military potential, uses in firefighting, or in treating burns or curing diseases.

In his continuous "tweaking" of his own profession, Dr. Gott closed his column as follows:

> . . . nobody — that's right, nobody — has the slightest inkling of how normal humans, after four hours of instruction, can walk barefoot across a barbecue pit. And no one seems to care about the explanation for this phenomenon, the implications of which are almost beyond

> comprehension. Isn't that a sardonic testimonial to the glory of medical research? I wish that some night soon, an upstart scientist would awaken with the novel realization that the mind is being ignored by medical-establishments technology worshipers. . . . I pray that he joins a firewalking seminar, studies the process, collates his data, writes a report and publishes his explanation of how it's done. Then the revolution will start — and we can begin.

Here then, is just what my good doctor ordered.

But other doctors seemed less enthusiastic. Some of them described having treated firewalkers with minor burns and others whose feet had been charred to the bone. "It's a dangerous practice," said one such doctor, "unless you are experienced and know what you're doing."

But isn't that the way of the world? The standard Catch-22 of every first job, every first horseback ride, every first dive off the high dive is that there's no experience without danger, no first-time anything without some leap of faith. True, the stakes in firewalking are substantial, but evidently, for most people it can be done safely, repeatedly and predictably. And for almost everyone who attempts it, even those who are burned, the firewalk seems to be a truly powerful, even transforming, experience.

For me, firewalking has been an extraordinary experience, but it is not for everyone. Despite the fact that the major American firewalking instructors boast of an extremely high success rate — some 95-99 percent of their students, they say, cross the coals without injury — I still would not recommend it to everyone. Actually, I would recommend it to no one. I am glad I did it, and I will likely do it again, but this is one you decide for yourself.

Walking the coals is no decision to be taken lightly, for one of the basic tenets of our reality is: *fire burns!* And to bring something this basic, this self-evident, into question raises questions about all of reality. As we shall see, this can be almost as unsettling as getting burned. Yet both my research and my personal experience have clearly shown that fire does not *have* to burn. To my amazement, it has been repeatedly confirmed to me that under certain circumstances, we are able to effect limited or even total immunity to the destructive force of fire. How this is accomplished by both body and mind — and what it might mean for us as human beings — is the subject of this investigation.

I begin, then, with a seeming miracle on 34th St. in New York, my first firewalk with Tony Robbins. Then I delve into the fascinating and magical background of Tolly Burkan, the father of American firewalking. In Chapter 3, I go back to the fire in New York, relating a very different firewalk from my first — this one at Public School #191 with a Thai martial arts and yoga expert named Mantak Chia.

Next, to get some perspective on the ancient ritual, I take you on a firewalk through history, exploring everything from ancient and biblical firewalking accounts to the great firewalking traditions of China, Japan, India and beyond. In this chapter, you'll see that men (and women and children, too) have walked and even danced over red-hot coals for numerous reasons: as a trial to determine guilt or innocence; as a test of faith; to insure good crops; to heal or empower; and even, on occasion, just for show.

In Chapter 5, I review all of the significant scientific investigations and expert opinions about the firewalk, searching for some logical explanation to the mystery. Here you can check out the findings of physicists, physicians, psychologists, psychiatrists, burn specialists, sociologists and others who have painstakingly (and sometimes painfully) gathered data to try to explain the firewalk enigma.

I take the scientific inquiry further in Chapter 6, closely scrutinizing several groups of Southern fundamentalist firehandlers and their centuries-old tradition of putting their faith to the fiery test. Then in Chapter 7, I go on to examine even lengthier contact with fire — including the almost unbelievable feats of two of America's longest-standing firewalkers, men who have repeatedly trekked through red-hot coals and occasionally even stood in fires for up to several minutes without even singeing the hair on their toes.

Having established that something extraordinary is going on here, that many people in certain states of consciousness do indeed exhibit varying immunity to burns, in Chapter 8 I delve more deeply into the psychology of physical immunity. I explain how faith connects to the fire and seems to prevent burns. I explore related examples of mind over matter, some commonplace, some perhaps even more astounding than firewalking. And finally, in Chapter 9, I offer you glimpses of an energetic field beyond the physical, a field that offers both a solid (though controversial) explanation for the firewalk — and most likely a new frontier for science.

Having drawn some conclusions about human immunity to fire, I return in Chapter 10 to the firewalk itself — this time, to America, center of the craze for hot coals. In the book's final chapters, I describe the social forces that fuel this craze, focusing on who has been caught up in it and why. I talk about how fire can be used to empower and heal instead of hurt. And finally, I offer some speculations about what the firewalk might mean for us as a luminous and still-evolving species.

This investigation, of course, is my own personal inquiry into the psychology of physical immunity; therefore, its conclusions and speculations are my own. Yet, as you will see from the evidence, it is not primarily wishful thinking that prompts me to believe we are far more than we think we are. Since that first night when I stood before the glowing coals on W. 34th St., the path of fire has led me — almost inevitably, it now seems — to the conclusion that we are all radiant beings, beings whose immunities and powers know no limits, beings capable of almost anything we can imagine.

Firewalk

1

Miracle on 34th Street

Faith . . . quenched the violence of fire.

Hebrews 11:34

It was just after Thanksgiving 1984, when a friend of a friend phoned with the word: she knew a firewalker, and we were all invited to meet him. Exactly what we would see or hear was never explained, but my interest had been piqued. Accordingly, the very next night, off I went to Manhattan Center on W. 34th St. to check out Anthony Robbins, firewalker.

Before seating myself in the ornate, seventh-floor auditorium, I assessed my feelings for firewalking. Like other miraculous feats, the ability to walk safely over fire had seemed noteworthy to me, triumphantly indicative of the power of the invisible over the visible. But until I personally witnessed such acts — and likely even afterwards, I thought — their relevance to me would seem minimal. I was most attuned to miracles of the heart, the passions of caring and loving, so psychic spoon-bending and the like tended to be little more to me than passing curiosities. Yet undeniably, there was something godly about walking over fire.

At first I teased myself about the weirdness of the endeavor, but the more I thought about it, the more it seemed this adventure might be an opening to a realm where anything is possible. It might not be a lasting state, and it might be of no ultimate import, I thought, but it seemed a potentially fascinating exploration. And besides, I had only come to *watch*; at this point I just wanted to see that such a thing was humanly possible. If any person can walk on fire safely, I reasoned, then all of us are potentially capable of doing so, and that was of far greater significance to me than whether I actually did it myself.

Within a matter of minutes after the presentation began, I saw a man walk on fire. Granted it was a televised fire; but there, up on the monitor, was big Tony Robbins walking across hot coals on the CBS news, then doing it again over NBC. Though the action on these network news clips seemed somewhat miraculous, it was still too distant to grab me.

Next, live and in person, came two young professionals from the Beverly Hills-based Robbins Research Institute, to introduce us to their work and their leader. In the vast ballroom of Manhattan Center, the air was rife with New Age razzle-dazzle.

Moments later, the theme from the movie "Rocky" erupted in all its corny glory, and down the aisle ran a bear of a man. Tony Robbins mounted the stage with lightness, turning to beam at us while clapping fiercely to the winning music. Soon we had all joined him in the clapping, and Robbins' smile looked as if it might tear his face, so wide did it stretch.

This was spirit-schtick at its height. Robbins' whole entrance routine resembled nothing so much as a dozen Johnny Carsons rolled into one; however, in place of Johnny's gentle, celebratory golf swing, Tony let out a cheerleader's war whoop, building and climaxing with one hand socking it to the other. Astoundingly, almost everyone at this introductory lecture joined in the pep chant, aping the star.

After the roar and the music had died down, Robbins filled us in on his background. Before he became a firewalker, he said, he was simply a personal development teacher, following in the footsteps of his Dale Carnegie-like model, Jim Rohn. Robbins characterized Rohn as a "goals-attitude-time-management" type, a no-nonsense salesman who sold people on themselves. "Attitude is everything" was a Rohn aphorism.

"The quality of my life is the quality of my communication," Robbins continued. "Write that down: 'The quality of my life is the quality of my communication.' And the way to succeed in communication is to find out people's needs and give it to them. People who succeed have personal power, the ability to take action. Remember the biblical saying? 'Faith without action is dead.' But how do you act? How do you get personal power?

"Here are the three keys to personal power," Robbins went on. "Write these down. Number one is energy. Without the energy, no matter how much you know, you can't do anything, and you don't feel like doing anything. So first off, you need energy, you need the vitality to make your dreams real. Second, you need the skills of power. Skill is knowing specifically what you want and having many strategies with which to get it." And the third key, Robbins told us, is transforming fear into power. This gives the ability to act, he said, to turn fears that are holding us back into the power to achieve.

"Fear into power is the third key," he repeated. "Fear into power means reprogramming all limiting factors. And remember, the 'Fear into Power Seminar' is not about firewalking. The firewalk is a metaphor. What I'm really here to teach people is a series of very specific skills to break through any limitations they have created in their lives. Fear of failure, fear of success, fear of rejection or of public speaking — what the fear is doesn't matter. I teach people to change the way they feel about themselves and how to operate effectively in their worlds. It's not about firewalking. I could teach you to firewalk in ten minutes, five if you're sharp."

After inviting us back to firewalk the following night, Tony Robbins ended his pitch by bounding from the stage and running up the aisle, ever the champ.

It was annoying to have Robbins on my mind the next day. I felt as if someone in the next room had left the television on. More than annoying, though, was a growing sense of fear, an all-over anxiety that began to crowd me out towards evening. Now that I knew anybody could walk over fire and that Robbins could show me how, would I chicken out? What was I trying to prove, anyway? The various characters in me argued with dramatic ferocity; fear roiled the seas of my stomach.

My perspective changed; my reporting becomes present tense.

I return to W. 34th St. early. Manhattan Center is mobbed. Hundreds of people are crammed into the lobby to sign up for the firewalk. I watch the elevator take up about 15 at a time, and my fear ignites an imaginary fire with hundreds of people trapped on the seventh floor and only one dinky elevator down. My fear conjures images of "Towering Inferno." During my own ride up, I am jumpy about everything. My mind is playing tricks on me.

Up on the seventh floor, registration for the firewalk is just like at college, with five wavy lines assembled alphabetically. My line doubles back on itself and seems to have at least three ends. The fee for the firewalk is $125, chargeable to MasterCard or Visa, and the price has apparently daunted few. Around me I see mothers and daughters, sons and fathers, teens and seniors, and skins of all known shades. Firewalking — or Tony Robbins, I think — must cut a broad swath.

The registration attendants are extremely accommodating and pleased to know I am writing about Robbins. In order to walk, we each sign an agreement releasing Robbins, his firm and the Manhattan Center from all liability should we burn, suffer psychologically or even die. The agreement pulls no punches, warning that "If I do choose to walk on the coals, I am fully aware that there are no guarantees regarding my safe passage and that there is a possibility that I may, in fact, receive severe burns to my feet requiring medical attention." People by the dozens sign the waiver as though it were a petition to increase the number of holidays.

Back in the ballroom, we are all seated. Once again, Robbins' Los Angeles lawyer introduces the show, telling us he has known Tony for a year and a half and has walked across hot coals 27 times himself. Then he asks us: "How many people here know that Tony has taken over 13,000 people across the fire?"

It has started; we are being programmed. The lawyer is not really asking, he is actively telling, "embedding," as Robbins himself might put it. Next he poses the question: "How many here wondered today if they're special, if they're the one who's going to burn?" Hundreds of hands fly up. It seems we're *all* special.

Seconds later, it's "Rocky" all over again, trumpets blaring, the champ dancing down the aisle, his legions on their feet in tribal ecstasy. On the stage, "Rocky" Robbins slides into his beaming hand clap, and in a moment the place is cooking.

The champ says hello and tells us this evening will break some patterns. He mentions a firewalk he arranged in a suburb of Seattle and how someone called the cops on him. It was then he learned that "not everybody's open to this piece." He also tells us about the "6:30 syndromers," those who have signed up and paid in advance but who don't show up for the firewalk. A fifth of the preregistrants are 6:30 syndromers who don't even ask for their money back. "It's a great scam," Robbins notes impishly.

Then he changes the tenor. He praises us for having come this far, for having taken the time, paid the money and sat with the intention to walk on fire. We have already conquered our fear, he tells us, and a ripple of relief washes over the room.

Robbins repeats that this is not a firewalking seminar and that firewalking could be taught in a few minutes. This is a seminar to change our ways of thinking, he says, and to learn some enjoyable techniques to break through fear. The firewalk is a metaphor for the impossible in our lives, for those too-frequent situations that feel like red-hot coals.

We are at the biggest firewalk in history, says Robbins. With over 500 present, we are far and away the largest group of firewalkers ever assembled in one room. He refreshes our familiarity with temperatures, reminding us the coals tonight will be between 1,200 degrees Fahrenheit (the temperature at which molten aluminum is cast) and 2,000 degrees Fahrenheit (the temperature at which they roll red-hot steel). So, lest we become complacent in our new-found group identity, he cautions us anew: there is real danger here — six people he knows of have been hospitalized with second-degree burns, three with first-degree burns, and three have died. That's the bad news, he tells us; the good news is that none of these injuries occurred in any of his seminars. Gales of tension-relieving laughter sweep the house.

Just as we are settling in, Robbins has us get up and walk *en masse*, clapping, down the seven flights of stairs to the street. The stereo blares with the voice of the late Jim Morrison, wailing, "Come on baby light my fire! Try and set the night on *fire*!" The stairs echo with hundreds of footsteps and handclaps. It feels like we're descending to the world of collective consciousness, moving from a quickly bonded tribe to a rapidly melding cult. Instead of resisting this loss of individuality, people here seem only too happy to hand it over to Robbins, the man who seems to have the keys to a safe passage over fire.

Out on the windblown north side of W. 34th St., we gather around four laid-but-not-ignited wood fires. As Robbins lights them up (on sod covering the sidewalk), he tells us to remember a fire that made us feel warm and secure. When we have made that association, he asks us to make a fist. As the blazes spring to life, we are all taken aback by their intensity all except Robbins, who steps forward to splash on more kerosene. The wind whips up the street. Flames shoot up the front of the building.

"Turn away if you have to," Robbins yells over the jet-like roar of the four fires. Like galaxies launched in a cosmic breath, clusters of sparks twist off their fiery pads, swirling in the blackness. Instinctively, every face turns quickly away.

"Turn to five others," yells Tony, "and introduce yourself. Tell them your greatest fear, what it would feel like if you conquered it and what your best feature as a human is. Then hug them."

I turn and, one by one, tell five people that I fear success, that it would be exhilarating to conquer it and that my availability is my best quality. In turn, Hillary is most afraid of what she doesn't know; Marcia fears failure; Gus also fears success; and Andrea also fears the unknown. Kate, the fifth person, turns to me with watery eyes and says her greatest fear is that she will never find the love she wants. The others' hugs are chummy; hers has a hunger.

These brief encounters concluded, Robbins asks us to go back upstairs with the strong belief that each us can and *has* walked on fire. To embed this conviction more deeply, he asks each of us to walk up using the "firewalker's strut," a step he claims we already know.

Back upstairs, Robbins tells us that this will be an experience to allow our "neurologies to be accessed." The coals are just a metaphor; what the evening is really about, he says, is *congruency*. In his lexicon, this word denotes a totally focused state in which all aspects of ourselves are in agreement with one another. It is this state that we need to achieve in order to walk safely over fire, and we can quickly achieve it, he says, with Neuro-Linguistic Programming (NLP). This new and evolving therapeutic discipline, he says, uses "embedding commands" to cause the conscious and unconscious to become synergistic. With it, he hopes to guide us to a place where we can remember who we are.

I am quickly forgetting. In the escalating barrage of information, both spoken and subtle, I am losing myself to the two-faced task of reporting and being indoctrinated — lest I be burned.

Congruency has value in every aspect of life, says Robbins into the tiny radio mike built into his jacket, and he's beginning to convince me. We're not good communicators with others because we're not good communicators with ourselves. What we need is *congruency*.

Robbins tells us he has guided people from five to 85 years old across the coals, that he's never had someone burn badly on him, but that he has had about a dozen blisterers. More significantly, he says, he has had spontaneous remissions with the fire, even a crippled man somehow finding a way to walk across. Walk with the stature you want, Robbins says, and change your belief about what's possible.

Firewalking theories are explained. Mass hypnosis, say some — and I believe them. Leidenfrost effect, say a few scientists, with sweat on the feet forming a vapor lock — and I believe *them*. Be in state, Robbins says, totally in state.

Death, public speaking and fire are some of our greatest fears, Robbins says, and personal power is all about taking action in spite of great fear. His goal, he says, is to leave New York in the trail of 500 newly awakened "monsters." "Monsters are good," he says. "They know what they want, and they go about creating value for others and hence themselves."

Robbins has us stand up and form a massive massage train, each of us massaging the person in front and snaking around the room to the hot beat of Billy Oceans' "Caribbean Queen." Then he tells us to sit, and a volley of maxims issues from the stage. There are no mistakes, he says, it's *all* all right. Positing an accidental universe is like saying *Webster's Dictionary* exists as a result of an explosion in a print shop. Success is what I want, where I want it, with whom I want it and as much as I want it.

"Write this down," says Robbins. "Knowledge is the key. Knowledge is the key." He pauses to allow us to reflect. "Now cross that out. Don't let your learning lead to knowledge, you'll become a fool. Let your learning lead to action, you'll become wealthy. Education has value only when it's used. Personal power is the key to success. And personal power is the ability to take action."

He gives us the example of Colonel Sanders, a man unsatisfied with his first retirement check, who took a not-too-spectacular chicken recipe from fast-food place to greasy spoon. He says it took Sanders two years and 1,009 "no's" before he got one "yes." Personal power means not only doing, but doing it until . . .

We all have talents and intelligences, Robbins says, and then he claims: "I can duplicate any form of talent or intelligence." To duplicate success, he says, you need to model the best — to copy their belief system, their mental syntax and their physiology. Robbins tells us of a contract he fulfilled for the U.S. Army in which he redesigned their pistol training program. The marksmen were skeptical about learning from a 24-year-old who had no gun experience, but after modeling them, Robbins says, not only did he become an instant marksman but he reduced their training time from four days to one and tripled their proficiency. Using NLP, he says, he can teach the same sharpshooter skills to anyone very quickly. He says he has linked this accelerated learning program to the firewalk, and that in several hours most of us will use it to perform the unthinkable.

All this rubs against my deeply ingrained belief that change is slow, frequently painful and usually incremental. Robbins is talking revolution — mind revolution. He's very convincing, a melange of Dale Carnegie, Werner Erhard, Johnny Carson and Carlos Castenada embodied in one sweet-natured hulk. He is the one-stop therapist, he says, a man who can cure even lifelong phobias in one session. If you go to your therapist and you have to go back, hey, you didn't get what you paid for; you didn't get fixed. It's one session with Tony, that's why he's a $1,000-an-hour man.

Robbins tells of a woman who was deathly afraid of snakes, noting that this woman could have had a heart attack from the mere suggestion that there was a snake in the bag he tossed her way. In one quick, on-stage session, he says, he had the woman handling a real live snake.

To try out his accelerated learning programs, Robbins claims, he became a karate adept in one afternoon, able to break bricks and boards with his bare hands. On stage he demonstrates, karate punching through two one-inch boards held by an assistant; and then, more impressively, from only inches away, punching through another two boards. He says anybody can do it, that he has even taught little kids in an hour or so.

When's he is breaking boards, Robbins seems truly fierce, bigger than life, snorting breath and focusing intensely. When he is communicating with words, he alternates between the teacher, the lover and the scamp. At his most impish, in the role of transcendental stand-up comic, nothing is sacred, and even that isn't a rule.

"Stand up!" he commands, as Ray Parker blasts out over the sound system singing the theme song from "Ghostbusters!" "We're Fearbusters!" Robbins shouts. "Sing: 'I ain't afraid 'a no fire!'" And as we sing, we embed commands in ourselves.

Song done, we seat ourselves while Robbins tells us we are here to integrate all the power we have ever had. "The people who come to my seminars never go home," he says mischievously. "They're different people who leave. And one of the ways we will achieve that revolution is through embedded commands to create total choice, to destroy all limiting factors.

"*Stretch*!" he says, in a slightly higher imperative. For an instant, many are unsure if he means literally, physically or metaphorically. "Stretch! Right? If you *can't*, you *must*! Right? If you're someone who doesn't believe in limitation, whatever you *can't* do, you *must* do! That's a life of adventure! You don't want security; that's what they've got prisons for. You want *freedom*!

"Take a clean sheet of paper and write down your main fear; under that, describe how it came about; under that, write what benefit that fear gave you . . . benefit, ya, there's always some benefit. Under that, write why you want to be free now."

I spell out my fear of success, how it might have come about through some alienation and how it allows me to lay low. Once again, I cite exhilaration as the expected result of freedom from such fear. We are further instructed to write the word "FEAR" and to note that it actually stands for "False Evidence That Appears to Be Real," or alternatively, "False Education That Appears to be Real."

"Reality is whatever we perceive it as," Robbins tells us. "Reality is a lie, a distortion, a belief system." He draws a curve on one of the oversize pads. "Concave or convex?" he asks. "Change your vantage point, you change your reality. It's all perception! People have gotten burned on *ice* when they thought it was hot. Set up the experience the way you want it to come out.

"Here are the five keys to fear," says Robbins. "These are metacommands. (1) Identify the fear. This will reduce its power over you. (2) Analyze it to death. Fear is usually of the unknown; anchor it to death, turn it around." Robbins then explains auditory anchors, finishing by stating that "Winston tastes good . . ." then listening while we complete the slogan with ". . . like a cigarette should." This is Pavlovian, he says. All we need to do is program ourselves, then say the magic word. (3) Be willing to accept the worst. This relaxes anxiety about possible disastrous failure. Robbins recounts a challenge he accepted in Hawaii, when a skeptical diver dared him to test his management of fear — with feeding sharks. In the pitch-black Pacific night, Robbins says, he threw himself overboard, proving both his and the diver's wisdom about sharks' indifference to the fearless. (4) Be will-ing to accept the best. Be willing to acknowledge that we are all "Masters." (5) Take disciplined action, for affirmation without discipline is lost.

Robbins himself certainly seems like a master — a master mechanic of personality. In my own evolutionary quest, I have found myself before many a powerful presence, before many "old souls" who are obviously communicating timeless virtues of cosmic significance, but Robbins is the first master mechanic of personality I've ever seen. Though I find his Los Angeles style glitzy and off-putting, and though at 24 he is a little heady with his newly won millions of dollars and his life in a coastal castle, I admire his communicative power, and I feel he is sharing and distilling some genuinely practical insight.

Now Robbins shifts into personal history, sketching his initiation into the rites of firewalking. In his pursuit of excellence, he says, he traveled to northern California, where a firewalker was reported to be practicing. That firewalker, unnamed this evening but who would turn out to be a man named Tolly Burkan, had learned the art from an American woman who in turn had learned it from a Tibetan monk.

Robbins learned firewalking by modeling, he says, by duplicating the belief system, mental syntax and physiology of the successful practitioner. Literally following his model across the red-hot coals, he says he was so awestruck that he picked up a handful of coals, held them for a moment, then tossed them away, completing his passage unharmed in any way.

"Here's how to walk on fire," announces Robbins, and everybody sits up. "First, walk at a normal pace." Some people try to run, others skip; best to walk real regular, that's the word. "Second, control or align with your inner dialogue. In India, they call this the *mantra*, and here we'll use the overload mantra, something to both occupy *and* suggest, something like . . . cool moss, cool moss . . . or we could use [illegible] you like that one? OK, cool moss, cool moss."

"The third thing to remember is to stay in physiology." He demonstrates how we are to walk: first sucking air down to oxygenate the cells and increase electrical activity; next looking up to place the mental syntax in visual memory; and finally clenching the hand to reawaken preprogrammed feelings of great power, love and security. We are to stay in this physical state, he says, traverse the coals, wipe our feet, then punch the air in celebration. We are told everything in terms of stimulus-response patterns. Like Pavlov's dogs, we will no longer feel our habitual or expected feelings, but rather those we have allowed Robbins and ourselves to decide upon for this occasion.

The leap of faith involved in subjecting myself to such conditioning seems at once important and a bit insidious. I find myself hoping that I can go through with this and still regain access to my "real" feelings when it is over. There is some hocus-pocus hypnosis going on here, but if I do not submit to it, I may get burned. Perhaps that's the gimmick: you work your way into a bind where you have to be reprogrammed in order to safely perform the firewalk that you weren't sure you wanted to do in the first place, or else you'll end up feeling yourself a coward. No wonder some people forfeit their deposit — why pay to get burned twice?

Robbins has us embed commands in each other, looking deep into a partner's eyes and affirming, "*I* can do this, and *you* can do it, too." Then we each lightly touch our partner's shoulder, a physical marker for the affirmation. Next, he tells us we can change instantly, that feelings are the same as ideas, and that even the deepest ones can be transformed in minutes. Every feeling is created by physiology, he says, and I feel my forehead furrow in disbelief. "Write this down," Robbins demands. "There is no mind; there is only body." He repeats it, then gives a new version. "Now write *this* down: There is no body; only mind."

Robbins has us all going, addressing most of his comments to our conscious selves, but aiming an even more significant part to our subconscious selves. The woman next to me giggles nervously every time Robbins changes tone and issues an embedded command. He has us repeat: "My body will do everything in its power to insure a safe and pleasurable firewalk." And once more, for the umpteenth time, "This seminar is not about . . . not about what? Firewalking! Right!"

He asks us to close our eyes. Are we ready? If there are any parts in us that are not in agreement with this firewalk, let them signal through some physical display. We don't have to do anything, our unconscious will do it all, he says.

He has us stand up, then sends us on a giant hug train. It is midnight, and we are dancing in kindergarten. An all-black conga band arrives, and the drumming starts. The room seems ready to lift off in a frenzy of circling, skipping, hugging and drumming. Robbins calms it down, cues the drummers to lighten up, then has us lie down wherever we can find a spot. Close your eyes, he says, as synthesized music filters in through the sound system.

Robbins' voice is the most soothing it's been all evening. He is charming us now, the way a snake charmer hypnotizes a cobra with a flute song. In a few seconds, he has us associating with images of the time when we were the most relaxed and secure ever. He even has us remember and duplicate our posture and breathing of that time.

For me, an early peak experience quickly comes to mind: an evening of childhood, fireside bliss in which all of me was "in sync." Drawing our attention to the tight fist he has asked us to associate with these thoughts, Robbins tells us we are now *a thousand times* more relaxed and secure than we were then, and that whenever we make a fist, we will "know and feel and be" all that relaxation and security.

I find this process surprisingly effective. In a room packed with strangers, I am extraordinarily relaxed, on the verge of becoming altogether tension free. The reporter in me blinks his eyes and looks about. All is calm.

Now Robbins has us recall the moment when we felt most loved. Once again I return to my childhood, to our grand country home where I was the center of much doting attention from a very extended family. Quickly I am asked to escalate that love a thousand times. Suddenly I am the radiant son, shining with a whole family's light.

Next, he asks us to recall our most powerful moment. For me, apparently, it was an afternoon when, at age 14, I pushed myself to win a tennis tournament in spite of heavy heat, dust and fatigue. Promising myself a special swim if I did it, I swam afterwards with awesome facility, bathing in my triumph. Again Robbins asks us to remember our posture and breathing as they were then. And again, through the clenched-fist cue, I make myself a thousand times more powerful than ever. Though the clenched fist is normally a sign of fear or tension, Robbins tells us in his most godly tones that it is hereafter our "anchor," our accessing tool to feelings of total relaxation, confidence, strength, love and resourcefulness.

I am being turned around. A new program is being punched in. I am still me; only my database and program have changed. Addressing any parts of me that still might not agree with this program, Robbins smoothly suggests that these parts will now agree and come into congruency for the benefit of the whole. Now, though we 500 prospective firewalkers are spread out over the whole ballroom, he says we are all congruent. "Good," he says, his words stroking our inner beings, "Good! Good! *Excellent!*"

At this moment, I recall hearing of an anesthetizing technique in which the anesthesiologist whispers into his unconscious patient's ear upon completion of the surgery: "Hello, there, this is God. The operation was a success. You will heal quickly and be in the best health of your life." If it works, I remember thinking, why the hell not? Now, with Robbins whispering in my ear and my doors of perception swung this way and that, there is only wonder.

Robbins calls us back from our altered state, but the feeling is one of empowerment: we are *still* in an altered state. And now is the time we have all come for. Now it is time to take off our shoes and socks, roll up our pants and march down the seven flights of stairs to the fire.

As if someone had shouted "*Fire!*" in a crowded theater, there is a great rush for the door. How odd, I think, that we are rushing *to* the fire, not *from* it. How very strange, this urgency to meet the fire intimately rather than to flee. Robbins asks us to clap, and we do — hundreds of barefoot, supercharged Americans on our way to a transforming, red-hot experience.

Over the loudspeakers, once again we hear the voice of Jim Morrison singing: "Come on baby light my fire! Try to set the night on *fire*!"

On the stairs, we are a pagan, clapping horde, eager for the heat of purification. We are Islamic fundamentalists questing for God; we are revivalist Christians shouting the gospel; we are Krishna cultists chanting to oblivion; we are Native Americans dancing into ecstasy. Bare feet slap the cool, metal-edged linoleum steps. Hundreds descend for what feels like the ultimate fire drill.

Normally I am very uncomfortable with spiritual group mind, feeling sullied by such a sustained effort at self-glorification. But such feelings tonight have long since passed. I no longer care where I am or whom I am with. Nor am I concerned that this possibly holy passion will take place on a strip of cut-rate clothing stores, right next door to Reverend Sun Myung Moon's New York compound. I will carry my own sacredness. I will see and hear Tibet.

It is 1:30 in the morning by the time we reach the street and the fire. The crowds have grown considerably since we were last here, and police are straining to keep the 500 firewalkers separated from the 500 onlookers.

"Are you Moonies?" asks a Hispanic boy.

"No-o," responds a Scandanavian participant named Inga.

"What is this?" asks the boy, eyeing the orange beds of coals.

"Neuro-Linguistic Programming," replies Inga.

"Oh . . . oh," says the boy, more confused than ever.

This is a firewalk, I hear myself think, a firewalk all dressed up in concepts.

Robbins is busy at the fires, raking the coals and directing others. The conga drummers have come down and begun serenading the entire neighborhood, drumming in the night. I am perplexed at the police protection; it seems to me that *we* are the rowdies — the firebuilders, firewalkers and late-night drummers. A cop nearby shakes his head in bewilderment, seemingly mirroring my own momentary impression of these New Age crazies given license by City Hall. It must have been some golden tongue that got us this protection, I think — no doubt Robbins himself, or one of his smooth-talking sidekicks.

"My body will do everything in its power to insure a safe and pleasurable walk." Robbins has us repeat the embedded command. He reminds us that no one is obligated to walk and that no one will be scorned for not walking. We will know if it's our time, he says. And then, like a big boy at his own birthday party, he gleefully recites a final important instruction, deeply coded in transcendental double-talk: "And remember to forget everything that will either get in the way or otherwise confuse you; *or* forget everything you don't or can't understand; *or* . . . smile, whichever comes first." Being attentive and eager to model our instructor, we all do precisely as he says.

I yawn — it feels like sleepwalking could also happen here. I shiver — at some level I am eager to get on the fire to warm up a bit. I search for my fear, but I am amazed to find it nowhere. Perhaps the movement of fear into power has already taken place. At this instant, I have no doubt that I can walk on fire.

Robbins walks first. Since we are supposed to model him, it is important for all of us to watch him cross the coals, a feat that is clearly a logistical impossibility. Necks are craned; hundreds stretch on tiptoes.

Robbins turns fierce. First he pumps himself up with oxygen, bellowing and seeming to grow bigger with each breath. Next it's eyes up, clenched fist and repetitions of "Cool moss, cool moss." In seconds he marches across, and the crowd roars. He has done it! But then, I have not really seen it. From my vantage point in the fifth row back, I have seen him move, but I have not actually seen him set foot on hot coals. I have no vivid image of his success. But I do not worry; I will see others walk who have seen what I couldn't.

One by one, the staff of the Robbins Research Institute crosses the glowing coals in their master's footsteps. Nobody cries out in pain, nobody leaves hopping with a hotfoot. There is only ecstasy . . . and the blinding flash of a photographer perched high atop her stepladder.

"No flash!" yells Robbins. "No flash!"

Now Robbins is standing at the start of the fiery runway. Before each walk, he checks each person's mental state, exhorting each to get stronger, breathe deeper, look higher. Before each walk, he also adds a light shoulder touch, another NLP cue that supposedly reminds the body that it can do this.

As I am watching all this, it occurs to me that since some scientists claim we are using only 10 percent of our brain's capacity at any given time, even if I *don't* know I can do this, the other 90 percent of me surely does. I feel in danger of getting cocky about this fire, but that is not the real danger. The real danger lies before me, glowing.

My turn is coming closer; there are only about a half dozen or so prospective firewalkers ahead of me. One fellow starts, then seems to shuffle to a halt only one yard out. Suddenly he realizes he is not going forward; and quickly, with Tony's help, he backpedals off the coals. This drama makes me momentarily forget my own. It is apparent that this student is back but not finished. Again with Robbins assistance, he rapidly rebuilds his confidence, clenching his fist and breathing extra deeply. To my amazement, after a 30-second pump-up and lots of shoulder-cueing from Robbins, the fellow starts out again and this time hustles across the fire apparently unharmed.

There are many firewalking styles here. Most people don't linger, simply aiming to get to the other side as quickly as possible. A few seem to delight in the intensity, sauntering across the glow as though it were their one ride in the heavens. Some stomp, others tromp, but no one cries out in pain.

Flashbulbs strobe the scene, now from the onlookers' side. "No flash! No flash!" screams one of the Robbins men. "People could get *burned* here!" But no one has, and no one does. The firewalk is just a metaphor, I remind myself. Can you get burned on a poetic device? It is my turn to find out.

I am now facing the fire, face to face with my greatest fear. After a short walk, either I will have conquered both the fire and my fear, or I will have been fool enough to follow a madman down an insane path to grave physical injury. In spite of the latter possibility, I find myself with the extraordinary feeling of knowing no doubt, of sensing fear only as a vague concept. I feel myself totally "congruent."

"Get stronger! Stronger!" Robbins yells at me, cueing me on the shoulder with his finger.

At this moment, I am as involved and as subjective as I can be. I want to be a good student. I sense that my future as an upright biped depends on it. I charge up my cells with oxygen and anchor myself with a clenched fist. This is my moment of truth.

"Eyes up!" shouts an assistant. "*Higher!*"

I am about to step off the edge of the world, this I know for sure. My mantra brings me back. "Cool moss" occupies my mind, seems to cushion my feet. With all the hot embers before me still swirling up into sparks on whirlwinds, "cool moss" is even on my lips and on the lips of those nearby. Suddenly the vivid image of cool moss replaces the hot reality before me. I recall the exquisite sensation of cool moss on my feet, cooling, cushioning. I am repeating the perfect mantra for this movement. But still, from somewhere, a question arises: Will it be mind over matter, or will matter assert itself and scream with a sizzle that there are limits, and that this is one of them?

"You're ready!" yells Tony, "*Go!*"

I go — out onto the red-hot coals, into the oven of fear . . . and power. It is everything I expected. I am walking on a radiant, pulsing life force that charges without wounding. I am equal to it, meeting fire with fire, glowing with my own radiance. Beneath my feet, crunchy warm objects rearrange themselves with my strides. I can feel other coals tumbling up and over my toes. Though my eyes are looking to the sky, I have the curious sensation of also being able to see where I am walking. While taking in the scene around me, it seems, I am also studying the coals.

Although the firebed is only a half dozen steps across, this seems like one of the longest walks of my life. I am not about to hurry, either. Without my fear to propel me across, I will stretch my own limits and the limits of the walks I have seen thus far. Furthermore, because each of my steps seems to empower me, I am eager for more. This fire is not like any other I have known. I rightly do not know where I am, what I am doing or why I am doing it. I am walking on a rainbow, a rainbow covered with cool moss that looks like a red-hot fire.

With another step, I am even higher in the sky, walking on the Milky Way, the stars beneath my feet. I am Lightfoot, the heavenly spangled walker. Glowing galaxies line my way. Every step is another miracle.

Either time has slowed down or I am out of time. I feel lost, as in ecstatic sex, aware and oblivious at the same time. I feel a warm tingling with each step, something much more akin to electricity than fire. I do not seem to weigh as much; out here my body seems lighter. I am all alone, and the whole world is watching. This is my moment of triumph, yet there is nothing to be proud of. I have connected with a fraction of my capability, realized only a speck more of my human potential.

On the other side of the firebed, I am waiting for myself, smiling patiently, watching me take my first steps. What a good little boy I am, following my teacher's instructions to a tee but adding my own little experiments, as well! I notice that I notice. There is no temperature now — none; all around me feels like body temperature. I am taking my time, but I can hear people screaming, "Go! Go!" I *am* going; in no time I will be there.

Too quickly, the timeless dissolves, and I am back on the ground again, whooping with delight as my unburned feet are hosed off. I have made it to the other side! I have walked on fire. I have turned fear into power.

Scores of firewalkers after me do the same, and Robbins is there, checking and exhorting each. Behind him, a second line feeds into the second bed of coals. Only a few of these walkers get the benefit of Robbins' send-off, being handled instead by an assistant. Over the glowing coalbed, a woman in a long dress runs. A boy seems to bounce. One young man boogies across, dancing on the hottest floor his feet will ever know. We are moving like an assembly line, turning out firewalkers every 20 seconds. The quality control seems excellent; nobody is burned.

By 2:15 the cops are getting antsy. One of them repeatedly tells Robbins to close up shop. Robbins turns down the volume on the music and sends the last few stragglers across the coals. He checks for any holdouts, asking them to step forward if now is their time. When no one responds, he asks for a show of hands of those who attended the seminar but didn't walk. A half dozen shamed hands struggle up.

"Let's have a hand," says Robbins, "for those six who knew what they wanted!" Suddenly we are all applauding the nonwalkers. Robbins has reframed their decision! Tony Robbins may not be a Master in the traditional sense, but he certainly is a master of many things — most assuredly of crowd control. Never is anyone diminished, always everyone is in some way celebrated. Ever the gracious host, Robbins forgets no one, marshaling students and onlookers alike to give another hand for New York's finest. A thousand people clap and cheer the police, and the men and women in blue bask in the warmth of the applause.

From a wheelbarrow, Robbins shovels out the last of the surplus red-hot coals, smooths the beds, then hoses them down. These fires go out, but not the ones inside the firewalkers. Charged and ablaze, we bound up to our seventh-floor home, different people from those who bounded down.

In the men's room, I meet an Oriental man who discounts the whole thing. Too short, he says; in Japan they walk 25 feet or more. We only took a few steps, he complains. The feet are tough and calloused; they need a long time to burn. I check my own cinder-stained feet, blackened but unburnt. I note in particular the thinness of the instep skin. My walk took me over glowing coals that made intimate contact with this baby flesh. Tough? Calloused? Hardly.

Back in the ballroom, the congas are pounding, the stereo is blaring and the air is charged with jubilant wildness. Everybody is a dancer. Everybody — even those who didn't firewalk — has met their fear. This is Woodstock in a highrise, a tribal liftoff in the land of suit and tie. There's a whole lot of shakin' goin' on, with the entire company cavorting "congruently."

After a good while, Robbins cools us down from the stage. "How many got blisters?" he asks his legions, counting the raised hands. "About 10. Ten out of 500. Not Bad. Tell you what to do: When you get home tonight, sit down, make your hand like this, like an arrow, and jam it into here, behind the knees. Do it with both legs even if you were only burned on one. Do it for about 25 minutes, the longer the better." Such a technique, he explains, healed his burns overnight, burns he incurred when coals stuck to his feet beyond the firebed. Someone asks if that arrow-behind-the-knee technique works for all burns. Robbins says no, and he doesn't know the other acupressure points. It is refreshing to hear this 24-

year-old say he doesn't know something.

Next Robbins calls for six people who "just have to speak," and a small band of eager beavers rushes the stage. Rita is disappointed that it was so easy. The gal next to her tells us we're always walking on fire. Another says that now every vision he sees must come true. These people are witnessing like Baptist holy rollers; we have reached the revival phase. Other born-again firewalkers continue the litany. A third-time walker testifies that for years she was afraid to sleep in the dark, but after a couple of firewalks, she turned out the light and slept well. A seasoned New Age journalist asks us to open our hearts and not be afraid of loving each other. And finally, a nine-year-old boy, fresh from his strut across fiery coals, reports that now he'll never be afraid of anything, except having to go to the laundromat with his mother. Tell it, brother!

Following the witnessing, we are treated to a bizarre bit of social welfare, as half a dozen Guardian Angels in red berets trot forward to share the stage with Robbins. It is getting toward three in the morning, and Robbins is telling us how, when he went to distribute food in the South Bronx on Thanksgiving, he was shocked to see that such a worthy organization as the Guardian Angels didn't even have a van. So tonight, with a small part of the profits from the firewalk, he is rectifying that, presenting their young training instructor with a check from Robbins Research. Robbins is practicing what he preaches, constantly creating value for others. The quality of his communication continues to impress.

After the Angels, Robbins tells us to form "hug trains," massaging the shoulders of the person in front of us. As our hug trains wind through the grand ballroom, we are once again in kindergarten, dancing just before nap time. From there, we meld into one huge ring, a thousand hands joining forces. Swaying in unison, we hear the emotion in Robbins' voice, praying: "May the rain fall behind you . . . the sun shine on your face . . . and may the road rise up to meet you."

So ended my first firewalk, another of thousands that has taken place in the United States annually since the father of American firewalking began shepherding people across red-hot coals in 1978.

2

The Father of American Firewalking

In this you rejoice, though now for a little while you may have to suffer various trials, so that the genuineness of your faith . . . is tested by fire.

I Peter 1:7

In many of the world's cultures, there lives a mythic creature, a fabulous man-bird called phoenix that recreates itself through fire. In the Egyptian myth, the phoenix lives for 500 years. When its time comes to die, it builds itself a nest of frankincense, myrrh and other spices, ignites it, and within the fire passes on to another life. With the body of a man and the wings of a bird, the new young phoenix then flies to Egypt, where it places the remains of its former self on the altar of the sun.

To the mystics of Persia, the phoenix was symbolic of immortality, the glory of a human soul reborn from its own dead body. For the medieval Hermeticists, this creature was the embodiment of the alchemical transformation, and "Phoenix" was the name given to initiates who were born again. [1]

Tolly Burkan, the father of the American firewalking movement, is in many ways like the phoenix. Burkan grew up in Parsippany, New Jersey, where he earned money and adulation as a clowning magician. But his seemingly normal, fulsome life began to suffer dramatic erosion in his late teenage years. The successes he had so easily achieved seemed increasingly meaningless, and he began to have recurring thoughts of suicide. Instead of killing himself, however, he hatched what he thought was a better plan: he would merely kill the identity of his old self, then run away and assume a new identity. As Burkan (he pronounces it Bur-KAN) describes it in his autobiography, *Dying to Live*:

> It was a disastrous plan from the start, since the cause of my problems was the very "me" I was taking with me, but in my deluded desperation, I concocted a scheme that would enable me to

> escape from New Jersey to California and to change my identity with forged papers. It seemed like the only possible choice if I didn't want to kill myself. I felt that I simply couldn't continue to live the life of Bruce Tolly Burkan; in order to continue living, maybe to find some happiness, I would have to be a completely new person in a new environment, where nobody had any expectations of me and where I couldn't disappoint anybody no matter what I did.
>
> I couldn't simply run away, however, because it would have been embarrassing to Mrs. New Jersey [his mother, who had won that title] and, furthermore, it might be assumed that I had been kidnapped. In any event, I didn't want people looking for me. So I decided to make it look as if I had drowned. As the plan took shape, I settled on the ocean beach at Asbury Park for the setting of my disappearance. In working out the details, I used every skill of deception I had learned as a magician. If I could pull this off successfully, my disappearance would be my ultimate magic trick. [2]

Still recovering from minor surgery, Burkan nevertheless went forward with his plan, telling his girlfriend he would meet her in the surf, then sneaking over to the bus station and making his getaway. As if by magic, a body was sighted near where Burkan had last been seen, but was swept out to sea before it could be recovered. Burkan was presumed dead, and his family held his wake. Actually, he was living in Los Angeles under an assumed identity, truly a man who did not know who he was.

He eventually returned home, as if from the dead, to a loving, supportive family and girlfriend, all of whom helped ease his transition back to his old self. But Bruce Tolly Burkan was a deeply disturbed man, and despite a good job as a cruise ship social director and magician, with complete access to the floating good life, his next three years were punctuated with pain. After a particularly opulent ball aboard the *S.S Rotterdam,* an event whose richness made it seem all the more hollow, Burkan decided for the second time to take matters into his own hands:

> Several days after the ball, I decided to return to that painless place from which we all come. I had tried to kill myself once before, but then it was because I was so overcome by sadness that I had impulsively seized suicide as a way to escape; this time, two years later, I arrived at the decision "rationally."
>
> While still aboard ship, in the middle of the Pacific, I calmly dissolved a supply of sleeping pills in half a quart of vodka. The last time, with the help of medical technology, the doctors had brought me back even after my heart had ceased to beat. [3]

This time, Burkan's heart didn't quite stop, but it slowed to such a degree that his legs began to decompose. Again the doctors brought him back from the dead.

Bruce Tolly Burkan had faked his death, then twice attempted to take his life, and still he lived on. He picked up the pieces, worked with human potential movement leader Ken Keyes and began to put his life back together. Soon he was helping Keyes in his workshops, then teaching a few on his own. He even co-authored a self-help book with Keyes, entitled *How to Make Your Life Work, or Why Aren't You Happy?*

Subsequently, Burkan retreated to the woodlands of Northern California, where he was visited by an old acquaintance, a woman named Linda. Linda had been living with Ajari Warwick, a Tibetan Buddhist master who taught near San Francisco. Though she had previously had a glorious mane of hair, now her head was shaved bald, part of her current spiritual work. In a matter of hours, her playful energy had spirited to Tolly, and soon he was shaved bald, too.

That night, Linda and Tolly made a fire in the cool darkness, and once more, as Burkan described it, the phoenix was reborn from the flames:

> An hour passed, maybe two. We sat in a close embrace, warmed by the dying flames. When the fire was gone, and the embers glowed red, my trance was broken by Linda rising, and snapping a branch from a nearby pine. She tossed the bough on the bed of red-hot coals and it immediately burst into flames. Without a word, she slipped off her shoes, peeled the socks from her feet, and proceeded to walk slowly across the coals.
>
> "Linda!" I screamed.
>
> She did not flinch but continued to put one foot in front of the other, setting it squarely down on the fiery path. I was numb. My heart pounded wildly. Was I dreaming? What the hell was this about, anyway?
>
> As she finished her walk, I suddenly blurted out, "If you can do it, I can, too . . . can't I?" She smiled. I knew in my heart that I could do it, and I knew Linda would have stopped me if she thought I couldn't.
>
> I ripped the shoes and socks from my feet and bounded onto the runway of fire. It was hot! It was very hot! Even as my mind shrieked and rebelled at the insanity of what I was doing, my heart thrilled with exuberance, my body tingled with delight, and I knew, I knew, my feet would not be burned. I half-laughed and half-shouted as I finished the walk. Before my mind had a chance even to demand that I check my soles, I made an about-face, and again strode the coals. A part of me died that instant, and another part of me was born. What died was a constricting belief system, and what was born was a sense of life's limitlessness.

"How? How is this possible?" I demanded when I finally inspected my unharmed soles.

Linda, ultimately composed, said simply, "I don't know. I really don't care. What does it matter? There's no need for an explanation. It's possible and it's healthy. What else matters?"

Burkan laughed and thanked her profusely for all she had taught him. Again, her reply was straightforward: "I haven't taught you anything. You simply saw me do something, you realized that there was no difference between you and me, and you gave yourself permission to do the same thing." [4]

It was a permission that seemed to fuse a chaotic jumble of talents into a cohesive whole, a permission that allowed a man to walk on fire and find his way. When Burkan returned to Berkeley from the woods, he brought with him an ancient ritual of empowerment, carrying it where all men carry rituals, in his being.

Soon, he considered adding firewalks to his human potential workshops. "The firewalk was the perfect metaphor to encompass all aspects of life," he wrote, "the full spectrum: from anguish to bliss. It was the perfect catalyst to raise fears and doubts as well as to challenge people's concepts about physical reality, what is possible and impossible." [5]

Like the legendary phoenix, Tolly Burkan had been reborn in the glow of the coals. Not only had he been healed and empowered, not only had he found an enthralling activity for his seminars and a new trick for his bag of magic, he had found his mission in life, his very reason for being.

When Burkan began to research the subject of firewalking, he found the data very contradictory. "There was no bottomline conclusion as to why ordinary people could walk on hot coals and not get burned," he concluded. "There wasn't even agreement as to why some people *did* burn!" He continued his personal experiments, firewalking by himself or with small groups of friends, and still continued to teach his human potential seminars. Very rapidly, the two began to mix.

Over a year passed, and in January of 1978, as I was conducting a seminar based on self-awareness principles taught in my books, I decided to introduce the entire group to firewalking. These were paying people who I had never met before, and it never even crossed my mind to use a disclaimer form! However, every member of the group, including an eight-year-old boy, walked without a singe or blister.

Thus was born the world's first firewalking seminar. At first, I only advertised my commercial firewalking courses in California. My personal observations were that anyone could do it, it was only fear that held some people back. Therefore, I made the theme of the seminar "Overcome Fear!"

Things went well until someone was horribly burned at one of these workshops. Until then, I was rather casual about the whole thing; actually believing people couldn't get burned. Barring accidents, I often had wondered about the people who reportedly were injured [firewalking] at different times through history. But the stark realization that I was playing with fire sobered me. The man who was burned in my class appeared to do everything in just the same manner as everyone else in his group and the same as everyone who had ever walked with me before. Yet both his soles were extensively blistered, with some of the skin receiving third-degree burns.

The shock of this incident made me reconsider whether or not to continue my firewalking seminars. Finally, I decided to continue, but with a different perspective. The firewalks would from here on out be themed with reverence and awe. I also initiated disclaimer forms, allowing no one to walk unless they signed.

In these seminars, I stressed the importance of Intuitive Guidance. Once it is plainly seen that walking unharmed on coals is possible for some people, it is only fear and uncertainty that prevents others from walking themselves. Yet fear must be acknowledged, for often its intention is to protect us. To discern between rational choice and irrational fears is the job of Intuitive Guidance. I asked people to listen to all the proposed theories and then to draw their own conclusions after having monitored their Intuitive Guidance system throughout the four-hour course.

Therefore, each individual participant was assuming full responsibility for walking or not walking. Most people walked, around 85 percent, but sometimes a few chose not to walk. After several thousand people had firewalked successfully at my seminars, another person got seriously burned. The second person burned much worse than the first, with skin badly charred on both feet. She was hospitalized for two weeks.

I felt sick. Despite a disclaimer form, my sensitivity caused me to suffer for months.

It was at this point in the evolution of my firewalking career that I decided it would be valuable to have active researchers in the field, besides just myself. During the next several years, I trained others to conduct firewalks with the public at large, reminding them all the time of the very real risks. I shared what I had learned from my own experience; I shared what I had learned about burns, fire laws, weather conditions; and I shared the written research I had complied. It seemed to me that as greater and greater numbers of people firewalked, there would eventually emerge enough data so that some conclusions could be drawn about the phenomenon.

Consequently, America, Europe and Australia were bombarded with advertisements for evening firewalks, and worldwide media

> took notice. By the time I appeared on the [Phil] Donahue Show, tens of thousands of people had walked across beds of hot coals at firewalking seminars taught by myself or someone else using my format. Physicists and engineers were doing it. Scientists, reporters and lay people were walking side by side across countless firepits almost nightly. [6]

Burkan met and married a like-minded human potential teacher, Peggy Dylan, and together they taught firewalking seminars and parented a child, Amber. Again, they retreated to the tranquility and beauty of the mountains of northern California, settling in Twain Harte. There they introduced thousands of ordinary Americans to the extraordinary possibility of striking up a new relationship with fire and, quite possibly, with life itself.

Questing for a closer look at the father of American firewalking, I viewed highlights of a typical Tolly Burkan seminar, captured on videotape in 1983. The tape begins in a lofty hall where, before the firewalk, Tolly and Peggy share their insights with several dozen seminar students. Outside, clearly visible through the floor-to-ceiling window behind them, a bonfire rages in the night. Tolly opens:

"In all the courses we teach, we always begin by asking people; 'What is your intention tonight?' Once you're really clear on your intention for being here, I can just do what I do and say what I say, and you will extract from the evening whatever it is that you need to get your intentions met. Once you know what you want, then my job's very easy. And if you *don't* know what you want, if you're not clear on what your intention is, then you're like a ship without a rudder . . . the wind can blow you this way, blow you that way . . . and the chances of you landing on target are rather slim."

It struck me, as I watched the video, that Burkan came across as a folksy camp counselor. What a different delivery from his modeler and firewalk rival, Tony Robbins, the slick salesman!

Continuing on video, Burkan asks his students to look inside and ask themselves why they came. Then he announces an introduction process in which each student will stand, say his or her name and state their purpose in coming.

One by one, the students stand and state their cases. One says he saw a firewalking poster and decided he wanted to get beyond all his fears and limitations. Another says she wants to master the illusions inside her brain. Others say they want to test their limits, grow, believe in miracles. And the last woman says something that touches everybody: "I want to learn how to trust myself," she says, "'cause it hurts so bad not to."

Burkan reminds those at the gathering that their greatest limitation is fear. "Nothing limits us more than *fear,*" he says. "The methods we're going to give you tonight are methods to overcome *fear*. Now, I'm not saying when you get out there, you'll be free from fear, but I'm saying the fear won't stop you. You will have tools that will enable you to *experience* the fear — and then walk right through it. And if you can do it tonight, and step out on that coal bed, you'll be able to do it the next time you want to ask for a job or a raise in salary."

Burkan continues. "The first technique we're going to introduce you to is so incredibly simple . . . that you might not appreciate the power it has . . ." And on a huge, oversize pad (very much like the one Tony Robbins uses, I notice) and with a magic marker very much like the one Tony Robbins uses, Burkan prints the words: "Pay Attention."

"Pay attention," he says. "We're not just talking about casual attention. I would like you to learn this evening how to pay attention *one hundred* per cent."

"It's quite magical," he goes on. "When you learn how to pay attention 100 percent, your whole experience of life is going to be transformed. This is a very ancient idea. Thousands of years ago, it was given the name *Tantra*." He writes the word on the board. "For example, if you smell a flower, and you pay attention to the smell of the flower, 100 percent, you become the smell of the flower. You *become* it! Can you imagine what your life would be like if you were able to pay attention like that every moment? There would no longer be any such thing as an ordinary moment. Everything would become magical. That's the essence of *Tantra.*

"Now, to help you remember the idea of learning how to pay attention 100 percent, I'm going to do a little magic show. The magic show is meant to be fun; it's not meant to be profound. First of all, I should tell you that I have no magical powers; everything I'm about to show you is a trick that can be learned from books. It's just to demonstrate False Evidence Appearing Real (FEAR); I'm going to make things appear, disappear, change shape, change size. And what it's going to do is remind you how frequently false evidence really does appear real. So often you go through life thinking you understand what's going on here, and so much of what you call reality is just an illusion."

Burkan makes a pencil disappear into a handkerchief. "Abra-cadabra!" he intones. "False Evidence Appearing Real," he repeats, writing "FEAR" on the pad. He continues, explaining the nature of fear and where it comes from. He speaks of the brain's "biocomputer" that stores information and makes decisions based on past experiences, and how those experiences create the fears, patterns, habits and judgments that dominate our lives. All of these, he insists, can be changed in an instant.

"You can change, right now!" he says. "If you believed all your life that walking out on coals at 1300 degrees would burn your feet, and then tonight you walk on these coals and you don't burn your feet, you're never going to go back to that old belief again. Through your direct experience of the truth, you will have reprogrammed your biocomputer.

"Right now, I'm going to give you the secret of firewalking. Here it is.

If you're sleeping, wake up now! Here it is: when you stand in front of the coal bed, if you can't take the first step and walk through that membrane of fear — if you can't take that first step — you're in the category of people that can't walk on fire." He pauses dramatically. "Did you get it?" he asks. "Did you *get* it? If you can't take the first step, you can't walk on fire. If you *can* take the first step, just keep *walking*! Because in that moment, when you take that first step, something incredible happens: the chemistry in your body changes."

Burkan explains some of the workings of the brain and the incredible variety of powerful chemicals that are produced in the body, all at the brain's direction. "My belief is that firewalking is not so different from the 90-pound grandma lifting the car off her trapped grandchild. Or remissions of cancer. Some process in here," he says, pointing to his head, "is able to affect physical form, physical reality. What we have just recently discovered is that neuro-peptides are released in response to the thoughts we run through our minds. When you think positive thoughts, you change the chemistry of your brain one way. When you think negative thoughts, you change the chemistry of your brain another way. If you change the chemistry of your brain, of course, you change the chemistry of your whole body.

"Now we're starting to discover, medically, something which yogis knew about thousands of years ago: Mind over matter. Where thought goes, energy flows. What goes on in here," he says, again pointing to his head, "affects what goes on out here." He rubs his arm. "So it's very important when you walk out on those coals to see what thoughts you're holding in your mind. See, if you believe that walking out on the coal bed is going to result in your death — if you have a picture in your mind of stepping out onto the coals, bursting into flame and melting back down to a greasy black smudge — then you're not going to walk out there. You're not stupid. So before you walk out there, you've already done something to allow yourself to take that first step. You've already decided that you're not going to burn yourself. The thought which allows you to take that step means you've already changed the chemistry of your body, and your body will protect itself. Obviously . . . *obviously*. So when you take that step, just keep walking! And that's the whole secret of firewalking: knowing, before you take the first step, that you're not going to burn your feet.

"Our job this evening," Burkan continues, "is to only assist you in taking one step. The Sufis say the journey of a thousand miles always begins with one step. Our three methods are only to help you take one step. . . . The first is: pay attention. The second actually has two parts to it. The first part is: imagine the worst that can possibly happen. If you can't accept the worst, if you're not prepared for the worst, then don't walk on the coal bed tonight. So the first part of this technique is: be prepared for the worst. And now, release those pictures . . . let them go. And now what I want you to do is: expect the best. It's just a matter of throwing a little switch in your head."

Before Burkan goes on to explain the last of the three methods, he mentions that no one will be allowed even to come outside to watch the firewalk unless they've taken off their shoes and socks and rolled up their pantlegs. As everyone does so, he says, "Notice what's going on in your body right now. When you go outside, this sensation might still be in your body. But you don't have to experience it as fear."

Finally he gets to the last part. "Now the last method has four points to it. The first point is: know where you are. Obviously, if you're going to take a trip to Kansas, you're going to have to locate your destination on a map as well as where you are or you're never going to get there. . . . Acknowledge your fear! That's the first step in overcoming it. . . . Number two is: know where you want to go." He writes with magic marker and repeats, "Know where you want to go. This means, set an intention. . . . Where do you want to go? Be specific! There's so much power that the mind has, once you focus it. Number three, choose a plan of action." He writes it and repeats it. "And the last point on this four-point method is, follow your plan. That means, go for it!"

After explaining that no one is obligated to walk the coals, and that sometimes it is wiser not to, Burkan takes his barefoot students outside to face the fire, arriving just as the fire breaks into orange coals. From the video screen and from accounts I have heard, it appears that Burkan's firebeds are considerably hotter than those of Tony Robbins.

His firewalking method is quite different, too. Instead of the slightly stiff, militaristic strides that Robbins takes across the coals, with eyes up and fist clenched, Burkan saunters across with love and openness, carefully watching where he is going. Effortlessly trodding a shifting mass of glowing coals, he makes it look easy — and fun. Others follow. There is a party spirit here, a mellow, good-time flavor along with a mystical, New Age flair.

Back inside, Burkan carefully and forcefully empowers the entire gathering: "Now, if you walked on the coals tonight, what I'd like to have you do is write on that card 'I walked on fire, I can do anything I choose.' If you didn't walk, on your card, write 'I can *always* trust my inner guidance!' Underline the word 'always' and put an exclamation point after that sentence!" [7]

By the late 1980s, the spark of Burkan's initial firewalking seminar had been fanned into roaring flames. He had trained hundreds of firewalking teachers, guided countless thousands of firewalkers over the coals, appeared in segments on all the major TV networks, authored books, lectured at major universities and was generally having the time of his life. His work had not only attracted public and media attention, but medical researchers also became intrigued by some of the implications of firewalking. Wrote Andrew Weil, M.D., author of *Health and Healing* and *The Natural Mind*, himself a firewalker:

> Americans, large numbers of Americans, learning to walk on red-hot coals: the idea would have been preposterous a few years ago. . . . Now we see people of all sorts learning to walk over beds of glowing coals after a few hours' participation in seminars taught by Tolly Burkan and by others who learned from him. . . . Tolly Burkan's main achievement is not his methods but his demonstration that firewalking is not foreign and not unattainable. . . . this has profound implications for health and medicine. [8]

By 1989, the flame of Burkan's firewalking had reached bonfire proportions. That fall, he founded the nonprofit Firewalking Institute for Research and Education (FIRE) near his home in Twain Harte. The first issue of the *FIRE* newsletter clearly spelled out the organization's aims: to investigate firewalking and the affect of mental states on the physical body; to sponsor firewalks for private and public groups; and to train firewalking instructors. [9]

The first issue of the institute's newsletter also announced free firewalks on the first Sunday of each month, as well as a week-long firewalking instructor training to be led by Burkan personally for a fee of $595. Subsequent issues announced an extensive national firewalking calendar, with dozens of firewalks offered by Burkan or his trained instructors in cities and towns all over the country. And one issue contained a plea for a research grant to conduct a thorough investigation of the firewalking phenomenon, including exactly what changes occur in the brain and body, to what degree the human mind contributes to immunity from burning, and potential applications of these discoveries to preventive health care, treating burn victims and bolstering immunity. [10]

In keeping with Burkan's latest aims for promoting the firewalk, more recent issues of the *FIRE* newsletter have offered an ever-expanding series of instructor's trainings (at prices from $1,000 to $2,500). Among the activities included in the week-long intensives are Greek firedancing, a Buddhist firewalking ceremony and a 40-foot firewalk.

In the mid-'80s, right after I firewalked with Tony Robbins, I heard of a firewalking seminar being offered by two of Burkan's trained instructors, Jon Webster and Mimi Katzenbach. One afternoon, at a rural home in Rhinebeck, New York, I attended their introductory lecture and stayed after the group broke up to talk with them.

Jon Webster, who knew that I had firewalked with Tony Robbins, was especially eager to hear my impressions of him and to share a few tidbits of gossip from the firewalker's world. First off, he said, Tony taped Tolly's workshop and stole it. Tolly's lawyer called and complained that it was copyrighted material. Tony reportedly paid a small fee and cooled their jets. Despite what he frequently claims, Webster continued, Tony Robbins never did really grab the hot coals in his bare hands the first time he walked at Tolly's. Damning too, was Webster's news that not only did Robbins steal Burkan's act, but Tony actually hired a clown to perform magic tricks similar to Tolly's. Shaking his head, Webster smiled as he estimated Robbins' income. Two hundred heads a night at a hundred bucks a head, times seven nights a week. A megabuck operation, Webster figured, all stolen from Tolly.

I told Webster I wasn't surprised, but that I remained impressed by Robbins, if for no other reason than that he seemed to me a man quintessentially himself, a young star who has wholeheartedly realized his own nature. I told him I also liked the context that Ribbons had spun out and the incongruity of his clean-cut, natty style contrasted with the savage messiness of the firewalk itself.

Still more dirt on Robbins rose to the surface. According to Webster, unlike Tolly, who trains teachers and then sets them free, Tony's trained instructors become his employees, teaching the firewalk *for* him. For this reason, Webster said, several of Tony's teachers have rebelled and set out on their own, regardless of their original agreements with him.

Still, I had to wonder whether I would have been burned had I not gone through all of Robbins' prep and modeling lessons. I still wondered about the possibly magical possibilities of Neuro-Linguistic Programming and what it had to do with firewalking. Burkan never mentioned it, nor was it likely that an African tribal chief or a Sri Lankan monk was familiar with it.

Tony Robbins and Tolly Burkan, two fired-up men with completely different styles, each encouraging others on their individual quests of self-discovery. I knew very well I would never cease in that search. Just how deep *is* my fear of fire? How deep is my responsive physiology, normally programmed to blister? Just what are the limits of my ability to transform fire into a pure energizer, a spiritual uplifter?

By this time, I had come to realize one thing very clearly: the firewalk is so hot that even my brief acquaintance with it had raised my psychic temperature. It had also raised a host of unanswerable questions about who I was — who *any* of us might be. I needed to experiment some more, take another walk, test my own limits again.

3

The Firewalk Comes to Public School #191

". . . he who realizes the truth of the body can then realize the truth of the universe.

The Ratnasara

After my initial firewalk with Tony Robbins, and after tracing the footsteps of Tolly Burkan's fascinating odyssey, I find myself eager for more, hungry for wider contexts and fuller explanations of the firewalking phenomenon. Consequently, when I hear of a Taoist firewalk on Manhattan's upper West Side, I find my feet quivering in anticipation.

I phone the Taoist Esoteric Yoga Center and Foundation. There, Maneewan Chia, the wife of Master Mantak Chia, reaffirms the time of the "MicroCosmic Orbit Meditation" and the master's upcoming firewalk. I phone twice more, once getting the master himself. He tells me the workshop centers on an old Taoist tradition of using fire to overcome fear.

Knowing that Master Chia attended Tony Robbins' firewalk the very night I did, I am somewhat suspicious. My suspicions increase at the master's frequent use of buzzwords like "firewalking workshop" and "fire to overcome fear." By utilizing an inner smile, the master says, it is possible to transform fear into power. When I ask if I can attend the workshop and take pictures, he says yes, providing we can come to some sort of an "agreement." I tell him truthfully that I am a Taoist myself and that I am sure we will have no problems.

That night, at Public School #191, on the upper West Side near Lincoln Center, I am slightly rocked by the registration scene. Though very sparsely attended by Tony Robbins' standards — there are only 60-70 people as opposed to 500 — the whole setup seems to be a clone of his. A dozen staffers; payments of $125; T-shirts; books (*Awaken Healing Energy Through the Tao* and *Taoist Secrets of Love*); and the workshop package, replete with firewalk pen — and, of all things, firewalk matches!

After passing through the receiving line, I take a seat near the rear of the school auditorium. I try to remain nonjudgmental, but something about this setup leaves me very disturbed. I am growing attached to the sacred possibilities of the firewalk. The more I investigate, the more I see a distressing pattern of Americanization. The event seems to me increasingly crass, if not profane.

Before I recover my journalist's equilibrium, an aide named John offers two of the master's books. He says he wants me to feel their friendliness, and I do. Then he tells me this evening is unique because it brings together the two highest teachers, Mantak Chia and Larry Short, of the two highest teachings, Taoism and Tantra. Over the years, I've heard this "My master is the highest and my way is the highest" rap so often it's coming out my ears. Consequently, it takes a great effort of will not to look away from this earnest salesman.

Following some intense and righteous proselytizing, John finally leaves, and I look at the literature. First, I peruse the mailer/preregistration form, showing Larry Short firewalking and announcing "The New York Step to Power." The back panel boasts: "Larry Short and Master Chia have shown hundreds of people nationwide the way to break through your belief systems about what you can and can not do. Learn to change STOPS into STEPS, and achieve outrageous goals in your life. The 'Steps to Power' workshop — an opportunity to experience changing fear into power by learning to walk safely across a bed of hot coals."

Inside, the mailer outlines "The Firewalk Beyond Belief." To the prospective firewalker, it beckons: "Learn how the Secret Power of an inner smile transforms your fear into power. Learn to conserve, recycle, and increase your healing energy for yourself and others. Experience personal power and master the impossible: walk barefoot across a bed of hot coals and not burn (only if you choose)."

To me, all this smells suspiciously like Tony Robbins' cooking (or possibly Tolly Burkan's) with the addition of a little smile sauce; however, the profile of Master Chia seems impressive. An energetic, 42-year-old Thai, Chia was once a copier salesman for the Gestetner Company of Thailand. More to the point, he has also been a teacher of kundalini yoga, Thai boxing, t'ai chi, chi kung, and Taoist sexual transmutation. In addition, he has studied Western medicine and anatomy. His books are dense and without fluff; he is apparently a wellspring of real Taoist esoteric knowledge.

After reading the mailer, I am feeling better about this firewalk. Maybe I will hear something new, I think, something that allows me to see how the whole process of fire immunity is controlled and affected. Maybe Master Chia will enlighten me, further empower me. Maybe his wisdom will help me take the evening beyond mere research.

Before the seminar begins, Master Chia's son Maxie bounces in. Maxie is a five-year-old dynamo, living testimony to his father's advocacy of the inner and outer smile. The little master impishly boasts about how he snuck in without his ID badge, and we revel in his mischief. He is as cute as they come, an advertisement for the glory of godly marriage. And he is fun. I entice him into a palms up/palms down handclap game. We touch palms, giggle and try to intuit the other's next move. It's slap, giggle, sense; slap, giggle, sense. And it is fun.

After a last bit of extra play, Maxie reluctantly leaves the action at his father's bidding. Momentarily, Master Chia is joined by his firewalk partner, American Tantric master Larry Short, a not-too-tall, stocky schoolteacher type. According to the "Steps to Power" flier, Short is the director of the Institute for Total Person Facilitation; founder and spiritual head of Grace Essence Fellowship; a member of Avanta, the Menninger Institute and the Lindisfarne Circle of Friends; and an NLP Programmer of 10 years' experience.

Master Chia begins, introducing us to the two energies: "fear energy" and "smile energy." Then he takes us through an "inner smile meditation," encouraging us to let our smile energy flow through our organs like a gentle waterfall, melting away all tension. If *we* don't smile to our organs, he asks us, who will?

Larry Short then picks up the ball, relating an Indian story about space beings who arrive on earth and ask how they can tell who is human. Humans, say the Indians, are the ones who sit around the fire, share food and tell stories.

We 60 or 70 humans are finished with stories for the moment; now it is time to light our own fire. This time, the coals will come from a single blaze no bigger than a large campfire. As we gather around it, Short asks us to celebrate its warmth and protection. Master Chia has us smile to the fire. If we smile to the fire, he says, it will be our best friend, our ally.

Back inside, Short suggests that we burn up our fears — better them than our feet, he says. Then on cards, he asks us to write down our fears and other things that tend to sabotage our lives. The writing, he says, can be in a very personal form, intelligible possibly only to us, because "I'm the one who has to know, I'm the one who has to let go."

At this point, I am a bit dizzy, swaying in my seat. Others are chatting or reading. I remind myself that this is an actual workshop; yet it is having less impact — at least on me — than the free introductory lecture put on by Tolly Burkan's students. I am a bit mystified. Supposedly, these men are heavyweights. They seem well meaning, but they are not even commanding the full attention of their audience.

While we write out our fear cards (mine remains curiously blank), I check over the workshop booklet. Entitled *The Healing Tao,* it is prefaced by the warning: "Respect the System and Respect the Master and You Will Naturally Receive True Transmission. Slight the System and Slight the Master and You Might as well not Waste Your Time."

How comforting, I think, that the booklet is addressing my current mindset. While I have great respect for the Tao and for the direction of both these men's efforts, the more I see of them, the less I think they should be leading this or any firewalk.

The firewalking instructions in the booklet only add to my growing uneasiness. Headlined "SMILE TO THE FIRE," the directions look like warmed-over Tony Robbins surreptitiously blended with a dash of Chia and a little Short. And considering that some of Tony Robbins may really be warmed-over Tolly Burkan, by this time Short's and Chia's personal qualities were becoming of critical concern to me.

Larry Short brings us up from our fears, relating his own firewalking history. "I first contacted firewalking about 20 years ago," he says. I perk up with the possibility that he has practiced it for years. But then he goes on to sketch out a vague Zen history, including such feats as taking icy baths and breaking boards. With each passing sentence, Short gets increasingly vague. Then, almost under his breath, he slips in the fact that the first time he actually firewalked was right here in New York, around the same time I did — with Tony Robbins!

Short goes on, but now I don't trust him. He says some interesting things, but they do not find their mark. We return to the fire outside, toss in our fear cards and watch them burn, endeavoring to see the fire as a respected and powerful friend. For the fire I feel great respect and friendship; for Masters Chia and Short, I feel a growing cynicism.

The countdown continues as Short and Chia wind up the preliminaries. If you're casual with the fire, Short says, you could be a casualty. A bearded lad asks Short what he will be looking for in people before he sends them out on the hot coals. Short hedges, then mentions a "certain state" that's "hard to describe."

Inside again, Master Chia has us take our smiles further, moving them around our bodies. We take our smiles through our navel, the place where energy is produced and stored. We men also take our smiles through the "sperm palace," while the women take them through the "ovary palace." The master chides us for our American habit of overeating, trying to shame us into realizing that we are "spending a lot of money feeding the toilet." Our gluttonous behavior, he says, makes the toilet the most expensive piece of furniture in the house. "Smile," the master exhorts us, "and feel the fear in the throat open like a flower blossoming."

Short takes over and reminds us that fire *can* burn but that it doesn't *have* to burn. He goes on to say that we can't *become* happy, we can only *be* happy. Then, to demonstrate fear into power and the inner smile, Short calls for several brave volunteers to come up onto the stage. The brave group onstage (and we less courageous ones who have stayed in our seats) then watch as Short places the feathered end of a wooden arrow against the wall and its sharply pointed tip in the hollow of his throat. Reminding us that the danger point is often also the breakthrough point and that the power of the inner smile is awesome, Short leans forward, bending and finally breaking the arrow. One by one, the brave volunteers smile, lean forward and break their arrows, too. A couple of them look like they have gotten their money's worth right there, clutching their broken arrow parts tighter than any boy with a big leaguer's broken bat.

Short talks to us about losing our "separateness" and takes us on some breathing exercises. Then, whipping this limp affair into its final count down procedures, he gives us the vital firewalk instructions: "See your success, see yourself on the other side."

With militaristic urgency, Master Chia commands us to "Smile! Smile! Smile! . . . Smile! Smile! Smile!" Then, strutting proudly across the stage, he exhorts us to "walk with elegance!" Short hastily joins him, upstaging the master by giving his own demonstration of how to walk ("don't hop, skip or jump"). We also might want to pray, Short says, or we might want to say something else, but don't say something popular like "Cool moss, cool moss." "Oh — and don't forget to wipe your feet," he blurts out. "Stay in state and wipe your feet!"

Now I am *really* thrown for a loop. Besides being a direct quote from Tony Robbins, this statement falsely implies that we have been taught how to access instantly some special state before stepping out onto the coals. Both "masters" also rush these instructions, as if they were mere afterthoughts. No matter, I think; not everybody is paying attention, anyway. The atmosphere now more closely resembles a singles cookout than a firewalk.

Finally we adjourn to the fire. To my amazement, the bed of coals is no more than four feet long. I am at a firehop! It will be a courageous and determined walker who manages to get three steps on these coals.

Short apologizes for the short bed and explains that the fire started the concrete exploding on the playground, so they had to make it smaller. A gent in a business suit hoses down the whole area. He continues hosing even after both masters tell him to desist, dousing the upper edge of the small, square coalbed. Now the coals are glowing orange hot. The fire is nothing to fool with, but its postage-stamp size has diminished the drama considerably. Joining hands with Master Chia, Master Short calls for the cameras. Though I am loaded with special film, lenses and a tripod, I have no interest in shooting this coalbed, so unimpressive does it seem.

Then they do it. Hand in hand, the "masters" traverse the hot coals, Short managing two quick contacts and Master Chia hopping across with one quick touchdown followed by a high-stepping bound. Elegance this is not; if the "master" is controlling anything here, I think, it is the duration of his contact with the coals. His high-step seems fearful and ungainly, his smile after seems nervous. Once again, the two "masters" hippity-hop across the coal square, and once again, they hardly make contact with it. The small crowd applauds, and the gurus bask in their apparently renewed power.

After this dubious display, I recall tales of Tony Robbins sending his students *elegantly* across 35 feet of hot coals. Personally, I have paid nothing for this firewalk; I am here as a guest. But somehow I feel gypped. I am not much in the mood for a firewalk and in no way exalted by these firewalk leaders. On the other hand, I am eager to use the fire for my own purposes. I am researching not only firewalking but also fire immunity, the ability to safely withstand long-term contact with red-hot coals. Toward this end, I advance in line for entry onto the little glowing square.

At the front of the line, Master Chia checks me over. I stare into the coals, but he demands that I lift my eyes up. The radiant firebed is so small and the level of the coals so much lower than the surrounding concrete that, without an accurate fix on the fire, I figure I could fall into it and clunk my head on the other side. The ground is also wet underfoot, and that doesn't feel right, either. In spite of these annoyances, I inhale deeply through my nose, access some of my accrued power, visualize myself already across, and slip into a silent repetition of "Cool moss . . . cool moss."

This time, it is not my intent to hippity-hop, to high-step or even to walk elegantly. In order for me to find out anything from this fire, I will have to stand in it for at least a few seconds. I remember that my recent visits to the Eileen Garrett Library at the Parapsychology Foundation have uncovered numerous, well-documented accounts of people who displayed the ability to maintain long contact with red-hot coals without burning. Although I have not been trained for this, it is, at present, my only avenue to the unplumbed depths of the fire. For a few seconds, I will trust flesh to intuition, body to spirit. At this moment, I have high hopes for my own "congruency" and feel a profound urgency that my being and body must cooperate. I am empowered with the knowledge that many others have done this before me, and that many of them did not know what they were doing, either.

Now is my moment of truth. The fire is waiting, toasting my face. I take a step into it, firmly planting my feet and digging them into the glowing coals. As I stand there, eyes to the night sky, my legs shuffle of their own accord. They are not burned; they are electrified. I am not in the heavens this time, not walking on stars or cool moss. This time I am in the fire square, truth or consequences. This time I am marking time, standing in place, at attention and at ease, on a treadmill going nowhere.

The little square of red-hot coals feels like velvet. Softly cuddled in radiant electricity, again I see everywhere as I fix my eyes on the night sky. I see my feet bathed in glowing, orange coals, more comfortable in this fire than they have been on many a hot beach. Then gradually I feel myself in a kind of quicksand; nature seems to be swallowing me. In the next instant, all is reversed; I am a messenger, a lightning bolt leaping up from the earth to the heavens.

Then the earth returns. Sensation returns. Heat rises rapidly into my right sole. I shift my shuffle into gear, take another step in the coals, then hop up and out. After my emergence from the glowing pit, the others congratulate me profusely, but I do not feel like claiming victory. On the contrary, I feel slightly burned in every respect.

Many others have yet to walk, and there is still the after-walk tally to come, but I am not interested. I have no room left for show and tell. I am too busy assimilating. Impressions are flooding me from the inside out. It is already clear to me that so varied are the firewalk preparations and so varied the attentions of individual firewalkers that the common thread of this phenomenon must be profoundly simple. Either we can all firewalk — or most of us can and always could — or firewalking is simply an act of faith.

I realize that I am still a long way from any conclusions, but at least now I am beginning to distinguish between limited and absolute fire immunity. My own burns — two minor, dime-sized blisters — are markers for my research now, strange signposts between realms, dividing the territory where fire burns from the land of total immunity.

Mysteries of the fire are flaring in front of me. Burning questions are raised in the brilliance, none yet answered. I need some distance from this feet-first approach. From the hot coals, I retreat for perspective, to heal and to ponder.

4

A Firewalk Through History

. . . strong in faith, we walk through the midst of fire, and press our footsteps in the glowing mass.

Virgil, *The Aeneid*

How on earth, I wondered, did humanity come to the notion that there might be some purpose in walking on fire? How is it that a host of poetic and inventive firewalking and firehandling ceremonies have evolved, all of apparently great power? After my own firewalking experiences, I was eager to know the answers to these and myriad other burning questions.

My curiosity led me to many a library, where for days and weeks I pored over every firewalking account I could get my hands on. I made many discoveries. I was fascinated to find that in many cultures and times, firewalking was (and still is) a ritual performed for a wide variety of purposes. Among Christian adherents, for example, it was frequently used to determine guilt or innocence. As a rite of purification, healing, initiation and devotion, it has long been a thread in the cultural tapestry of dozens of countries worldwide. And most recently, of course, it has surfaced in the United States and other industrial nations as a ritual of empowerment.

Not until recent years has firewalking ever been practiced by great numbers of people in any one country. For centuries, though, it has been purposefully woven into the religions and cultures of many places. I was also startled to discover that some cultures have developed a tradition of dancing on fire — and astounded to run across a number of well-documented accounts of individuals who seemed to have complete immunity to fire. Some of the highlights of my personal firewalk through history and around the world follow, a search that served to push me even deeper into the mysteries of the coals and the marvelous workings of the human mind and body.

ANCIENT AND BIBLICAL REFERENCES

Writers of antiquity, including Virgil, reported on firewalking. In his 1890 book, *The Golden Bough*, Scottish anthropologist Sir James Frazer devoted a whole section to the "fire-walk," noting:

> At Castabala, in Cappadocia, the priestesses of an Asiatic goddess . . . used to walk barefoot through a furnace of hot charcoal and take no harm. Again, at the foot of Mount Soracte, in Italy, there was a sanctuary of the goddess Feronia, where once a year the men of certain families walked barefoot, but unscathed, over the glowing embers and ashes of a great fire of pinewood in the presence of a vast multitude, who had assembled from all the country around about to pay their devotions to the deity or to ply their business at the fair. [1]

There are numerous references to firewalking in the Bible. The Old Testament story of the fall of King Tyre about 600 BC in ancient Phoenicia, for example, is highlighted by a firewalk: "I had provided you with a guardian cherub, you were on the holy mountain; you walked amid red hot coals." (Ezekiel 23: 14-16) King Tyre was destroyed after walking on fire, because, as Ezekiel implies, God was displeased with him for pretending to be a god.

Another instance of the Jewish prohibition on firewalking is found in Deuteronomy 18:9-12. Says the Old Testament: "When you come into the land Yahweh your God gives you, you must not fall into the habit of initiating the detestable practices of the natives. There must never be anyone among you who makes his son or daughter pass through fire . . ." This prohibition was apparently necessary because many Hebrews had incorporated Assyrian forms from the cult of Moloch into their own religious practices, and one of these practices was sending their firstborn children through a furnace of fire. [2]

In the New Testament, part of the book of Hebrews actually recounts stories of Old Testament faith. Most remarkably, the Book of Daniel recounts the story of Shadrach, Meshach and Abednego and their clash with Nebuchadnezzar, the King of Babylonia. In the 6th century BC, this conceited, domineering ruler put down a revolt in Jerusalem, practically destroying the city. Thereafter, he made an "image of gold," 60 cubits by six, and commanded all in his kingdom to worship it. At the dedication ceremonies, a group of Chaldeans came forward and informed the King that several Jews whom he had appointed to watch over the affairs of the province of Babylon were not worshipping the image he had set up. These men were Shadrach, Meshach and Abednego. In a furious rage, Nebuchadnezzar commanded that the willful trio be brought before him. He gave them one more chance to bow down and worship, warning them that if they did not, they would immediately be cast into a "burning fiery furnace."

Shadrach, Meshach and Abednego replied, "O Nebuchadnezzar, we have no need to answer you in this matter. If it be so, our god whom we serve is able to deliver us from the burning fiery furnace; and he will deliver us out of your hand, O king."

Nebuchadnezzar was enraged. According to the Bible, he ordered the furnace to be heated seven times hotter than usual. Then he ordered the three men bound and cast into the fire. The fire was so hot, it immediately incinerated the soldiers who threw the men in, but the three themselves remained unscathed in the midst of the furnace.

King Nebuchadnezzar was astonished, saying to his counselors, "Did we not cast three men bound into the fire?" They answered him, "True, O king." And he replied, "But I see four men loose, walking in the midst of fire, and they are not hurt; and the appearance of the fourth is like a son of the gods."

Nebuchadnezzar went to the door of the furnace and called to Shadrach, Meshach and Abednego to come out. They did so, and all who were gathered there saw that "the fire had not any power over the bodies of those men; the hair of their heads was not singed, their mantles were not harmed, and no smell of fire had come upon them."

Nebuchadnezzar was so mightily impressed that he cried out, "Blessed be the God of Shadrach, Meshach, and Abednego, who has sent his angel and delivered his servants who trusted in him, and set at nought the king's command, and yielded up their bodies rather than worship and serve any god except their own God." Moreover, he gave all three promotions in the province of Babylon and decreed that anyone who spoke ill of their God would be torn limb from limb and their houses laid in ruins.

This fascinating story operates on many levels. On one level, it is the story of Nebuchadnezzar's pagan idolatry and egocentricity; on another, it is the story of Shadrach, Meshach and Abednego's abiding faith in Yahweh, god of the Hebrew prophets. It is also a parable about the power of faith to deliver us from the hottest fires into which life throws us. Most fascinating of all, as I was soon to discover, there is strong historical evidence that this story might have operated on a literal as well as a figurative level.

The Bible itself suggests other references to firewalking and fire immunity. In the book of Isaiah, Chapter 43, is found the following message to the faithful: "Fear not," says God to Jacob and the people of Israel, "for I have redeemed you; I have called you by name, you are mine. When you pass through the waters, I will be with you; and through the rivers, they shall not overwhelm you; when you walk through fire, you shall not be burned, and the flame shall not consume you."

In a related vein, Proverbs 6:28 asks the provocative question: "Can one go upon hot coals and his feet not be burned?" Here, however, the question is asked in the context of the faithless sinner, the implied answer being that if one walks on hot coals (or plays with fire), one will inevitably be burned.

A figurative trial by fire is the subject of several New Testament passages in the First Letter of Peter, as well as Paul's letter to the Corinthians: ". . . and the fire will test what sort of work each one has done. If the work which any man has built on the foundation survives, he will receive a reward. If any man's work is burned up, he will suffer loss, though he himself will be saved, but only as through fire." (1 Cor 3:12-15) Here, then, the fire test is sanctified, and only through it, can a man or his works be proved.

In the gospel of Luke, when the multitudes ask John the Baptist if he is the Christ, John answers them, "I baptize you with water; but he who is mightier than I is coming, the thong of whose sandals I am not worthy to untie; he will baptize you with the Holy Spirit and with fire . . ." (Luke 3:16). Since John is baptizing people with real, literal water, which has symbolic connotations, it is not farfetched to imagine that he means Christ will baptize with real, literal fire, equally symbolic.

This theme is repeated frequently. The apocalyptic vision of the Bible and of other holy books, for example, depicts the world coming to a climactic close in a fury of fire, with the faithful somehow surviving. Similarly, according to the ancient Persian prophet Zoroaster, in the final war between good and evil, fire will cast the deciding vote. "Fire and death will swirl over all" he says, and everyone will have to pass through boiling lava. To the just and righteous, the lava will be "as warm as milk," but to the wicked, it will be "scalding and fatal." [3]

THE CHRISTIAN TRIAL BY FIRE

Until fairly recent times, a literal trial by fire was a fixture in many cultures, serving as a kind of red-hot lie detector test. In the Hindu religious epic, *The Ramayana*, the wife of Rama proves her purity by walking unharmed over red-hot iron. In early times, under the influence of Germanic law, most nations throughout the Indo-European region also employed an ordeal by fire as a method of ascertaining guilt. Soon, the Christian Church began to adopt the trial, as well.

One of the Christian fire tests documented recounts the exploits of the Bishop of Smyrna in the year AD 155. Condemned to be burned at the stake because he would not recognize the Roman emperor, the 86-year-old bishop was led into the stadium at Smyrna (in what is now Turkey) and set atop a pile of logs. Just how he died is the subject of a long letter from the members of the church of Smyrna, all of whom witnessed the event:

> When he had offered up the Amen and finished his prayer, the firemen lighted the fire. And a mighty flame flashing forth, we to whom it was given to see, saw a marvel, yea and we were preserved that we might relate to the rest what happened. The fire, making the appearance of a vault, like the sail of a vessel filled by the wind, made a wall round about the body of the martyr; and it was there in the midst, not like flesh burning but like gold and silver refined in a

> furnace. For we perceived such a fragrant smell, as if it were the wafted odor of frankincense or some other precious spice. So at length the lawless men, seeing that his body could not be consumed by fire, ordered the executioner to go up to him and stab him with a dagger. And when he had done this, there came forth a quantity of blood so that it extinguished the fire, and all the multitude marvelled that there should be so great a difference between the unbelievers and the elect. [4]

Because of the miraculous nature of his martyrdom, the bishop was subsequently canonized, known forever after as Saint Polycarp.

In later centuries, the Church routinely sanctioned the ordeal by fire as a legal means of adjudication, sensing an ecclesiastical neatness in determining guilt or innocence by sending the accused for a firewalk over red-hot iron. But there would hardly have been a point to the test if no one could pass it safely.

The trial by fire grew so significant in Church practices that a special liturgy was developed for it between the 9th and 11th centuries. In its final form, this liturgy included a celebration of the Mass, interspersed with a great number of benedictions, exorcisms and oaths. Everything and everyone involved was first blessed: the fire, the iron, the accused (liturgically called the "probandus") and his or her accusers. In the *benedicto ferri*, as it was called, fire was addressed as a creature of the Lord and was blessed with a prayer from the Easter Saturday liturgy, sanctifying it for the purpose of determining the truth. [5]

According to 20th century German historian Ernst Benz, not every defendant was put to the test.

> . . . the accused is sentenced to the [fire] ordeal only after careful consideration and often only at his own request. The decision to invoke God as judge and helper in a hopeless situation for the accused, who is without witness and compurgators, is for the probandus an extremely significant decision which profoundly affects his whole spiritual life. It amounts to a decision to deliver himself over to the judgment of the living God and thus to agree to an anticipation of the Last Judgment while still being alive in this world. [6]

According to Benz, all those directly involved, including accused, priests and witnesses, abstained from food, drink and sex for varying periods of time prior to the test. At the ordeal itself, when the fire had heated the iron sufficiently, Benz reports that "two neutral parties who are sober and who have not slept with their wives the preceding night should come from both sides of the nave of the church and confirm that the iron is red hot." [7]

After the final exorcisms, entreating the devil to keep his magic at bay, concluding prayers were said, repeating the request that God reveal guilt and lead innocence to victory, and calling for the red-hot iron to be a refreshment for the innocent but a burning hellfire for the guilty. Generally, the iron was brought from the fire into the nave of the church for the ordeal. In especially prominent cases, the accused was required to walk barefoot across a series of red-hot plowshares, usually nine in number, stepping on them firmly with the entire sole. The plowshare itself was considered to be imbued with magic, a power that could fend off evil and which was only increased by making it red hot. This form of ordeal by fire was used especially by women of nobility who had been accused of adultery. Since they usually had no significant defender of their innocence, the trial by fire offered a way out.

Accused of adultery by her husband, Heinrich II, German Empress Kunigunde is reported to have chosen just such a course in the year 1007. In the Cathedral of Bamberg, the fire was lit, the Mass said and the iron heated. Accompanied by two bishops, the empress carefully and deliberately walked over nine red-hot plowshares, stepping off the last one with no injuries whatsoever. One report hints that she was in a kind of trance during the ordeal. Empress Kunegunde's successful firewalk was considered a divine miracle by the Church, one of the rare instances in which ecclesiastical authorities recognized an ordeal as such. [8]

Queen Emma of England is said to have faced the same marital crisis of confidence in the year 1043. To prove her innocence, she underwent a trial by fire in Winchester Cathedral. Nine red-hot plowshares were placed on the freshly swept stone floor of the church, spaced according to the length of her step. Barefoot and coatless, her outer garments tied high up, the queen walked across the glowing plowshares, her lips muttering prayers, her hands guided by two bishops. She, too, finished her firewalk unscathed. [9]

In these patriarchal societies, men were never called to account for themselves sexually, so the only times they faced a trial by fire was for some everyday crime, or a crime against the Church. The accused did not have to emerge completely free of injuries; if he or she did not die, the wounds were observed; and if healing was rapid, a judgment of innocent might also be rendered. In most cases, however, the fire was so efficient it meted out its own justice, with the officials relieved of any further judicial responsibility.

There were dozens of variations on the Christian trial by fire, among them an ordeal in which the accused was dressed in a shirt saturated with wax, then sent to walk through the fire. But as the Middle Ages gave way to the sensibility of the Enlightenment, all sorts of arguments against the trial by fire arose. There were theological arguments quoting the Bible ("You shall not put the lord your God to the test." Deuteronomy 6:16); and there were strong statements that the trials were incompatible with the laws of reason and nature. Most significantly, the religious structure of the fire ordeal was called into question; for if the accused had just received absolution, could God really damn him or her in the fire? And what, then, of the priest's pronouncement of the accused's sin-free status? Moreover, wouldn't many of the truly guilty go into the fire with a totally clear conscience because of this absolution? And despite the numerous exorcisms in the Mass, there were strong suspicions that the devil's magic often entered into the trial. [10]

Even so, more than a few Christian monks and priests spontaneously stepped into blazes and walked out smiling. In 1062, after the death of Bishop Gerard of Florence, a duplicitous bishop bribed his way into succession, thereby provoking the local citizenry. As a means of restoring peace, it was decided to appeal to heavenly judgment. St. John Gualbert, Abbot of Vallombrosa, instructed one of his monks, Peter Aldobrandini to submit to a fiery ordeal so that local rule by divine right might be established.

Two great walls of wood were piled, with only the narrowest path between them. The woodpiles were set ablaze, burning fiercely and quickly strewing the path with glowing embers. Having said Mass and divested himself of his chasuble, Peter slowly walked down the straight and narrow path, the fires raging all about him. As with his Biblical predecessors Shadrach, Meshach, and Abednego, not a hair of his head was singed, nor were his vestments even scorched. The people were satisfied; the pretender to the bishop's position was deposed, and he subsequently gave proof of sincere repentance. Years later, Peter was ordained a Cardinal, and eventually he was canonized as St. Peter Igneus, patron saint of firewalkers. [11]

Some two centuries later, another Italian monk, Giovanni Buono (John the Good) went for a short firewalk that stunned his fellow monks. Apparently, a monk named Jachim was passionately tempted to give up his vocation and leave the order. While standing around a great fire one cold winter's day, the other monks intensely debated Jachim's fate. John Buono began orating on the supreme importance of one's religious vows. Monks should fear nothing, he said. Then, ". . . stepping into the fire, he began to shuffle the embers about just as if they were water, and there he remained standing for as long a time as it would take to say the Miserere halfway through." He too, walked out of the fire beaming, completely unscathed. [12]

This type of ecclesiastical firewalking continued in Italy in 1435, when a friar named Francis oversaw the construction of a monastery near the city of Paolo. According to the friar's biographers:

> Perhaps the most amazing of all the miracles during the building of this monastery was one of the first, related to the furnace built to prepare lime for mortar. Shortly after it was completed, workers noticed that some of the stones making up the wall had come loose, either from faulty construction or from the tremendous heat of the fire. Alarmed, the workmen tending the furnace ran to tell Francis, expressing fear that the furnace would collapse. Francis examined

> the damage and advised the workers to be of good spirit and to trust in the help of God. When all the workers had left for lunch, Francis stood in front of the furnace entrance, lifted his arms in prayer, made the Sign of the Cross over it, then entered into the roaring flames. He assessed the condition of the furnace, then calmly walked back out, his clothes completely unharmed by the fire. [13]

At Francis' canonization hearings in 1519, no fewer than eight eyewitnesses testified to the miracle, and many others verified numerous other incidents of fire immunity displayed by the friar who would come to be known as St. Francis of Paolo.

France was the setting for another dramatic and voluntary trial by fire, this one being witnessed by over 600 men. In 1685, King Louis XIV of France completely undermined Protestantism, revoking the religious and civil liberties of the Huguenots. One of the most faithful of these was Claris, who soon was among the leaders of the ensuing Camisard rebellion.

At the height of the conflict, amidst guerilla warfare, Claris called for a great fire to be laid. In a state of apparent possession, he climbed onto the lattice of logs and, despite terrified shrieks from his protesting wife, ordered the fire to be lit. The flames rose up all around him, but Claris, secure in his religious ecstasy, addressed the crowd with fervor. His was a compelling testimony to faith in action. The fire rose over his head, and still he spoke with unfaltering voice as his wife wailed in panic.

Claris continued to declaim for a considerable while, until the wood was quite spent and there was no flame. Then, stepping through the glowing coalbed, he finally emerged unhurt in any way, with clothes and hair completely intact. Colonel Cavalier, the leader of the 600 troops who surrounded the fire, later confirmed the event to many who were not there. [14]

FIREWALKING IN THE ORIENT

In his *Golden Bough*, Sir James Frazer described the Chinese solar festival of fire enacted every spring, where, he says, the main performers are laborers who have refrained from sex for seven days and fasted for three.

> On the eve of the festival, an enormous brazier of charcoal, sometimes twenty feet wide, is prepared in front of the temple of the Great God, the protector of life. At sunrise the next morning, the brazier is lighted and kept burning by fresh supplies of fuel. A Taoist priest throws a mixture of salt and rice on the fire to conjure the flames and ensure an abundant year. Further, two exorcists, barefooted and followed by two peasants traverse the fire again and again until it is somewhat beaten down. . . .
>
> Wild music now strikes up, and under the excitement caused by its stirring strains, the procession passes thrice across the furnace. At

> their third passage, the performers are followed by other peasants carrying the utensils of the temple; and the rustic mob, electrified by the frenzied spectacle, falls in behind. Strange as it may seem, burns are comparatively rare. [15]

In Japan, Frazer reported that the firewalk was performed as a Shinto religious rite at a temple in the Kanda quarter of Tokyo. One of these performances was witnessed in September 1903 by the wife of an American Naval officer. She noted that the bed of charcoal, fanned into a red glow, was about six feet wide, 18 feet long and two feet deep. She also noted that, curiously, the white-robed priests who calmly walked the coals first rubbed their feet in salt that had been poured onto mats at both ends of the fire. The priests were followed by numerous others, including some boys and a woman with a baby in her arms.

Explained Frazer, "The Shintoists claim that, having been perfectly purified by their prayers and ceremonies, no evil has any power over them. Fire they regard as the very spirit of evil; so twice a year, I believe, they go through this fire-walking as a kind of outward and visible sign of inward spiritual grace." [16]

According to another witness, those who have faith to brave the coals are said to receive special protection through the coming year. Moreover, this Shinto Hi Watari rite is also performed on burning wood, with the celebrants moving in single file across a narrower path of burning logs. [17]

Singapore has a long tradition of firewalking for healing and purification, and a particularly massive firewalk there was featured in *National Geographic* in 1931. Wrote L. Elizabeth Lewis:

> The devotees, including quite a number of women, approximated 400. Some were kneeling and touching the earth with their foreheads, while others, more devout, were literally grovelling in the dirt. While these zealots were proceeding with their tasks, a bed of coals was being prepared. Great piles of wood were burned to embers; then the ashes were raked into a neat bed about 24 feet long. It seemed hours before it reached this stage, as the atmosphere was rendered almost unbearable by the intense heat. . . . At the end of the mass of live coals was dug a pool which was filled with milk brought to the spot in earthenware jugs. . . . Finally, the priests who held back the devotees began to lash them with whips, and one by one they made a dash, barefooted, across the red-hot coals into the pool of milk. . . . The women seemed much calmer than the men. Some of them carried babies in their arms. . . . Walking on fire has become a custom for the curing of bodily ills or the overcoming of other calamities. [18]

In Singapore, walking on fire may also be something of a spiritual test by which the advancing adept may mark his or her progress. Such a psychological structure may have been in place at the very demanding and unusual firewalk observed by travel writer John Dingle and relayed by chemist Mayne Reid Coe in 1957. Dingle reports seeing a yogi in Singapore heat iron sandals red hot in a furnace, strap them to his feet and then walk across the temple courtyard. After the yogi removed the red-hot sandals, Dingle examined the soles of his feet and found them to be unburned in any way. But when the writer touched one of the still glowing sandals, he burned his hand badly, bearing the scar for life. [19]

James McClenon, a contemporary sociologist who has firewalked in Japan and observed the modern version of this ancient rite, reports that the ceremony was initiated in AD 744 as a means of training mountain priests of the Buddhist Shingon sect. According to McClenon, lay people were forbidden to observe or participate in the *hiwatari* until 1950. Modern *hiwatari* rituals, he concludes, are thought to contribute to world peace, sustain the health of those crossing the firebed, and reduce the number of automobile accidents in the prefecture for the coming year. [20]

Another contemporary American who has firewalked in Japan is New Yorker Richard Leavitt. In a 1973 *New York Times* Travel Section article entitled "To Walk on Fire You Must First Master Yourself," Leavitt spelled it all out:

> The secret is concentration. Most of those who walk chant Buddhist scriptures as they go. Actually, any short, clear, easily recited formula will serve to keep the mind steady and the pace regular. It is dithering, distraction and hesitation that cause trouble.
>
> Step out confidently but not too fast, plant your feet firmly, rolling them evenly from heel to toe, and walk with a steady gait. That's where a good chanting rhythm helps. The hardest thing to accept is that you must press your feet firmly down into the glowing coals as you walk. The walker who skips about or goes on tiptoe will get burned . . . But . . . if you walk more than once, often enough to get past the deluding veils of quaintness and gimmickry, of cliche and ego-tripping, so that you can both produce and observe the conscious state required, there is something to be learned. [21]

Something indeed! For if you could learn to consciously control your body's immunity to fire, who knows what other immunity-control you may be able to muster?

THE GREEK FIREDANCERS

For centuries, firewalking has been part of Greek village life. Some researchers trace the practice to antiquity and the orgiastic dramas of the

Dionysian cults. More popular is the belief that Greek firewalking was born in the 13th century in a village named Kosti, in what is now Bulgaria, when devout villagers rescued icons from a burning church without being burned themselves.

To this day, annual festivals honoring Saint Constantine and Saint Helena are celebrated with firewalks in the Greek villages of Lankadas and Ayia Eleni. Holding the icons of the two Saints aloft, the firewalk leader traditionally dashes back and forth across the glowing coals in the pattern of a cross. Dozens of men and women take after him, some trudging in apparent delirium, others jumping or dancing on the fiery bed. At Lankadas, a 1980 report by Nicholas Gage in *The New York Times*, describes "a prim young woman" bending down, heaping smoldering ashes on her feet and then picking up the live coals and appearing to wash her hands with them. [22]

For these small Greek sects and the onlookers they attract, this semiannual firewalking festival, called the Anastenaride, creates quite a spectacle. Writes anthropologist Loring Danforth, who has studied the Greek firewalkers for the last three decades:

> Other Anastenarides entered the fire, running and dancing back and forth across the bed of coals, stirring up showers of sparks and glowing embers. Thodoros scooped up some coals in one hand, squeezed them in his fist, and scattered them in the air. . .
>
> The climax of the festival of saints Constantine and Helen occurs when the possessed Anastenarides enter the fire and dance back and forth over the glowing coals until they are extinguished. For the Anastenarides, the firewalk is an act of faith, a miracle they perform every year that ritually confirms their belief in the existence and power of Saint Constantine. As the Anastenarides themselves say, the firewalk is a "trial by fire"; it demonstrates whether people enter the fire with the power of the Saint (in which case they will not be burned). [23]

THE BULGARIAN NISTINARES

A related sect is the Bulgarian Nistinares, firedancers recently reported on by researcher Svyatoslav Slavchev:

> The night before, several adult women locked themselves up in church in order to pray for the entire night. In the morning, several men arranged and lit the firewood to the sound of special music played by folk instruments. Later that day, in the evening, the men slowly raked the coals into an enormous, glowing circle. When the church doors opened, the women walked out barefoot onto the coals, walking in a spiral toward the center and taking quick, short steps. The women seemed to be lost in a pagan dance to the frenzied music. Then they would come out of the red-hot disk unharmed. [24]

Slavchev later goes on to describe the mystifying and amazing dance of a young girl named Nevena:

> At this point, Todor, a Bulgarian of about 40 with sparkling black eyes, came over and gathered Nevena up into his arms and carried her over to the fire. He let her down gently into the disk of burning earth. She began to fly across the coals, her arms outstretched and her eyes half-closed, walking the way that I imagine sleep-walkers do at the edge of a roof. The music played faster, wailing even more wildly. I myself was even tempted to take off my shoes and fly across the coals with the rest of the village.
>
> After a period of time which to me seemed like hours, the ritual ended. I found Nevena sitting near the platform, and asked to see her soles. No protective ointments, no calluses, no burns on the delicate soles of her feet.
>
> "How are you able to do this, Nevena?" I asked her.
>
> "I don't know. As soon as the music starts, I feel the blood leaving my legs and my soles becoming numb. I feel like I am in a dream, flying over the red earth." [25]

NATIVE AMERICAN AND SHAMANISTIC FIREHANDLING

Though Native American firewalking and firehandling undoubtedly predates recorded history on this continent, written note of it first appears in a 17th-century letter from a French Jesuit missionary stationed on the St. Lawrence River. In 1639, Father Le Jeune wrote to his superior in France, telling of a healing firewalk he saw among the Indians:

> In the cabins of the savages, which are in length and form like garden arbors, the fires are in the middle of their breadth, and there are several fires along its length, according to the number of families and the size of the cabin. . . . It was through the very middle of the cabins and through the very middle of the fires that the sick woman marched, her feet and legs bare — that is to say through two or three hundred fires — without doing herself any harm, even complaining all the time how little heat she felt. [26]

Some 30 years later, Father Marquette reported similar firewalks among the Ottawa Indians of the upper Great Lakes, noting, in one healing, "there were only the juggler (medicine man) and the sick man, who was made to pass over some large fires that had been lighted in all the cabins. They said he did not feel the heat." [27]

About a hundred years later, Jonathan Carver witnessed the feats of the Indians living west of the Great Lakes. Among the astounding sights noted in his 1802 *Travels in North America* was the parade of warriors who would "walk naked through a fire . . . with apparent immunity." [28]

There were scattered, sketchy reports of other Native American firewalks. In particular, the Blackfeet have a medicine legend that speaks of such things. The legend, among their many "Trickster Tales," features a recurring character called "Old Man," who is an amalgam of strength, weakness, wisdom, folly, childishness and malice. Called "The Fire-Bed Game," the tale begins as follows:

> Another day, just wandering, Old Man heard some really queer singing. He had never heard anything like it. He searched and at last discovered a circle of rabbits making medicine. They had built a fire and produced a bed of coals on which all but one would lie down together and sing, while the remaining rabbit covered them. After a short while, the guardian would uncover them and they would all jump out, and this apparently was great fun.
>
> "Little Brothers," said Old Man, "it is wonderful, how you lie there without getting burned. I wish you would teach me to do that." "Come on, Old Man," they said. "We'll show you. You must sing our song and not stay too long; for those coals are really hot." Old Man began to sing, lay down, and they covered him with the coals which did not burn him at all. "Why this is very nice," he said. "You have powerful medicine."

As the story continues, Old Man tricks the rabbits into lying in the red-hot coalbed while he covers them with the entire fire, keeping them there until they are roasted. But then the trickster himself gets tricked by a wily coyote. The coyote intentionally loses a footrace with Old Man, then beats him back to the rabbit roast, downing the last rabbit just before Old Man returns. [29]

In my research into the firewalk, I also came across many accounts of shamanistic firehandling. Among other things, a shaman is a specialist in ecstatic trance, an otherworldly state that he or she reaches either through psychoactive drugs such as peyote or, just as often, through some rhythmical, percussive sound such as drumming or rattling. Though in many ways shamans are very grounded individuals, they are nevertheless separated from other community members by the very intensity of their religious experience.

At the core of that religious intensity is fire. Fire, both spiritual and physical, is the energy by which a shaman heats and tests himself. "Fire, of whatever kind, transforms man into spirit," says Mircea Eliade in his masterful study *Shamanism: Archaic Techniques of Ecstasy*. "This is why shamans are held to be 'masters over fire' and become insensitive to the touch of hot coals." [30]

In Eliade's comprehensive survey, firewalks and firehandling abound, especially in the context of shamanic initiation. "During the Araucanian shaman's consecration festival," he notes, "the masters and neophytes walk barefoot on fire without burning themselves and without their clothes catching fire." [31] He also reports that "the Maidu initiators put candidates in a hole full of 'medicine' and 'kill' them with a 'medicine-poison'; after this initiation, the neophytes are able to hold red-hot stones in their hands without hurting themselves." [32]

In almost every tribal shamanic repertoire throughout the world, mastery over fire is a central element. In Polynesia, Eliade saw the transmission of shamanic power as hereditary:

> Finally, it should be mentioned that certain shamanic powers are transmitted by heredity in certain families. The best-known example is the power to walk on burning coals or stones heated white-hot, an ability confined to some Fijian families. The genuineness of such feats is beyond doubt; a number of competent observers have described this "miracle" after taking all possible measures to ensure objectivity. What is more remarkable, the Fijian shamans can confer insensibility to fire on the entire tribe and even on outsiders. [33]

In many shamanic traditions, the firewalk appears as an initiation ritual. In North Asia, Eliade notes, "Among the Manchu, the public initiation ceremony formerly included the candidate's walking over burning coals; if the apprentice had at his command the spirits that he claimed to possess, he could walk on fire without injury." [34]

Similarly, north of China, the Lolo shamanic initiation includes a ritual in which a "number of plowshares are also heated white-hot and the shaman must walk over them," just as certain members of the medieval gentry were occasionally called upon to do. [35]

In examining the fire rituals of Far Eastern shamanism, Eliade appears to view the firewalk as a path to complete mastery over fire:

> Like the shaman in Fiji, the *sai-kung* directs a fire-walking. The ceremony is called "walking on a path of fire" and takes place before the temple; the *sai kung* walks over the coals first, followed by his junior colleagues and even by the audience. It is believed that spiritual preparation before the ceremony makes it possible to walk on . . . fire unharmed. In this case, as in innumerable examples of mediumship, spiritism, or other oracular techniques, we encounter an endemic phenomenon of spontaneous pseudoshamanism, which is difficult to classify but whose most important characteristic is its easiness. [36]

This last comment struck me as particularly insightful. Chances are, I thought, you could ask any firewalker — Fijian, Indian African or New Age

American — and he or she would tell you: once you make the decision, once you are committed, once you step through that membrane of fear, a firewalk is in many ways like a stroll in the park; nothing could be easier.

Yet for the shaman, handling fire is not an end in itself but more of a physical touchstone, a practical, down-to-earth affirmation of the ecstatic state needed in order to do as the shamans do — to heal or to visit other worlds:

> Mastery over fire, insensibility to heat and, hence, the "mystical heat" that renders both extreme cold and temperature of burning coals supportable, is a magico-mystical virtue that . . . translates into sensible terms the fact that the shaman has passed beyond the human condition and already shares in the condition of the "spirits." [37]

Among the North American Indian tribes, the Fox and the Menomini had shamanic traditions that included firehandling. (38) And among the Zuni and Keres in particular, there were and may still be small secret societies that specialize in firehandling, with various members walking on fire, handling red-hot iron and swallowing red-hot coals. [39]

Around the turn of the century, American ethnographer Matilda Coxe Stevenson made an extensive study of the Zuni, subsequently published by the Bureau of American Ethnology and the Smithsonian Institution. In it, she included several of her own eyewitness accounts of paranormal firehandling. In a chapter on the Zuni esoteric fraternities, Stevenson devotes a section to what she calls "the great fire fraternity." Attending one of the ceremonies, she herself is shocked into an altered state by what she sees:

> Soon after the order assembles, one of the theurgists, who is also a member of the Fire division, stands before the altar and dips the quill ends of his eagle plumes into the medicine water and presses the quills to his nude breast to receive the charm of the medicine, when he becomes extravagant in his beastlike performances and dancing. He raises first one foot, then the other as high as possible, each time stamping firmly on the floor; leaps about in the wildest manner; throws himself upon the floor, maintaining the most graceful attitudes; then suddenly rising, dances before the altar.
>
> After some minutes, he runs into the back of his belt the two eagle-wing plumes he carries, and dashing forward to the fireplace takes a large coal and, dancing with it first in one hand and then in the other a moment or two, puts it into his mouth, where it remains thirty seconds, during which time he indulges in extravaganza. He is soon joined by other men and women, whose dusky forms, moving beast-like in light or shadow, according to the uncertain light of the embers in the fireplace, their eyes almost as bright as the coals in

> their mouths, which scintillate with every breath, carry one in imagination to the regions of Pluto. The longest time a coal is held in the mouth is one minute; the shortest, thirty seconds. There is considerable rivalry at such times, each one aiming to outdo the other, yet all are filled with spirit of good nature.
>
> When the coal is removed from the mouth, it is tossed into the fireplace with a peculiar quick and graceful motion. . . . Again the theurgists come forward two or three at a time and pelt the members of the choir with live coals, and then lighting large bunches of corn husks, shower the choir with the sparks, and each one runs the burning mass into his mouth. [40]

The heyday of the fire fraternities has surely passed, but individual shamanistic activity still goes on. As recently as 1921, a sacred fire ceremony was performed in public. At the Morongo Harvest Moon Festival, celebrated at the Banning Reservation near Palm Springs, California, a 67-year-old Cahuilla shaman from Torres called on the Great Spirit to remove the heat from the bonfire before him and to protect his "burning heart." Stripped to his loincloth and waving feathers in the air, he stepped out on the glowing coals, then scooped some up with his hands. He tilted his head back, looked to the sky, then filled his mouth with the red-hot coals. Closing his eyes, he held the radiant coals in his mouth until they had lost their glow. A doctor who witnessed this exhibition subsequently examined the shaman's feet, hands and mouth, finding them to be uninjured in any way. He could offer no explanation. [41]

FIREWALKING IN INDIA

India has a great tradition of firewalking, and there the ceremony is called "Agni Yajna." Around 1900, Henry K. Beauchamp, editor of the *Madras Mail*, witnessed the Agni Yajna and reported that the coals were fanned close to white heat. The firewalk itself was preceded by an elaborate ritual, including incantations, pantomimes, processions, sword brandishing, incense scattering, coconut smashing and plume waving — "all intended to subdue and render temporarily harmless the demon of the fire. When all the rites had been finished," he continued, "the chief performer, attired in gorgeous silks and huge turban, and holding a sword aloft, walked barefooted, calmly and with apparent ease, down the entrance slope, across the glowing floor of the pit, and then up the exit slope." Beauchamp explained that such firewalkers claimed to be exempt from burning by virtue of supernatural powers they acquired through fasting, pilgrimages and prayer — and that their immunity was automatically transferred to anyone who followed them through the fire. [42]

So deeply is the firewalk embedded in Indian culture that it can carry a variety of meanings depending on the locale and sect performing the rite. For example, in northern India, at Barsana, the faithful expect the local village priest to walk through what is called the "Holi bonfire" without being burned. In return for his demonstrated incombustibility, he is entitled to use land without paying rent. [43]

Another East Indian sect, the Bhuiyas, "worship their tribal hero Bir by walking over a short trench filled with fire, and they say the man who is possessed by the hero does not feel any pain in the soles of his feet." [44] To the south of India, at Akka in Bangalore, "one woman at least from every house is expected to walk through the fire at the village festival." [45]

Near the end of Colonial rule, one Monsignor Despartures, a Catholic Bishop of Mysore, India, was given a formal invitation to a firewalk by a maharajah, and in the interest of public relations, Despartures accepted. The ceremony was held at the maharajah's summer palace outside the city, and by all accounts held little religious significance, being more of a demonstration for the assembled guests. Despartures later wrote of the firewalk in great detail, describing how throngs of people marched through the fire unscathed:

> They marched into the fire, three by three. At this juncture, several cartloads of dried palm-leaves were brought down and thrown upon the embers. They blazed up at once, breaking into tongues of flame higher than a man's head. The Mohammedan induced others of the palace servants to pass through the flames and they did it without harm. The bandsmen went through a second time, carrying their instruments in their hands and with their sheets of music on top. I noticed that the flames which rose to lick their faces bellied out round the different parts of the instruments and only flickered round the sheets of music without setting them on fire. There, must, I think, have been two hundred people who passed over the embers, and a hundred who went right through the middle of the flames. [46]

Less than a month later, Despartures witnessed another firewalk led by the Mohammedan, this one within Mysore proper. Again, many people passed through the fire unharmed. But toward the end, after the Mohammedan warned that no others must make the attempt, three people pushed their way in, walked on the fire and were badly burned.

Some people maintained there was some mass hallucination involved, but the bishop rejected such a claim:

> I was in full possession of my faculties. I went round the trench before the proceedings began; I went back to it again after it was all over; I spoke with those who passed through the fire, and I even said a Hail Mary or two with the view of arresting any exhibition of diabolic power. . . . It was beyond doubt a real burning fire . . . I do not

think that any material cause can explain it. . . . I am forced to believe in the influence of some spiritual agency which is not God." [47]

AFRICAN FIREWALKERS, FIREDANCERS

As venerable as the subcontinent's firewalking tradition is, Africa's may be even older. As early as the 1920s, British missionaries in Southern Africa realized they had a curious problem. When they explained to the natives of Natal that damnation and hellfire awaited all unconverted sinners, the locals seemed decidedly unperturbed. After all, the African-born Hindus walked on fire regularly. Reported a local paper on March 5, 1928:

> A representative of the *Natal Advertiser* attended the special invitation of the Hindu priest, and after witnessing the fire-walking, examined the *soutris* carefully. Six tons of firewood were used in making the fire over which the worshippers walked, but they suffered no harm to their feet, although the embers were white hot. Two medical men, Dr. Goldberg and Dr. Witkin, also examined the *soutris*, and the former said he could offer no physiological explanation of the normal condition of the Indians after their terrible ordeal. [48]

In the Kalahari desert of Southern Africa, the !Kung bushmen have walked on fire since their tribal beginnings. Entering an altered state of consciousness they call "*!kia*," the !Kung routinely walk and dance on fire as a means of performing cures. [49]

The firedance is a high-energy community healing that empowers both individuals and the tribe as a whole. When the mood is right — quite possibly when a problem has arisen or a triumph been realized — a great fire is built and the tribe gathers around, singing and playing musical instruments. The tribal healers dance around the fire, circling with such frenzy that they wear a deep groove around its periphery.

In 1977, anthropologist Laurens van der Post published an account of his travels to Africa to study the !Kung. Here are some of his observations:

> How the dancers found the power to go on ever faster and faster, hour after hour, seemed beyond explanation or belief. They danced so hard and long that the circle in the sand became a groove, then the groove a ditch high up to their calves. Long before the end, they seemed to pass into a dimension of reality far out of reach of my understanding, and to a moment and a place which belonged only technically to the desert in which we were all gathered. Indeed, so obsessed did the men become by this search for fire that they were drawn nearer and nearer to the flames. . . . Then, suddenly, they halved the circle and went dancing with their bare feet through the middle of the flames. [50]

After dancing on the blazing fire, the newly re-empowered !Kung seek out their sick folk to share with them the force of their healing energy.

Harvard psychologist Richard Katz also went to the Kalahari to study the !Kung, reporting in 1982 that "as the dance intensifies, *n/um*, or energy, is activated in those who are healers, most of whom are among the dancing men. As *n/um* intensifies in the healers, they experience an enhanced consciousness called *!kia*, during which they heal all those at the dance." [51]

According to Katz, the !Kung believe there is also *n/um* in the fire:

> . . . the !Kung work with the fire to help heat up the dancers' *n/um*. The singers will rub coals in their hands before they work on a dancer whose *!kia* has fallen. Dancers will go in the fire, walk in it, put their heads in it, pick up coals and rub them over their hands and body. . . . When the *n/um* in the body is boiling and as hot as the fire, they will not be burned. [52]

FIREDANCING IN THE SOUTH SEAS

In the South Sea Island of Bali, it is not the mature males who firedance, but the young girls — some of them beginning at seven years of age. [53] Like the !Kung firedance, the Balinese dance is a formalized ritual in which each participant knows her part by heart, trained through long social indoctrination. But in Bali, the rite is less spontaneous, and untoward events experienced by the !Kung — like a dancer's burning or having to be restrained from the fire — would never occur. Instead, according to psychologist Peter van der Walde, the trance state these islanders achieve automatically leads to behavior that is predictable, yet astounding in the demonstrated immunity to burning. [54]

In an ironic spiritual twist, the children become the guides for these dances. According to Van der Walde, "most of these trance-dances are performed by children, and in Bali, the gods are thought of as 'children of the people.'" [55]

An eyewitness of the 1983 Balinese trance dance gave this account of the spectacle:

> In a small open area stood an open white umbrella. This meant that a priest was present. Everything necessary for the ritual stood on a small table, particularly incense in burners. Two young girls were already dressed in festive attire; the priest moved the intoxicating fumes of the incense toward the girls, who began to breathe them in. They both began to go into a deeper and deeper trance state. The priest gave them fans and they, now in deep trance, began to perform an incredible dance . . . The girls rested a little without coming out of their strange state. Then they were given the fans again, and they resumed their dance.

> One of the attendants lit the fire and the girls began to dance around the fire with their eyes closed. We were literally numb with fear, afraid that they would accidentally wind up in the flames. They spun in circles around the fire, approaching it closer and closer, until finally one of them ran and with bare feet leapt into the fire. The second girl followed. The girls turned round and round in the fire, stamping the burning wood and coconut husks. The dancing and the music reached its climax — I wanted to pinch myself to prove it wasn't a dream. . . .
>
> Suddenly, the dance stopped. The priest led the exhausted, trembling girls to some low benches and lit the incense again to bring them out of their trance. When we came up to see the girls, we realized that they were only children. They were both smiling weakly; there was not a single trace of any burns on them. [56]

HOT WALKS IN THE PACIFIC ISLANDS

The Pacific Islands have a long history of firewalking, and there the event often takes place on hot rocks. The first vivid accounts of the feat began trickling back to the West in the late 19th century, with the performance of a Tahitian firewalker named Papa Ita stirring particular interest. The Honolulu correspondent for *The Boston Evening Transcript* reported the events of that March 20, 1891 as follows:

> On the vacant land swept a year ago by the Chinatown fire, a great elliptical pit was dug and a large quantity of wood placed therein, on which were piled the lava rocks. All day the fire burned till the stones were of white heat; then the white-haired native from Tahiti approached the fiery furnace dressed in a robe of white tapa, with a girdle and head-dress of the sacred ti leaves and a bundle of leaves in his hand for a wand. Striking the ground with his ti-leaf wand, he uttered an incantation in his own language, which was a prayer to his gods to temper the heat and allow him to pass; then calmly and deliberately, with bare feet, he walked the length of the pit, bearing aloft the ti-leaf wand. Pausing a moment on the other side, he again struck the ground and returned over the same fiery path. This was several times repeated, and he even paused a few seconds when in the middle of the pit to allow his picture to be taken. . . . It was a fact that others followed with shoes on, but no one could be found to accept the standing offer of 500 dollars to anyone who would, with bare feet, follow Papa Ita. [57]

In the coastal town of Viti Levu, Fijians who would walk on fire prepare for ten days, immersing themselves in study, meditation and purification. They live in a cloistered environment, abstaining from drink, smoke and sex. Early on the morning of the firewalk, the participants wash themselves in a stream, then sit in a circle around their leader, praying, meditating, gradually entering the psychic state they believe essential to a safe walk over the red-hot stones. [58]

As Frazer described it, this rite has strong agricultural ties. On the Fijian island of Mbennga, he explained, the root of the fibrous, sugary dracaena plant is harvested and baked on hot stones for four days in order to render it edible. When the flames have died down and the stones are at white heat,

> . . . the members of a certain clan called Na Ivilankata, favored of the gods, leap into the oven and walk unharmed upon the hot stones, which would scorch the feet of any other persons. . . . The immunity thus enjoyed by members of the clan in the fiery furnace is explained by a legend that in former days a chief of the clan . . . received for himself and his descendants this remarkable privilege from a certain god, whom the chief had accidentally dragged out of a deep pool of water by the hair of his head. [59]

In his youth, ethnologist William Tufts Brigham walked over semi-molten lava in Hawaii along with three *kahunas*, or native priests. Before stepping onto the lava, the *kahunas* took off their sandals, tied ti leaves around their ankles and chanted in archaic Hawaiian to the goddess Pele. Barefoot, one *chain* trotted out onto the black-skinned, red-hot lava, and as Brigham watched openmouthed, he was shoved out onto the lava pool himself. Still wearing his socks and boots but nevertheless broiling in the intense heat, the doctor ran for the other shore, which he reached safely. The soles of his socks and boots were burned through, but his feet were fine. None of the *kahunas* blistered or burned, although their ti leaf anklets burned up quite quickly. [60]

This very rational doctor, at a loss to objectively explain what he had seen, attributed the *kahunas*' firewalking ability to . . . magic! "No, there is no mistake," he said. "The *kahunas* use magic in their fire-walking as well as in many other things. There is one set of natural laws for the physical world and another for the other world. And — try to believe this if you can: The laws of the other side are so much the stronger, that they can be used to neutralize and reverse the laws of the physical." [61]

Some of the largest firewalks ever held were staged in early 1949, when Tunui Ariipeu from the Society Islands came to Hawaii and arranged for a series of five public firewalks. Four were held in the University of Hawaii amphitheater and the fifth at Wailuku, Maui, with an average of 600 people attending each performance. At the Honolulu walks in the amphitheater, 567 people crossed over the hot stone oven. Many of these firewalkers had no preparation and many were mainlanders. About 50 were injured, three requiring hospitalization.

Interestingly, the firewalk leader, Tunni Ariipeu, had warned those in attendance that the ceremony was a religious rite and should be performed as such. Anyone who was afraid, skeptical or inclined to show off, he suggested, was likely to be burned. One such skeptic was James Engle, a radio engineer who believed the stones in the center, unlike the red-hot ones at the edges, were actually quite cool. Setting out to prove his theory, Engle walked rapidly to the center, cried out in pain and was rushed in agony to Queens Hospital, where he was treated for second-degree burns.

Reverend N. Vanora Wattson of San Francisco also burned, but not seriously. Her burn was incurred after slipping, falling and cutting herself. Up until that point, she had been firewalking successfully. But as she fell, she sensed a mental change and thereafter burned. "It seems to me," she said, "that the secret lies . . . in allowing a mental state of a rather definite sort to withdraw the consciousness from the self, and that when something happens unexpectedly to bring this self-consciousness back into function, the fire-immunity momentarily or permanently fails." [62]

At about the same time, the American writer Wilmon Menard observed a firewalk on the Tahitian island of Raiatea. The firepit, he reported, was 30 feet long, 15 feet wide and four feet deep, and the fires had been burning for two days. Chief Terii-Pao crossed the pit four times, followed by his assistants. Then, across the 30-foot expanse of glowing stones, the chief *crawled on his stomach*, uninjured. Inspired by this performance and encouraged by Chief Terii, Menard removed his shoes and socks and marched out across the stones. Lungs heavy with superheated air, feet tingling, the writer walked across the oven without pain or injury. [63]

During the early 1950s, researcher Clement Stone visited the islands and witnessed the firewalk over red-hot stones. The firewalk is performed predominantly by men, he reports, but some women also participate. Here, the firewalk is a cultural marker, a coming-of-age ceremony with profound social and psychological ramifications. Says Stone: "The islanders still have a simple belief that no man is truly a Beqa man until he becomes a fire walker — and they all do." [64]

In 1969, surgeon, writer, lecturer and world traveler G.M. Feigen accompanied his friend R. Buckminster Fuller to a Raiatea firewalk. This was a serious firebed. Reported Dr. Feigen in *Saturday Review*, "The cinder bed was white hot, and the bottom two-thirds of the rocks were beginning to show a constant ruddy blush . . . the firebed was an orange ruby, darkly radiant."

Though both came as observers, Feigen suddenly decided to join in:

> Tanetoa greeted me, blessed me, and I felt myself grasping the palm of one of the initiates as he helped me step onto the firebed. From my legs up, I was aware of a frighteningly intense, though bearable heat; my legs and feet felt cold. I moved along steadily, looking down, unaware of any special pathway. . . . The rock sur-

> faces felt like sandpaper and made my feet tingle. I saw no one. At last I had stopped reasoning! I stepped off as if awakening from sleep; then I recognized Fuller. "Bring me some water," I said, "and I'll turn it into wine!" [65]

Fifteen minutes later, however, the pain in his feet was severe, and it became evident that he had burned.

Travelers to today's Fiji can still enjoy the spectacle of the firewalk, within walking distance of their hotel in Viti Levu. Reports Joan Gould in the "Sophisticated Traveler" section of the October 1, 1989 issue of the *New York Times*:

> At the Hyatt Regency, I sat outdoors in the bleachers and watched a bonfire send up sparks against the black hills. After a long wait, a man introduced as the high priest entered. He was followed by a dozen firewalkers, both men and women, wearing skirts of banana leaves and wreaths, armlets and anklets of pandanus fibers. The electric lights went out and the timbers that covered the fire were removed, revealing a bed of red-hot stones. Members of the audience hushed their jokes about toasting marshmallows.
>
> Under the direction of the priest, the stem of a tree fern was laid across the fire, to "transfer the spirit to the rocks." Then the pile of stones was levelled with vines. At last, the firewalkers approached in single file, climbed up onto the rocks one at a time and crossed the fire. . . .
>
> As soon as the firewalkers finished their performance and made their exit, I walked over to the fire — nobody tried to stop me — and laid a finger on a stone. My finger wasn't blistered. But it was definitely burned. [66]

AUSTRALIAN FIREWALKERS

If self-consciousness inhibits fire immunity, as some have suggested, what a great advantage so-called "primitive" people must have in launching into the psychological state required to safely enter a fire. Consider several of the tribes of Southeast Australia, as described by anthropologist A. W. Howitt in his 1904 account:

> In the center of this circle was a fire of moderate dimensions, and attended by one of the men. Shortly, there was a stir when a detachment entered the circle, and with dancing, yelling, and gesticulations, and brandishing of arms at intervals, all made a rush to the fire, yelling and jumping on it, until it was extinguished . . . [67]

Later, in describing an initiation among the Chepara tribe, Howitt describes a similar situation. In this case, while the young initiates are sleeping, the men make a long, narrow fire. When the fire is ready, the boys are roused and sit on one side of it in a sleepy state. At this point,

> . . . the men pretend that it is stormy and that it rains, and make noises to represent the wind. Then a number of boys hop about and croak like frogs. Finally, the men all dance and then extinguish the fire by jumping on it with their feet. The method differs from place to place, yet they all have in common the fact that people do it and do not get burnt."[68]

SRI LANKAN FIREWALKING

Sri Lanka, the large island south of India formerly known as Ceylon, has a colorful firewalking tradition that has been described by a number of Western reporters. According to sociologist James McClenon, each year a festival occurs in Kataragama, including a procession on 10 consecutive evenings during July or August. The processions include elephants, dancers, and various forms of ceremonial defiance of pain. People thrust metal skewers through their cheeks and arms, some hang from wooden frames with hooks in their backs and some engage in firewalking.[69]

In the late 1950s, professor of English, Leonard Feinberg reported on one of these firewalks in the *Atlantic Monthly*. As background to the ritual he witnessed, Feinberg was told of a young English clergyman who reasoned that the faith of a Christian was at least as strong as that of a Hindu and accordingly volunteered to walk the fire with the others. He did, and spent the next six months in a hospital, where doctors barely managed to save his life.

Possibly with that in mind, these Ceylonese firewalkers underwent serious, long-term preparation, living ascetically for three months. Reported professor Feinberg:

> The men and women nearest the pit had held their places for days, eating and sleeping in one spot. A wave of malevolent expectation permeated the air, a powerful undercurrent of suppressed sadism that made intruders like ourselves feel dilettantish, uncomfortable, and slightly ashamed. Fire walking is far more than just a spectacle to most of these people; it is a concrete symbol of intimate identification with a supernatural power. . . .
>
> Among the eighty persons who walked the fire that night there were ten women. But in the mad excitement of the crowd's cheers, the drumbeats, the odors, the tension, it was difficult to identify individuals. Some men skipped lightly through the fire, as if doing a restrained version of the hop, skip and jump . . . some marched through, determined, somber. Some ran through exultantly, waving spears. One man danced gaily into the center of the pit, did a kind of

> wild jig for a few moments, then turned again and danced on through. Another man stumbled suddenly and the crowd gasped; he fell forward, hung for a ghastly moment on the coals, then straightened and stumbled on.

Others were no so lucky. Reported Feinberg: "On the night we watched fire walking at Kataragama, twelve people were burned badly enough to go the hospital, and one of them died." [70]

Nearby, in the Sri Lankan village of Kolonnawa, not far from Colombo, firewalks are a regular occurrence. In the mid-'60s, *National Geographic* publisher Gilbert Grosvenor described one such walk and some accompanying scientific observations:

> At 4 a.m. my friend Ed Lark, an American movie photographer and lecturer, measures the temperature of the coals with an optical pyrometer from the Ceylon Institute of Scientific and Industrial Research. The pyrometer registers 1,328 degrees F. Since Ed is also a trained engineer familiar with this precise instrument, I trust his measurement. Crowds perching on banks fall still as a young man dances across the 20-foot carpet of coals, twisting his body and feet as he moves. Then another man follows, scooping up handfuls of embers and throwing them over his shoulders. Nearly twenty men, women, boys and girls firewalk, not once, but two and three times, believing that the longer they stay on the coals, the more merit they gain. Mohotty crosses the fire four times, twice with his young son on his shoulders.

Like some other Third World firewalkers, Mohotty set his own stage for the firewalk by piercing his flesh with steel skewers, which, when removed, left no bloodstain and no visible wound cite. When asked what his secret was, Mohotty replied, "My secret? Faith. Total faith in my gods." [71]

A few years later, a correspondent for *Harper's Magazine* attended a firewalk in another Ceylonese village near Colombo, Udappawa. At one point in the firewalk, the reporter noted: "The entire male population of Udappawa, six or seven hundred, have walked across the pit at least once." How did the fire feel? one firewalker was asked. "Not bad," he replied, "like warm red flowers." How did he do it?" he was asked. "Preparation and also faith," he replied. "With faith, anyone can do it." [72]

RED-HOT RELIGIOUS SPECTACLE IN ARGENTINA

Firewalking was nearly transformed into a spectator sport in 1962, when 15,000 eager onlookers filled a soccer stadium in Buenos Aires, Argentina, to watch 30 members of the cult of St. John the Baptist walk barefoot over a bed of fiery wood coals. The group, including two teenage girls, walked the firebed after their leader, Angel Ali, whispered "secret words" to them. No one suffered any burns, a phenomenon inexplicable by attending doctors and university professors. [73]

INCOMBUSTIBLE SPANIARDS

One of the few remaining European firewalk traditions continues in Spain. For centuries, certain Spanish firewalkers were employed to help put out fires. Notes Andrew Lang in his book *Magic and Religion*, "There is a family or caste in Spain, who from father to son, have the power of going into the flames without being burned, and who, by dint of charms permitted by the Inquisition, can extinguish fires." [74]

In the Spanish village of San Pedro Manrique, the firewalk is still the highlight of a midsummer solstice festival. When one of the firewalkers was asked how he could walk over glowing coals without getting burned, he said that he had faith in the Virgin of La Pena, who would protect him. One eyewitness in 1969 reported, "Narciso carried the mayor across the embers, a hefty middle-aged man. One man carried his wife across, another crossed with a man on his back, and a boy on the back of that man." [75]

Throughout Europe and America, incombustible men and fireproof women began to appear on stages and in sideshows with increasing frequency in the 18th and 19th centuries. Some of these performers protected themselves from the fire with special preparations, and some prepared only mentally. Among those who apparently faced the fire protected only by their faith was Jean Chacon, "The Incombustible Spaniard." Among many other feats, Chacon would run red-hot iron over his tongue, hands, arms and head — without even singing his hair — and would stand over lighted candles for 15 minutes. [76]

FIREHANDLING IN GREAT BRITAIN AND AMERICA

Until recent years, firewalking has not been especially popular in either England or the United States; however, there are numerous, well-documented accounts of 19th-century firehandling in both countries. During England's golden age of mediums and spiritualistic phenomena, a Scottish-American named Daniel Douglas Home performed feats of fire immunity that were not only witnessed, but in some cases even shared, by many of the country's more prominent figures.

Reports abound, commencing with Lord Adare's 1868 account of a D.D. Home seance at Norwood. After some preliminary poking at the fire, Home seemed to entrance himself. Next, in the most casual manner, he performed some feats that would astound most modern-day firewalkers. Reported Lord Adare:

> . . . he went back to the fire, and with his hands, stirred the embers into a flame; then, kneeling down, he placed his face right

> among the burning coals, moving it about as though bathing it in water. Then, getting up, he held his finger for some time in the flame of the candle. Presently, he took the same lump of coal he had previously handled and came over to us, blowing upon it to make it brighter. He then walked slowly round the table and said, "I want to see which of you is the best subject. Ah! Adare will be the easiest because he has been most with Dan [Home]. Mr Jencken held out his hand, saying, "Put it in mine." Home said, "No. Touch it and see"; he [Jencken] touched it with the tip of his finger and burned himself. Home then held it within four or five inches of Mr. Sarl's and Mr. Hart's hands, and they could not endure the heat. He came to me and said, "Now if you are not afraid, hold out your hand." I did so, and having made two rapid passes over my hand, he placed the [red-hot] coal in it. I must have held it for half a minute, long enough to have burned my hand fearfully; the coal felt scarcely warm. Home then took it away, laughed, and seemed much pleased. [77]

This combination of fire immunity and conferred fire immunity was a Home speciality, and he repeated the feat frequently. Reported Lord Lindsay to the Committee of the Dialectical Society in 1869:

> I have frequently seen Home, when in a trance, go into the fire and take out large red-hot coals, and carry them about in his hands, put them inside his shirt, etc. Eight times I have myself held a red-hot coal in my hands without injury, when it scorched my face on raising my hand. Once, I wished to see if they really would burn, and I said so, and touched a coal with the middle finger of my right hand, and I got a blister as large as a sixpence [about the size of a dime]; I instantly asked him to give me the coal, and I held the part that burnt me, in the middle of my hand, for three or four minutes, without the least inconvenience. A few weeks ago, I was at a seance with eight others. Of these, seven held a red-hot coal without pain, and the two others could not bear the approach of it; of the seven, four were ladies. [78]

Home's most renowned display of fire immunity and conferred fire immunity occurred in a session with his friend Samuel Carter Hall, editor of *The Art Journal*. Home drew from the fire "a huge lump of live burning coal" so large he had to hold it in both hands, and then deliberately placed it on the head of his aged friend. Someone asked: "Is it not hot?" and Mr. Hall answered, "Warm, but not hot." Then, according to the most vivid account, written by Hall's wife, Mrs. S.C. Hall,

> [Home] proceeded to draw up Mr. Hall's white hair over the red coal. Mr. Home drew the hair into a sort of pyramid, the coal still

> showing red beneath the hair; then, after, I think, four or five minutes, Mr. Home pushed the hair back, and taking the coal off Mr. Hall's head, he said, addressing Mrs. Y: "Will you have it?" She drew back and I heard him murmur, "Little faith." Two or three attempted to touch it, but it burnt their fingers. [79]

Home appeared to confer with spirits before his fire handling. Fellow medium W. Stainton Moses described another such scene, on April 30, 1873, a fiery drama also witnessed by physicist-chemist William Crookes, among others.

> Home then went to the fireplace, removed the guard, and sat down on the hearth rug. There he seemed to hold a conversation by signs with a spirit. He repeatedly bowed, and set to work to mesmerize his head again. He ruffled his bushy hair until it stood out like a mop, and then deliberately lay down and put his head in the bright wood fire. The hair was in the blaze, and must, under ordinary circumstances, have been singed off. His head was in the grate, and his neck on a level with the top bar. This was repeated several times. . . . He then came to all of us to satisfy us that there was no smell of fire on his hair. There was absolutely none. [80]

In other seances in the British isles and America, several different mediums displayed distinct talents for fire immunity. In June 1882, a London woman, Mrs. William Tebb, wrote that during a seance with five others, one of them fell into a deep trance and "put his hands over a flame and held them for some time without apparent injury. He also held the flame close to his eyes, to our horror, and we had to beg for the fire test to be dropped." [81]

During a Glasgow seance at the home of author James Robertson, near the turn of the century, London shoemaker John Hopcroft is reported to have lifted a huge, red-hot coal from the fire and walked about the room with it. The coal was described as being so hot that "its glow was reflected by the pictures on the wall." [82] And at public seances in Chicago, a Mrs. Suydam handled red-hot coals, super-hot lamp chimneys and red-hot iron. Reported the *Religio Philosophical Journal* of Chicago, "While she is under the control of the 'Fire Queen,' her hands are cold and clammy; as cold as ice." [83]

Also in America, at about the same time that D.D. Home was carrying red-hot coals around during seances, a freed slave named Nathan Coker was safely handling fire in a variety of everyday situations. Coker was born into slavery in the town of Hillsborough, Maryland, about 1814. In his early teens, he was leased by his second owner to a lawyer named Purnell. Purnell mistreated the boy, frequently depriving him of food. Coker was therefore always hungry, a painful experience that nonetheless prompted the discovery of his rare gift. In reflecting on his experiences later, he remembered:

> I shied around the kitchen one day, and when the cook left, I shot in, dipped my hand into the dinner pot, and pulled out a hot dumpling. The boiling water did not burn and I could eat the hot dumpling without winking; so after that, I often got my dinner that way. I has often got the hot fat off the boiling water and drank it. I drink my coffee when it is boiling. . . . [84]

When Coker obtained his freedom, he moved to Denton, Maryland, where he became a blacksmith. In his daily work, his early immunity to fire assumed a significant role. "I often take my iron out of the forge with my hand when red hot, but it don't burn," Coker explained. "Since I was a little boy, I have never been afraid to handle fire." [85]

News of Coker's fire immunity spread, first to surrounding towns, then, via a report in *The New York Herald*, to the big city. In 1871, a Dr. Stack of Easton, Maryland arranged for a demonstration by Coker. In the doctor's office, before a number of the town's prominent citizens — including two local newspaper editors and four physicians, Coker gave a convincing display of his abilities. According to the account in the *Herald*:

> A brisk fire of anthracite coal was burning in a common coal stove, and an iron shovel was placed in the stove and heated to a white heat. When all was ready, the negro pulled off his boots and placed the hot shovel upon the soles of his feet, and kept it there until the shovel became black. His feet were then examined by the physician, but no burns could be found, and all declared that no evidence of a heated substance having come in contact with them was visible. [86]

Coker then licked a red-hot shovel until it cooled. Afterwards, he poured molten lead first into his hand, then into his mouth, where he held it until it solidified. Examination by the physicians revealed "nothing upon his flesh to indicate that he had been in the least affected." After this display, Coker put his hand into the stove, taking a handful of hot coals, passing around the room to show the other men. Again, "not the slightest evidence of a burn was visible upon his hand after he threw the coals back into the stove." [87]

There was a great resurgence of Western interest in firewalking in the mid-1930s when a Kashmiri magician named Kuda Bux got his act together and took it on the road. First stop: New York, New York. First promoter: Robert Ripley, of "Believe It Or Not" fame. First venue: Radio

City. Not exactly the Music Hall, mind you, but there, in Radio City's parking lot, on August 2, 1935, before a chic crowd, Kuda Bux walked barefoot over a bed of red-hot coals, hopping out after he'd crossed just half of the 20 foot long firebed. His walk appeared calm and deliberate until he hopped out, and his hasty exit seemed not to be accompanied by pain. Dr. E. Spire, who had examined the Kashmiri's feet prior to the firewalk, also examined them after, and could find no burns or blisters. Said Kuda Bux in explanation, "It is the accomplishment of the power of perfect faith." [88]

MODERN FIREDANCING IN AMERICA

Firedancing is an offshoot of American firewalking that seems particularly close to the spirit of several Third World rituals. Though it appears from Tolly Burkan's autobiography that firewalking in the United States was indirectly inspired by a Tibetan monk, there can be no doubt that some of the new American firewalkers have also been infused with the firedancing spirit of the !Kung bushmen and the Greek Anastenarides.

One of these is Ken Cadigan, a globetrotting Maine resident who has led firewalks in Europe and America and who has danced on fire in Greece with the Anastenarides. Like so many of America's new firewalk leaders, Cadigan first firewalked with Tolly Burkan. And though there is no doubt much of Burkan's influence in his firewalking workshops, Cadigan has chosen to emphasize the firedance. For Cadigan, the firewalk is a spiritual, goal-oriented activity aimed at breaking through a barrier of fear, while firedancing is more of an ecstatic communion.

"I've stayed [barefoot] in the fire for five minutes," he says. "You can dance in the fire for as long as you can dance outside it. The only limitation is how long you can keep it up physically with the proper attitude." [89]

Another Burkan-trained firewalker who has gone on to develop his own firedance is Michael Sky, of Eastsound, Washington. Sky's book, *Dancing with the Fire*, details his observations, feelings and conclusions based on over 100 firewalks. After leading a simple ceremony of music and song, Sky has seen some mind-boggling sights:

> People have done cartwheels through the fire, and have walked across on their hands. Some people have walked very slowly, others have stood still, and still others have reached down to pick up coals. I have watched one person sit down in the coals, and another lie completely flat on them, his hair included! And I have watched lots and lots of dancing. [90]

Though he, too, has had his share of burns, Sky says he can never forget those moments when he knew what it was like to be "able to do just about anything with the fire — dancing, slow dancing, standing still, laughing through it all and feeling no heat whatsoever." [91]

FIREWALK FEVER IN BRAZIL

The same sort of astonishment permeates a modern American's firewalk report from Brazil. On the Buddha's birthday, in the city of Sao Paulo, the large Japanese colony there celebrates annually with a firewalk. In 1982, Dick Gunther, a successful Los Ángeles businessman, accompanied a film crew to document that event. Reports Gunther:

> There was a pit with red-hot coals giving off a terrific blast of heat. The priests and other participants went through an elaborate ceremony with swords, sticks and pinches of salt. The priests walked across. And then some of the older men began to get up from the audience and walk across — and they walked, they didn't run; in fact, some of them were grinding their feet into the fire.
>
> I was sitting with my son, who is a medical student at the University of California. I said, "These aren't priests, these are people just like us." We took off our shoes and socks and walked over to where the people had lined up to walk across the coals. The people waved us to the front of the line. Then I was facing the pit. There really was a tremendous blast of heat.
>
> . . . I was enormously focused, so focused I felt I could walk through a brick wall. I went right across. I could feel the roughness of the coals. Then my son did it, and then a guy from the TV crew with a camera, and then some other cameramen. . . . If I had to tell you what the experience did for me, I would say it made me aware that we limit our own potential ourselves, because we exclude it by our beliefs. We can do far more than we think we can. [92]

As firewalking continues in traditional settings and proliferates into New Age contexts, it becomes the increasing object of social and scientific scrutiny. From a Western history limited to anecdote and speculation, a new and even more participatory rite is emerging, one that draws people from amazingly diverse backgrounds. What was once principally a non-Western religious ceremony is now a popular facet of human potential training, exciting the interests of both medical and psychological researchers. As a result, the firewalk's history is being rewritten daily.

It seems abundantly evident that firewalking and firehandling have been an integral part of the human experience for hundreds, if not thousands of years. It also seems evident that the coals, flames or red-hot iron nvolved probably vary greatly in temperature and that direct physical contact with these surfaces might vary from a second or two to as long as five or ten minutes. Most amazingly, it appears that in some cases, not only the feet but *the entire body* might be immune to the burning effects of fire.

What could possibly account for it?

Obviously, you don't need NLP; you don't need to be in a trance, self-induced or otherwise; you don't need swords, sticks or pinches of salt. Over and over, incredibly, the common denominator seems to be . . . faith!

Yet it seems very likely that few in the scientific community would agree with this conclusion. So, I must delve even deeper into the coals, to give the scientists their due and to trace the social and emotional storm created by "the impossible." I need also to fuel or quell my growing suspicion that we humans are much more than we think we are, capable of achievements unimagined.

Firewalk Illustrations

BRIAN GARLAND

Firewalker leader Peggy Dylan strides the red-hot coals with a confidence sparked by her former husband, Tolly Burkan.

DAVID GORDON

With eyes upward and fist clenched to cue a power state, a Tony Robbins student is escorted across the coalbed.

BRIAN GARLAND

Founder of the American firewalking movement, Tolly Burkan safely crosses a red-hot firebed. He has made over a thousand such passages in the last ten years, suffering minor blisters on only a few crossings.

HARRY KNOBEL

With "cool moss" in mind, and hot coals underfoot, Tony Robbins demonstrates his firewalk technique for a gathering of attentive students. Robbins says he uses Neuro Linguistic Programming and other mind control techniques to insure safer firewalks.

In Christian iconography, St. Anthony is one of the many saints depicted safely standing on fire. This illuminated miniature is from the 15th-century French Kildare Hours.

RIPLEY'S ENTERTAINMENT

Firewalking initially came to New York City in the 1930's, when Robert Ripley of "Ripley's Believe It or Not" fame hosted the Kashmiri magician, Kuda Bux. In a parking lot near Rockefeller Center, on August 2, 1935, Kuda Bux walked half of the 20-foot long, glowing trench, then hopped out — reportedly unharmed, but quite cautious.

COURTESY OF THE TIMES OF LONDON

Among the many significant British scientific investigations of the firewalk was this one at Carshalton, England, on April 7, 1937. Under the direction of Harry Price, this test took East Indian firewalker Ahmed Hussain and three volunteer Britons across coals with a surface temperature of 575 degrees C. (1,067 degrees F.). Hussain had made an earlier pass unharmed and claimed he could confer his immunity to others. It proved not to be the case, as each of the British volunteers was burned to some degree, although the Indian professional — a magician by trade — again walked across without injury.

THE BISHOP MUSEUM, HAWAII

Society Island firewalker leader Tunni Ariipeu walks over glowing red-hot stones in a 1949 public firewalk at the University of Hawaii Amphitheater. Hundreds of native islanders and mainlanders attended, and after hearing the leader tell them they could safely follow in his footsteps if they walked as part of a religious rite, many of them did. In a series of five public firewalks, 567 untrained, unprepared people walked the hot stone oven, testing their faith — or their foolhardiness. About fifty were injured, three requiring hospitalization.

To be reborn, the legendary Phoenix builds a fire and steps onto it, then dies and passes to a new incarnation. In just such a manner, many firewalkers walk on fire, die to old, limited views, and feel psychologically reborn.

COURTESY OF THE U.S. TREASURY

With its hovering, radiant eye, the American one dollar bill may mystically allude to the very process that protects firewalkers: the generation of a force field whose intensity increases as a being becomes focused in the third eye, the single eye, the single-minded congruency of one "I". "If thine eye be single," says the Bible, "thy whole body shall be full of light." In such a focused, radiant state, an individual is truly individual, indivisible, and immune to many diseases, most insults, and a variety of injuries, including burning to varying degrees. The motto "Annuit Cœptis" appears in the great seal above the eye; in Latin, this means "He has favored our undertaking." Underneath the pyramid appears "Novus Ordo Seclorum," Latin, for "A new order of the ages."

WHAT CAUSES SOME PEOPLE TO ACHIEVE THEIR ULTIMATE GOAL WHILE OTHERS MERELY WISH FOR CHANGE?

AN INVITATION TO MASTERY

ANTHONY ROBBINS LIVE UNLIMITED POWER™ WEEKEND

FEATURING THE FIREWALK EXPERIENCE™, THE PSYCHOLOGY OF SUCCESS CONDITIONING™ SEMINAR, & THE LIVING HEALTH™ SEMINAR

What sets certain men and women apart from all others and what allows them to take their dreams and turn them into reality? What are the key foundational tools to be able to influence yourself and others? Anthony Robbins' work has powerfully impacted over a million people to make major changes in their lives: to lose weight, to overcome self-sabotage, and to assist them in the process of changing limiting beliefs and developing a consistent plan of action. Now you have the chance to learn from Anthony Robbins in person in his live Unlimited Power™ seminars. Here's your chance to condition your mind and emotions for life-long success. Success doesn't come from doing things once in awhile; it comes from doing it consistently. Consistency comes from developing conditioned patterns for personal excellence.

The Firewalk is a metaphor. What I am really here to teach people is a series of very specific skills to break through any limitations. Fear of failure, fear of success, rejection or public speaking -- what the fear is doesn't matter. I teach people to change the way they feel about themselves and how to take control of their lives, now."

ANTHONY ROBBINS

ANTHONY ROBBINS' THREE STEPS TO PERSONAL POWER

LIVE IN PHILADELPHIA MARCH 22-25, 1991

WYNDHAM, FRANKLIN PLAZA

THE FIREWALK EXPERIENCE™

This is an opportunity to join the over 150,000 people who have walked across a bed of hot coals as a demonstration that even the seemingly impossible becomes possible when we overcome limiting belief systems. You will learn to eliminate the fears that block you from realizing your goals, and begin to master the break-through technology of Neuro-Associative Conditioning™. You will also learn to transcend your limitations and turn fear into power to achieve whatever you want while developing yourself for lifelong success.

THE PSYCHOLOGY OF SUCCESS CONDITIONING™

Skill is knowing specifically what you want and having many strategies with which to get it. You will learn to gain access to the parts of your brain that will allow you to be successful in any desired context and to perform with elegance and clarity in every area of your life. In addition to relationship and persuasion strategies, you will also learn to specifically define your desired goals so that they are more easily accomplished, and to transform unresourceful emotions into resourceful ones...instantly.

THE LIVING HEALTH™ SEMINAR

The Living Health Seminar is a synthesis of the most advanced research of nationally recognized scientists, nutritionists, medical doctors, biochemists and exercise physiologists. It is a simple, scientifically based program you can easily incorporate into your life now for a balanced, energy-filled and disease-free lifestyle. You will learn how to dramatically increase your energy levels, and to naturally activate your immune system. You will also learn how to combine foods in proper sequence for greater nutritional value, and a nutritional approach to disease prevention.

To enroll in this exciting 4-day program, call Robbins Research International now, or contact your local representative.

1-215-569-3940

$695.00 in Advance* -- $895.00 at the Door -- Seating is Limited

*Group rates are available as well as special rates for lodging at the host hotel. Please call for more information.

ROBBINS RESEARCH INTERNATIONAL, INC., 9191 TOWNE CENTRE DRIVE, TOP OF THE GATEWAY, SAN DIEGO, CA 92122

COURTESY ROBBINS RESEARCH INTERNATIONAL, INC.

A 1991 Tony Robbins advertisement offering a variety of weekend courses in Philadelphia, among them, his trademarked Firewalk Experience.

Tolly Burkan's World Famous

FIREWALKING SEMINAR

An inspiring presentation on achieving full potential

TOLLY BURKAN
Founder of the Firewalking Movement

Sunday, March 19
Virginia Beach, VA
Radisson Hotel, 1900 Pavilion Drive
(804-425-0996 – Information)

Tuesday, March 21
Charlottesville, VA
Sheraton Hotel
2350 Seminole Trail (off Route 29)
(804-425-0996 – Information)

Wednesday, March 22
D.C./Baltimore Area
Columbia, Maryland
Wilde Lake Interfaith Center
10431 Twin Rivers Road
(804-425-0996 – Information)

Saturday; April 8
Philadelphia, PA
(215-627 5683 – Information)

Saturday, April 15
New Paltz, NY
Unison Learning Center
68 Mountain Rest Road
(914-255-1559 – Information)

". . . the idea is to overcome your fear. In other words, Tolly is saying that if you can do this, its's amazing what else you can do . . ." — **Phil Donahue**

This seminar is for everyone who wants to make life an excellent experience. The evening consists of practical demonstrations and applications of recent mind/body discoveries for peak performance in your life as well as self-induced healing. As you absorb methods for affecting your state of mind and emotions, you will be overcoming fears and limitations that have prevented you from realizing your goals. The evening culminates in a walk across a 10-foot bed of 1200 degree coals. Participation is voluntary. Whether you choose to participate in the firewalk or not, this seminar will provide you with success strategies for both personal and professional power.

All locations 7 to 11p.m. Rain or shine. (6:30 p.m. registration) **COST: $75.** Preregistration by March 15 / **$95.** after March 15. **Register Now – Limited space available**.

COURTESY *FIRE*

A Tolly Burkan advertisement for his spring 1989 East Coast firewalk seminar tour.

BRIAN GARLAND

Seattle firewalker Dan McHale tests his immunity to burning in a variety of ways, among them, walking across red-hot firebeds on his hands. Repeatedly, he has been able to make such passages without any injury whatsoever, and, in the process, has challenged the skeptics' theory that the firewalk can be safely performed only because the feet are tough and callused.

SARA RAINTREE, COURTESY CHALLENGES UNLIMITED

Steve Bisyak of Renton, Washington, making the Guinness Book of Records world record firewalk, over a highly-fanned, 15-foot long firebed whose coals measured 1,546 degrees F. In the presence of University of Washington scientists, he and a few others completed the remarkable walk unharmed in any way.

SARA RAINTREE, COURTESY CHALLENGES UNLIMITED

Laura Bisyak, Steve Bisyak's wife, safely crosses the fan-intensified fire that became the path to the Guinness Book of Records world record firewalk. The firewalk program was called "Challenges Unlimited."

Another "Challenges Unlimited" student accomplishes the world record hottest firewalk, without injury.

SARA RAINTREE, COURTESY CHALLENGES UNLIMITED

5

Scientific Studies, Expert Opinions

What is true in the lamplight is not always true in the sunlight.
Joseph Joubert

Since humans first strode across firebeds with intention, hoping to heal or empower themselves, hoping to ward off evil or strengthen their crops, there have been those who longed to explain such rites in concrete, scientific terms. Few scientists could enter such a hotbed of controversy without having some predilection, some preconceived world view that might dramatically influence the track their research would take. Most scientists are very skeptical of so-called paranormal phenomena, seeing themselves as defenders of the faith, a logically based canon of the laws of physics. Consequently, the history of scientific investigation of the firewalk is, in great part, a history of skepticism, of humans and their instruments assaulting the sacred notions that God or man could alter human physiology in miraculous ways.

Many researchers have been much more than debunkers. These men and women would have loved nothing more than to "discover" some uncharted phenomenon, some natural occurrence so odd and intriguing that it would cause the textbooks to be rewritten. But in all honesty, their interpretation of the data they recorded led them to refute the miraculous nature of the firewalk. As a result, the great majority of scientific reports conclude that the safe walk over glowing coals can be explained by the conventional laws of physics.

But there are other reports, too — those whose conclusions amount to big question marks, those that suggest we might be dealing with something far beyond our understanding. These are the reports that intrigued me most, not just because they remained open to the miraculous, but because they expressed a willingness not to know, to step beyond the safety of convention. In all endeavors, this takes courage. And, as the work of all great scientists eloquently testifies, the courage to imagine the unimaginable is science at its best.

EARLY FIREWALKING RESEARCH

Around the turn of the century, Professor Samuel Pierpont Langley, secretary of the Smithsonian Institution and a professor of physics and astronomy, traveled to Tahiti to study Papa Ita, the Tahitian high priest of firewalking. Before meeting the firewalker himself, Langley studied every available newspaper account of the firewalk over red-hot stones. Later, the scientist went to the beach and observed the stones that Papa Ita was to walk on. His report described them as "rounded water-worn stones, weighing, I should think, from forty to eighty pounds apiece. They were, perhaps 200 in number, and all of porous basalt, a feature the importance of which will be seen later." [1]

Langley carefully observed every detail of the firewalk, making special note of the color and apparent temperature of the stones with which the bare feet of the walkers actually made contact. After Papa Ita and his acolytes had all walked across the bed of glowing stones four times, Langley "secured Papa Ita's permission to remove, from the middle of the pile, one stone which from its size and position every foot had rested upon in crossing, and which was undoubtedly at least as hot as any one of those trodden on."

His assistants hefted the large stone into a wooden bucket half filled with water. The water boiled violently for about 12 minutes, after which Langley measured the amount of water left in the bucket and calculated the amount of evaporated water to be about 10 pounds. The stone, composed of vascular basalt and one of the hottest in the pile, Langley found to weigh 65 pounds. Later, he took a piece of it to Washington, D.C., where he conducted further experiments, including determinations of its specific gravity and specific heat. He concluded that the stone was extremely nonconductive. "One end of a small fragment could be held in the hand," he wrote, "while the other was heated indefinitely in the flame of a blow pipe, almost like a stick of sealing wax." [2]

From his research, Langley deduced that the mean temperature of the stone must have been about 1,200 degrees Fahrenheit, but that its surface temperature must have been indefinitely lower. "It was a sight well worth seeing," he concluded, "a most clever and interesting piece of savage magic, but from the evidence I have just given, I am obliged to say (almost regretfully) that it was not a miracle." [3]

Crude as Langley's scientific methods might have been, they presented the first dispassionate view of the hot materials on which the firewalkers walked — in this case, porous basalt. Still, Langley's conclusions raised as many questions as answers. Though he observed Papa Ita on stones that were not glowing, many other reports have him walking — and even standing still — on stones that *were* glowing. How, I wondered, would Langley explain Papa Ita's 1901 appearance before Hawaiian Queen Lilioukalani, when the firewalker was observed by many reporters to walk to the center of a red-hot stone pit and *stand* there, smiling for photographers?

And how to explain another Fijian firewalk leader who had been observed in a red-hot firepit for half a minute? [4] Furthermore, other scientific investigators had found that even porous basalt, when red-hot, possesses sufficient thermal conductivity to inflict burns when touched for half a second or longer. [5] To me, Langley's conclusions seem calculated to explain away a phenomenon they only partially addressed.

Fiji was also the site of the next significant scientific inquiry into the firewalk, this time in 1935 by David Watterson of St. Andrew's University in Melbourne, Australia and Sir James Purves-Stewart of London. They did not agree on their conclusions. Watterson stated that it was the Fijians' frequent exposure to high temperatures that accounted for their immunity to burns, while Purves-Stewart concluded that the ability lay in strong suggestion. After noting that artificial inflammation, blistering and even immunity to pain can be induced in good hypnotic subjects, Purves-Stewart wrote: "Similar marked abnormalities of vascular reactions in the skin and deeper tissues when subjected to painful stimuli have repeatedly been verified in patients under hypnotic suggestion." [6] This was the first scientific hypothesis connecting the firewalk with previously-observed, psychosomatically-induced immunity to pain.

That same year, back in England, there was another attempt to reveal the firewalk's mysteries, this time under the direction of psychic investigator Harry Price. Price assembled a team of physicists and physiologists, under the auspices of the University of London Council for Psychical Investigation, and orchestrated an experiment focusing on a young Kashmiri named Kuda Bux, the same fellow who had firewalked for stuntmaster Robert Ripley at Rockefeller Center in New York the month before. Once a suitable subject had been located, Price and his team of scientists set about establishing their testing methods.

Frank L. Hopwood, a physicist at St Bartholomew's Hospital Medical College at the University of London, suggested X-raying Kuda Bux's feet to insure that they were not impregnated with any metallic salt. Another physicist proposed taking the temperatures of the soles of the firewalker's feet before and after he walked. A third physicist suggested holding a cold mirror near the soles of Bux's feet to see whether they were covered with any liquid that might act as an insulating layer. Still another physicist suggested a "cotton test," arguing that any heat which scorched cotton ought also to scorch Bux's feet. Finally, to assess the surface the firewalker would be contacting, the scientists measured the surface temperature of the fire trench as well as the temperature of any potentially insulating ash. [7]

In an overview of the event he was about to stage, Price found so many variables that he decided to hold a test walk. Wrote the investigator: "The first test was held on Monday, September 9, 1935. Two tons of oak logs, ten gallons of paraffin, twenty-five copies of *The Times* — and a box of matches. This was the incendiary material used in the first fire-walk ever seen in Great Britain." At a suburban estate in Carshalton, a raging inferno 25 feet long and three feet wide erupted from the carefully laid oak log fire. After several hours of burning, it was reduced to a firebed of glowing, orange coals 12 inches deep. Bux tested the fire with one bare foot. Price described the final preparations:

> At 12:55, the Kashmiri again stepped into the trench and pronounced it "fine." He then said it was time to put on the top layer of forest-burnt charcoal, which we did. The charcoal was the purest we could find, and to test its quality, Kuda Bux ate a piece and said it was "good."
>
> The fire was now a mass of red-hot glowing logs, and one could not stand near it for more than a few seconds at a time. We had a staff of helpers, raking and smoothing out the embers, and they had to use wooden shields to protect their faces from the intense heat. At one o'clock, a piece of white paper dropped into the trench burst into flames upon contact. [8]

The party adjourned for lunch, and by the time they returned, they were all disappointed to discover that the firebed seemed shallower, perhaps just three inches deep, but a mass of glowing red-hot embers nevertheless. According to Price, Bux was most upset of all, saying he liked

> . . . at least nine inches of embers in which to bury his feet. He could give no clear reason for this, but said it was much more difficult to walk on a thin layer of fire. It appears to be part of the technique of fire-walking, and is a very important point for future research. Curiously enough, unless the bottom of the trench is completely covered with live embers, Kuda Bux cannot walk on it; it just burns him, though an observer would imagine that the bare base of the trench was not nearly so hot as the glowing embers. In order to make the layer of fire thicker, we raked the embers from one end, piling them onto the center of the trench, which was now shortened to about twenty feet. [9]

At 2:45, the Kashmiri's feet were carefully examined and photographed by several attending physicians. Before Kuda Bux stepped onto the firebed, he used a fan to carefully brush away the ash from the embers. Commented Price: "Whatever else we proved on this historic afternoon, we proved quite definitely that ash plays no part in forming an insulating layer between the feet and the fire. Kuda Bux will not walk on ash; he prefers the red embers." [10]

Bux walked the firebed four times, with a maximum of four steps on each passage. His feet did not burn, but the thinness of the fire worried him: "I must have thick fire," he reiterated.

The investigators carefully examined Bux's feet and found them unaffected in any way, without even the suspicion of a blister. Performing a cotton test, with a swatch of calico covering a wooden shoe last, the scientists found that the fabric scorched in one second and burned completely through in two-and-one-half seconds.

After the cotton test, an observer named Digby Moynagh removed his shoes and socks and momentarily placed a bare foot against the red-hot embers. Pronouncing them hot, he asked the investigators for permission to try the firewalk himself. They consented, and "after a moment's hesitation [he] stepped boldly into the fire and walked two paces before jumping out," his feet badly burned. [11]

The investigators learned a number of things from their first test walk. One, they discovered that ash as insulator between fire and feet plays no role. Two, they found out (from having lunch with Bux just before his firewalk) that fasting was unnecessary for successful firewalking. Three, they concluded that a firewalker "does not have to work himself up into an exalted or ecstatic condition." And four, they agreed there had been no trickery in the Kashmiri's performance. From all this, they could deduce three possible explanations for the successful firewalk: either it was faith, callous feet, or "a knack in placing the feet." [12]

A second test was planned for the following Tuesday, again at Carshalton. Once again requesting a thick bed of coals, Bux also expressed an urgency that there be no cow dung in the fire. One piece in the fire, he said, would make it "unclean" and, hence, impossible for him to do the walk.

This time, Price and the others used seven tons of oak logs, one ton of firewood, a load of charcoal, 10 gallons of paraffin and 50 copies of *The Times* to make the fire. [13] Reported Price:

> . . . by one o'clock, the trenches were a mass of red embers, radiating a terrific heat. The wind shifted every few seconds, and with each gust, showers of sparks and ash nearly smothered the helpers, who were blinded by the heat laden wind which made stoking impossible. The wearing of goggles relieved us somewhat, but I had a raincoat scorched through merely throwing on a log. The heat could be distinctly felt at a distance of sixty-five feet. . . .
>
> After lunch, the red embers just filled the trenches flush with the ground. It was still blowing half a gale, and as the wind swept across the fires, they were fanned almost to white heat. It reminded

> me of a mighty blacksmith's forge at full blast. At 2:30, Kuda Bux had a look at the fires, said they were satisfactory, and instructed us to tip on the load of forest-burnt charcoal. As each sack was tipped on to the trench, a man raked the charcoal evenly over the surface. It will give the reader some idea of the heat of the trenches when I remark that every minute or so, the handle of the rake caught fire and had to be extinguished! [14]

By three o'clock, according to Price, the charcoal was red-hot. Once again, Bux's feet were examined by a doctor and his skin temperature found to be 93.2 degrees F. Once more, the Kashmiri summoned up his faith and resolutely strode the firebed, staying in the trench a total of 4.5 seconds. When the skin temperature of his feet was measured after this walk, it was found to be just 93 degrees F, slightly *lower* than before his passage. Bux's feet were neither burned nor blistered.

Once more Kuda Bux walked the fire, and again he was uninjured in any way. Dr. R. E. Gibbs, one of the attending physicists, measured the temperature of the fire with a thermocouple. Its main body was 2,552 degrees F, with a surface temperature of 806 degrees F. Following this second test, Digby Moynagh — who still had not recovered from the blisters received from his earlier firewalk — stepped out on the coals again, took a single hop, then bound out in pain. Another onlooker named Maurice Cheepen stepped into the trench and took two short steps, but he too was badly burned.

Curiously, at one point in the second test, Kuda Bux said he could not walk on the fire again; that the scientists had upset him and he had lost his faith. Wrote Price:

> His sudden breakdown after the second walk seems to indicate that, after all, "faith" (or confidence) plays some part in the performance. I think that may be secret of the fire-walk. After that "faith" had broken within him, nothing would induce him to do the walk. In addition to the part that faith and nerve control may have played in Kuda Bux's fire-walking, I think there is a certain technique to be learnt. He said he first practiced fire-walking in India when he was fourteen years old (he is now thirty). We proved the immunity from burns is not due to callosity of the skin, as Kuda Bux has soft skin, which is not callous. We exploded the theory that ash acts as an insulator between feet and fire, as the wind and our rakes removed it all. We have proved that it is a fallacy that "anyone can do it." [15]

Price's conclusion after these tests?

> We have not completely solved the mystery of fire-walking, but we are very near to a solution. I think the secret of immunity from burns lies in the fact that, in the case of Kuda Bux, there is some obscure relationship between physical and mental forces, and this helps to make him immune from injury. I think he also works himself up into a semi-hypnotic state. Apparently, that state is easily disturbed, witness how he broke down after the second attempt on our experiment on September 17, 1935. The scientists upset him. He told professor Pannet that the physicist who placed the thermocouple in the pit had "desecrated" it. He said that his was a religious act of faith and that it had been rendered impossible by the thrusting of the instrument into the burning embers. [16]

The press was intrigued. In England, *The Observer* reported: "This is a genuine 'miracle' in the original sense of something to wonder at from the standpoint of ordinary experience and reasoning. . . . Unless some better explanation emerges, a state of mind would appear to have influenced the behavior of matter through channels of which we have no knowledge." [17]

The council's much-publicized firewalk stirred the world's interest in this strange rite. According to Price, accounts of the experiments appeared in every principal newspaper in the world, and in India, Kuda Bux was hailed as a hero.

Bux's feats inspired another Indian fire-walker named Ahmed Hussain to offer his services in early 1937. Reported Price: "Through his agent, I offered him a 50 pound fee. He wanted 100 pounds, which I said I would pay him if he successfully passed our tests. . . . Like Kuda Bux, he is a 'magician' by profession, and has walked on fire in India on many occasions. Also like Kuda Bux, he claimed to impart his alleged immunity from burning to others." [18]

Price advertised in the *The Times* for volunteer "walkers" to be used as controls. To his surprise, he received 40 replies, including a young lady undergraduate. Again the tests were held at Carshalton, and once more a bonfire was built, this time consisting of "four tons of oak logs, one ton of firewood, five hundredweight of forest-burnt charcoal, ten gallons of paraffin, and fifty copies of *The Times*." The addition of *The Times* was not merely ceremonial; old copies of the paper were crumpled and laid in the fire as tinder, starting the inferno with news of the past.

The news of the present had Price seeking out even more sophisticated instrumentation, together with a host of physicists, physicians and other assorted men of science. With even more precise thermocouples, they measured the temperature of the fire, as well as the temperatures of Hussain's soles before his firewalk.

Dressed in turban and belted jacket, Hussain recited a prayer from the Koran. Moments later, at 3:45 p.m. on April 7, 1937, the barefoot magician stepped into the fire and took three quick strides in 1.3 seconds, emerging completely unburned on the other side of the pit. Remarkably, when the temperature of the soles of his feet was taken this time, it was found to be *10 degrees lower* than before he had walked!

Next, Hussain walked across with four volunteers, the amateur walkers following behind with hands linked to their leader. All the volunteer walkers were burned to varying degrees, showing that Hussain was *not* able to confer his immunity to others.

Two days later, another test was held, with the BBC broadcasting live commentary. According to Hussain's requests, the first firebed had been only 12 feet long; however, the researchers felt that this limited not only the duration of contact with the fire and the potential heat buildup on the firewalkers' feet but also their own window of scientific observation. Thus, with Hussain's consent, they built a bigger fire and raked out a longer firebed, this time using 10 tons of oak logs, a ton of firewood, 500 pounds of charcoal, 10 gallons of paraffin and 50 copies of *The Times*.

After muttering his prayers, Hussain entered the 20-foot-long firebed and quickly took six steps across it in a total of 2.3 seconds. This time, the magician was slightly burned, receiving six small blisters on his feet. All the amateur walkers who followed were also slightly burned.

As the final test of the day, one of the amateur walkers, Reginald Adcock, walked the firebed in a pair of dry, rope-soled shoes, taking seven steps in 3.6 seconds. The soles of his shoes were unburned, only the frayed strands of rope at the edges being slightly scorched. Concluded Price:

> The results of the tests on April 9 were enlightening. It was quite clear that, whether amateur or professional, the limit of walking on a really hot fire was two steps per foot with contact time of about one half-second each. Also, it was quite obvious that "confidence" had a great deal to do with it. Most of the volunteers floundered more or less. Reginald Adcock, who walked the most steadily, was burned the least. And the fact that the rope-soled shoes were not damaged made it clear that the low thermal conductivity of the hot ash and wood embers injures neither normal skin nor other objects if the contact-time is about half a second. [19]

After reading this, I couldn't help wishing Price and his crew had dropped one of the rope-soled shoes onto the coalbed to see how long it took to scorch or catch fire. Over and over, I had heard reports (and on occasion even seen evidence) that firewalkers' clothes are as immune to burning as the soles of their feet. If Adcock's shoes had scorched or caught fire in less than half a second when he was *not* wearing them, what might the scientists have concluded then?

Final tests were held in the grounds of Alexandra Palace on April 20,

1937, with reports going out over radio and, for the first time, over television. This was also the first televised, remote outdoor event in England, and for the few TV sets in and around London, the pictures were of startling clarity and content. They showed Ahmed Hussain taking four steps over a 12-foot long firebed, followed by Reginald Adcock, the plucky English amateur. Neither was burned in any way.

From the 1937 experiments, the council concluded that the secret of firewalking lies in: "(a) the short contact-time of each foot with the embers, with a limit of immunity of two steps per foot . . . (b) the low thermal conductivity of burning or burnt wood embers; (c) confidence and steadiness in walking. . . . The experiments proved once and for all that no occult or psychic power, or a specially induced mental state, is necessary in a fire-walker." [20]

Together with Kuda Bux and Ahmed Hussain, Harry Price, and the London Council had taken a giant stride forward in revealing the firewalk's mysteries. But their experiments and conclusions still did not explain reports of longer firewalks and firedances, much less long-term contact with coals and other red-hot objects.

There were reports of routine, 30-foot firewalks in India and South Africa. Writer Arthur Miles and others had told of 50-foot firewalks in India and Burma. And London author-traveler Bindon Blood had described two Moslems who calmly walked barefoot and uninjured over 88 feet of red-hot coals at Nawanagar, India. [21] Still, mainstream science continued to debunk the feat.

CONTINUING SKEPTICISM

In 1939, for example, *Scientific American* gave an historical overview of firewalking. "The solution is simple," it stated. "The feat is stripped of its atmosphere of mystery and hocus-pocus. Probably you could do firewalking — simply by doing it." [22]

Besides giving a cultural and scientific perspective, the report essentially summarized and quoted the work of the London Council firewalks with Kuda Bux and Ahmed Hussain. Of particular note were some of the slightly condensed conclusions of Dr. G. Burniston Brown, author of the London Council's report:

> The fire-walk is no sense a trick: the walk is performed in a normal manner with bare and chemically unprepared feet. The fall in the temperature of the surface of the soles of the feet during the experiment was possibly due to a number of steps being taken on the grass after leaving the fire, before the place of examination was reached. The fact that no signs of burning were found on the dry rope-soled shoes (which can hardly be supposed to be affected by the mental state of the wearer) leads to the view that the secret of

> the fire-walk lies in the low thermal conductivity of the burning wood. The thermal conductivity of copper, for example, is about 1000 times greater than that of oak wood. [23]

Summarizing the London Council's arguments, the *Scientific American* article closed by stating that "brief contact, few contacts and a poor conductor of heat — seem sufficient to account for the ability to do fire-walking." [24]

THE LEIDENFROST EFFECT

Riviera Beach, Florida was the site of the next significant "scientific" firewalk, this one a ritual-free performance by American chemist Mayne Reid Coe, Jr. In the early 1950s, Coe believed he had discovered "the answer to a mystery of the ages, the secret of the firewalkers." In an 1890 physics text, he had found the buried treasure, a statement to the effect that "liquid in a spheroidal shape does not actually touch the red-hot surface on which it dances; it is buoyed by an insulating cushion of its own vapor. And its temperature is always below its own boiling point as long as the spheroidal state remains." [25] As long as contact with the hot surface is brief, Coe theorized, this vapor barrier protects the skin from injury.

Actually, Coe had come across what is known as the "Leidenfrost effect." The phenomenon was first made public in 1756, when the German physician Johann Gottlieb Leidenfrost published a paper entitled *A Tract About Some Qualities of Common Water*. Taking a red-hot spoon from the fire, Leidenfrost placed a single drop of water in it and observed its movement. Counting the swings of a pendulum, he noted that his first drop on the spoon danced for 30 seconds before evaporating; a second drop on the same spoon danced for only 10 seconds; and further drops lasted only one or two seconds.

Leidenfrost might have been the first to write about the phenomenon that bears his name, but he never really understood it. It was his theory that the hotter spoon sustained the drops longer because the heat increased the watery surface tension. In fact, a Leidenfrost drop is supported by a layer of its own vapor approximately .09 millimeter thick, if the surface over which it is dancing is sufficiently hot. As one scientists describes it, "The drop dances and skims about in reasonable safety from the hot plate because of this protective vapor layer, which is constantly supplied by evaporation of the bottom of the drop. Eventually enough heat is conducted and radiated through the vapor layer to vaporize the remaining drop, and then the dancing is over." [26]

To test his hypothesis, Coe subjected himself to a series of bold experiments. After trying instantaneous foot contact with hot sheet metal, he drove to the beach near his home and prepared a firebed of wood coals. Facing the fire, at first he found it difficult to walk; however, certain of his principles, he pushed through his fear and took two steps before hopping out in pain. After immersing his foot in a bucket of water, he examined it and found it undamaged in any way. Summoning his courage again, he made a second attempt, this time crossing the bed in four steps without pain or burning. Then, doing an about-face, he crossed again without incident.

Coe explained that the act of walking, of placing one foot and then the other gives the spheroidal state a chance to operate. "As one [foot] is raised, it must sweat instantly," he wrote. "Then, as the foot descends and contacts the hot surface, it is insulated from it by the spheroidal state of the moisture. The faster one crosses the fiery pit, the more fleeting the moment that foot touches the incandescent object." [27]

Among a wide range of other fire-immunity experiments, Coe also successfully firewalked on red-hot rocks and ran barefoot across red-hot iron. Just what he proved, besides his own bravery, is open to question; for again, his conclusions do not explain the documented cases of longer contact with fire. But as far as Coe was concerned, all his firewalking successes were due to brief contact combined with the protection of water vapor in the spheroidal state, the Leidenfrost effect. As we shall see, this was to become (and still is) a popular explanation for injury-free firewalks.

TESTING THE FIRE IN CEYLON

Ceylonese firewalking was the stimulus for the next serious study of the phenomenon, this time by physiologist C. Fonseka of the Colombo Medical College. Fonseka had lived in Ceylon all his life, and in the early 1970s, asked himself how these local devotees, whose amazing feats he had often witnessed, kept walking through fire without getting burned.

To gather data, Fonseka observed a firewalk at Kataragama. Using a thermoelectric pyrometer, he made careful measurements of the fire's temperature, then carefully watched and timed 100 firewalkers as they crossed the coals. He found that the fire varied several hundred degrees in temperature, from 572 degrees F. to 842 degrees F, and that the average contact time for a single step was .3 seconds. [28]

After assessing the heat (which he called the "stimulus") and the duration of contact with it, Fonseka measured the "responding" surface, the soles of the feet. Using a variable heat generator in the laboratory, he established some clear thresholds for the perception of warmth and pain. Not surprisingly, people who had worn no shoes their entire lives had tougher soles and a correspondingly higher point of perception for both warmth and pain. Similarly, cold, wet feet took significantly longer to communicate pain than did warm, dry ones.

From all this, Fonseka reached his hypothetical explanation — once again, that the firewalk can be safely performed because of short contact with the coals. To test his hypothesis, he prepared an experimental firewalk, with firebeds approximating the one he had observed at Kataragama. Reported the doctor: "With no special preparation — physical, mental or spiritual —

five healthy adult men walked these fires with a maximum of four steps taken in a maximum time of 2 seconds. They did not sustain any burns." [29]

THE FIJI EXPERIMENT

The perennial inquiry returned to Fiji in 1974, this time with West German nuclear physicist Friedbert Karger directing. A member of the prestigious Max Planck Institute for Plasma Physics, Karger applied sophisticated temperature-indicating paints to one of the Fijian firewalker's feet. Despite the 600-degree F temperatures recorded over the firepit, the firewalker's foot never became hotter than 150 degrees F. Not long after the walk, Karger placed a piece of calloused skin from one of the Fijian's feet on one of the red-hot rocks, and it turned to a blackened crisp almost instantly.

How to interpret these seemingly contradictory bits of data: the piece of foot skin charring and a live firewalker's foot skin under much greater pressure withstanding repeated contact without burning? For Karger, the data suggested two possibilities: either some sort of insulating effect or something dramatically reducing the firewalker's weight. (Fijian firewalkers often reported being "lifted" over the hot rocks.) Whatever is happening underfoot, Karger concluded, it cannot be explained "within the realm of known physics." [30]

LEIDENFROST REVISITED

Several years later, the defenders of the faith at *Scientific American* vigorously disagreed. In 1977, they published the report of physicist Jearl Walker, who once again focused on the vapor barrier, the Leidenfrost effect. Walker takes us to a pancake griddle, noting that if the surface is hot, but not yet hot enough, a test drop of water will hit the griddle and evaporate in a couple of seconds. If the griddle is hotter, though, a test drop will not evaporate right away; instead, it will dance on the hot surface, vibrating and skimming over the griddle for 30 to 100 seconds. [31]

Walker reported that of all the demonstrations of the Leidenfrost effect, firewalking is the most amazing. After describing several firewalks, he wrote:

> In none of these cases is there any reason to invoke unusual powers. Although somehow shutting off pain information to the brain, having a deep seated religious faith or just being dumb enough to try the stunt might help, the primary protection on the walker's feet comes from the natural moisture on them. Each step places parts of a foot in contact with the coals, and moisture at those places partially vaporizes to give momentary protection. Sweating between footfalls can replenish some of the moisture, but eventually most of it is depleted and the foot begins to warm up perceptibly. The walk usually ends then unless the walker has an unusual tolerance for pain. A thick layer of ash and heavily calloused feet might also lengthen

> the walk somewhat, but running does not help because the feet are then slammed down into the coals. [32]

Now that Walker had his hypothesis worked out on paper, he had only to put it — and himself — to the test.

> Having been amazed by stories about people walking on hot coals, and having now become a firm believer in the Leidenfrost effect, I set up a five-foot bed of hot wood coals for such a walk. I suddenly found it remarkably easy to believe in physics when it is on paper but remarkably hard to believe in when the safety of one's own feet is at stake. As a matter of fact, walking on hot coals would be such a supreme test of one's true belief in what one had learned that I have suggested graduate schools might substitute it for the Ph.D. examination in physics. On one side of a pit of red-hot coals would be a line of fresh Ph.D. candidates. On the other side would be the department chairman with a handful of certificates. If a graduate student really believed in physics, he would stride across the coals without hesitation. If, however, he had any serious doubt, he would not be able to bring himself to do it.
>
> I had to try it myself. Clutching my faded copy of Halliday and Resnick's *Physics* in one hand, I strode over the five feet of hot coals. Apparently I am a true believer in physics. I have to report, however, that my feet did get a bit hot. Oh well, I am almost a true believer. [33]

Again, it seemed that Walker's conclusions did not account for prolonged contact with fire. Moreover, his experiment seemed to me more a testimonial to faith than to science. When faced with the fire, like Ahmed Hussain before him, Walker clutched his holy book as he crossed the hot coals.

No doubt Jearl Walker would respond, "No, not faith; the Leidenfrost effect saved me from burning." Perhaps. But after several more successful firewalks, Walker made a passage that failed, suffering third-degree burns on both feet. He stayed off the coals after that but maintained his belief, stating that the Leidenfrost effect would indeed protect a walker for a "short" firewalk. [34] Just how short such a walk might be, he did not specify.

STUDYING THE GREEK FIREDANCERS

Throughout the 1970's, another Max Planck Institute staff member, a Greek neurologist named Christos Xenakis, studied the firedancing Anastenaria of Lankadas. His extensive tests indicated that the dancers are not in a trance, but in a high state of self-induced concentration. Through movement, music and visualization, combined with a special way of walking, he concluded, firewalkers can somehow produce a state in which they are insensitive to pain and, even more miraculously, unaffected by burning temperatures. "The firewalkers are normal people," he wrote, "but show what can be done through strong belief and concentration." [35]

For 10 years, Xenakis and two fellow researchers studied the Anastenaria. In order to obtain the most precise data, they used such sophisticated instruments as tele-EEGs, tele-EKGs, blood tests and movie films. The EKGs proved normal, while the EEGs showed low-voltage theta rhythms (a highly relaxed state of consciousness usually associated with the dream state) during the preparation stages and normal rhythms during the actual firedance. Neurological, psychiatric and lab tests (blood, urine and electrolytes) also were in the normal range. Xenakis was mystified by the lack of burns. Unable to account for it, he concluded that ". . . present knowledge is not adequate to explain the phenomenon." [36]

But in other research papers, published in German psychiatric journals, Xenakis seemed to draw different conclusions. In one, he suggests "a psychological component with specific effects on the physical regulation of temperature." [37] In a second, he suggests a special technique of walking combined with a surplus of pain-dampening endorphins produced by "the long, stressful period of preparations." [38] In these papers, Xenakis and his associates seem to be saying that unusual things do occur in a Greek firedancer's physiology, but nothing outside the scope of known biophysics and biochemistry.

PSYCHOLOGY, SUPERCONDUCTIVITY AND BIOENERGY

In their book *Anomalistic Psychology: A Study of Extraordinary Phenomena of Behavior and Experience*, published in 1982, Leonard Zusne and Warren Jones describe the firewalk and the various explanations that have been advanced for the seemingly miraculous immunity to burns.

> These include mass hallucination, chemicals applied to the soles of the feet, the use of pain-deadening drugs, callous feet, autohypnosis that induces analgesia and a bio-chemical modification of skin surface, hydration, and the spheroid state. Although some of these factors may be involved some of the time, none of them in itself is the complete explanation. [39]

The authors examine each possible explanation, eliminating mass hallucination, chemicals on the feet and pain deadening drugs; but they do find a measure of immunity-impacting capability in all of the others. They conclude that physical factors play the primary role and psychological factors a secondary role:

> Fear . . . translates into sweating, including the sweating of the feet, which may cause hot ashes and small cinders to adhere to the skin and cause burns. Fear also affects the way we walk. Inexperi-

> enced volunteers who are uncertain about their ability to do the walk and become apprehensive as they feel the heat radiating from the trench, attempt to jump or run, dig their heels too heavily into the embers, and get burned as a consequence. Confidence in oneself manifests itself in a confident posture and a confident walk. Confident walking, in turn, leads to the least damage in fire walking. [40]

These scientists seem to be on to something but they don't go far enough. *Why* does confident walking lead to the least damage? Perhaps it's because fear not only influences the way we walk, it destroys faith. And faith, I still suspect, is the magic ingredient that creates immunity. As far as digging one's heels into the embers, apparently these scientists hadn't read Harry Price's accounts of Kuda Bux, the Kashmiri who refused to firewalk on anything but a deep bed of red-hot coals.

Giovanni Iannuzzo, an Italian psychologist reporting in the paranormal investigating *Psi Research* magazine, has reduced the firewalking mystery to concepts of physiology and psychology. Noting that mammalian tissues cannot stand temperatures higher than 140 degrees F without burning, but that some people have an immunity to such temperatures, he notes three possible hypotheses: trickery, paranormal phenomena or psychophysiological explanations. [41]

His own preference, however, is different. "A more plausible assumption," he writes, "is that participants of firewalking ceremonies are in trance-like altered states of consciousness which can be transferred from one individual to another. Therefore, perhaps, it is not the ability of fire immunity that is transferred, but rather the trance-like altered state." [42]

Along with a few other researchers, Igor Guberman, also writing in *Psi Research*, speaks about the skin's "superconductivity," made possible by changes in the nervous system. In this state, the skin is the medium for a variety of electrical energies. Then, finally staring squarely at the firewalk riddle, Guberman writes, "All these theories cannot explain why the protein of life cells is able to withstand temperatures many times beyond its limits, or why no burns occur." [43]

Greek psychiatrist Vittoria Manganas also believes that the skin has superconductive abilities. In a December 1983 article for *Psi Research*, she further states that firewalking is correlated with an increase in "bioenergy" and the formation of a "bioenergetic, protective field" around the body. [44]

Manganas is a specialist in adapting Kirlian photography to psychiatric research. Kirlian, or high-frequency photography, is also known as "corona discharge" photography, as it is said to visually record the vital force field around animals and plants. Appearing somewhat like the halo around the sun, this force field apparently dims when an organism becomes ill and disappears altogether when the organism dies.

Kirlian photography is not yet generally accepted by the scientific community, many researchers feeling that the small electrical charges used to enhance the streamers, or corona images, may in fact be *causing* them. After examining a number of Kirlian photos of firewalkers' feet, I had to conclude that the imagery was impressive, but open to a variety of interpretations.

In relating her study of the Greek firedancers, Manganas is clear about her reasons for using the controversial technique. "Anastenarides have been subjected to almost all current medical and psychiatric tests, even injections of endorphin antagonists, without conclusive results. In this study, high frequency photography was used as in previous psychiatric research, because of its potential for revealing bioenergetic states and changes in living organisms." [45]

Accordingly, she took Kirlian photographs of the hands and feet of 11 Anastenarides during preparation for the firedance, during the dance itself and during situations in everyday life, then compared these images with those of people in special states such as hypnosis, meditation and autogenic training (AT). "In all the above conditions, including fire dancing," she reports, "an increase in the corona discharge can be observed, compared to the corresponding rest conditions. . . . The Kirlian photos of the feet show a remarkable increase of the length and density of the streamers and sparks of different colors. This is not dependent on the mechanical act of dancing, since the same image was given while at rest." [46]

Manganas' conclusions are sure to be startling to some scientists, sheer hogwash to others:

> At this point, I would like to express the hypothesis that in firewalking not only is there an increase in bioenergy as in other special states, but that a kind of biogenetic protective shield is formed. Victor Inyushin and Alexander Romen postulate that, in special extreme conditions, man can display exceptional capacities by increasing (voluntarily or not) his amount of "biological plasma," as can be seen in a high frequency field. In the case of fire dancers, the "bioplasma" protects from burns because the charged particles or free electrons that form it produce a state of superconductivity of the skin. [47]

Despite some enduring scientific skepticism, the notion of a bioenergetic force field appears in many esoteric traditions — and even in modern biology. Beginning in the 1930s, science had to reconcile itself to acknowledging at least a part of the mystics' vision, when it was scientifically verified that all living things emit an aura or force field of some sort. Between the ivy-draped quadrangles of Yale University, biologist Harold S. Burr monitored a series of trees with electrically sensitive detectors, measuring a subtle electrical field surrounding the tree trunks. The existence of Burr's discovered "Life Fields," or "L-fields," as he called them, was confirmed by other researchers. They also confirmed his finding that the L-field is affected by changes in the organism's environment, and that changes in the organism's health can be detected in the L-field. [48]

Burr's student and colleague, Leonard Ravitz, carried on his work. Ravitz has focused on humans, charting the L-field effects of environment, weather, and lunar phases, as well as the effects of various mental and emotional states. One of Ravitz's significant conclusions: "Both emotional activity and stimuli of any sort involve mobilization of electrical energy, as indicated on the galvanometer, hence, both emotions and stimuli evoke the same energy. Emotions can be equated with energy." [49]

By changing our emotional state, Ravitz seems to imply, we can affect our force field. By affecting our force field, Vittoria Manganas seems to imply, we may well affect our immunity to fire. We'll return to these researchers and this force field for a closer look in Chapter 9.

MENTAL-EMOTIONAL STATES OF FIREWALKERS

Psychologist Julianne Blake is probably the only firewalking investigator to have statistically examined the mental and emotional states of those who cross the coals. In 1985, she interviewed and administered a battery of psychological tests to 98 first-time firewalkers and 13 veterans, aged 14 to 73. These were close to equally divided between participants in a Tony Robbins workshop and those following Tolly Burkan. Sixty-four percent of the firewalkers showed no physical evidence of their contact with the coals, while 36 percent burned or blistered.

Blake found that nonblisterers were generally more predisposed to anxiety and that they experienced more anxiety in anticipation of the firewalk than those who blistered. She also found that those who had little belief in chance or in the power of others tended to blister. In her study, the successful firewalkers felt the most important factors were group energy, the power and charisma of the leader and visualization of a successful walk. Significantly, 100 percent of the nonblisterers (as opposed to 33 percent of the blisterers) thought that faith was involved in the firewalking process. Blake concluded that in order to walk on fire without burning, a healthy anxiety is necessary and appropriate, coupled with a strong belief in powerful outside forces. [50]

MIND-INDUCED PHYSICAL IMMUNITY

Physician Andrew Weil is a former Harvard research associate who has become a popular authority on psychophysiology. In his book *Health and Healing*, a study of conventional and alternative medicine, Weil zeroes in on firewalking as possible evidence of mind-induced physical immunity. He suggests a number of different mechanisms that might contribute to the immunity to burning, among them changes in blood circulation, changes in the functions of local nerves and "some as-yet-undiscovered capacity of the nervous system to absorb potentially harmful forms of energy, transform them, and conduct them away from the body surface." In any case, he asserts, successful firewalking is the result of "using the mind in certain ways . . . and so allowing the brain and nerves to alter the body's responsiveness to heat." [51]

For Weil, this medical mystery was an avenue for discovery, so he walked down it himself — on a bed of red-hot coals. After his own experience, he was convinced that firewalking is made possible by extraordinary states of consciousness, and he was inspired by the prospect that such states might also be used to cure or prevent disease:

> Firewalking demonstrates the reality of using extraordinary states of consciousness to modify the body's responses to ordinarily harmful external stimulation. If you don't have to get pain, redness, and blisters on exposure to a certain range and type of heat, then you don't have to get infections on exposure to germs, allergies on exposure to allergens, cancer on exposure to carcinogens. What an exciting and largely uncharted territory in which to discover powerful new techniques to bolster natural resistance to disease!
>
> I make this request of medical professionals who consider themselves scientists: Do not ignore firewalking. Scrutinize it and put the conclusions you come to about it to work in your daily practice of the healing art.[52]

Here is a man of science with an open mind; a man with no fear of losing his bearings by acknowledging the unknown. Another man of science with an open mind is sociologist James McClenon. McClenon has not only studied and written about firewalking, he has personally walked the glowing firebed numerous times — in Sri Lanka, in Japan and here in the United States. Drawing on his range of cross-cultural experience, McClenon speculates that there may be a host of contributing factors to successful firewalking. But he believes the greatest factor is the power of the mind to alter the body's normal perceptions and reactions to pain.

"I believe that firewalking is a kind of borderline phenomenon," he told me in a telephone interview. "It doesn't necessarily require the paranormal, but people who are involved in this kind of thing probably have more unusual experiences . . . It could be paranormal." [53]

In his continuing quest to explore the unknown, McClenon organized a series of nine firewalks himself, on the island of Okinawa, Japan, while he was teaching sociology there. Did he have a ritual? "Yes," he said, "but in my mind, it was basically hypnosis. The ritual was: hypnotize the people and give them the suggestion that when they saw me walk over the coals, they would be able to do it also."

And had he himself engaged in a bit of self-hypnosis prior to his leading walk? "Yes, I believe in self-hypnosis," he said. "But it's not really necessary. Just the thought that you will be protected, just that realization . . . would do the trick." [54]

Being a man of science, McClenon was trained to be skeptical, dubious of any data that does not fit into the historical norm. At one point, he said, he came to agree with the growing scientific consensus that firewalking was not the least bit paranormal and that anybody could walk across glowing coals without being burned, because the coals were so low in thermal conductivity. That is when he got badly burned, on his second firewalk in Sri Lanka. "It was a very hot coalbed," he explained, "and I had thought that this low conductivity business would protect me." [55] The sociologist laughed, in retrospect, the absurdity of the scientific puzzle and the pain he suffered swirling together in his mind. The reality of low thermal conductivity of wood coals should have protected him, but instead there was almost instantaneous pain and burning.

As a result of the third degree burns he received, McClenon was unable to walk for three weeks. Since then, he has firewalked a dozen times, but he still hasn't faced a fire like that Sri Lankan fire, the one that burned most of the day and half the night before it turned to a radiant walkway, shimmering in the darkness. Nor has he felt the searing, screaming heat he did that night.

I asked him what he would do differently, were he to face such a fire again. "I would stick with the master firewalkers and obey anything that they said to me," he replied. "I don't believe the skeptical scientists understand it. If I were to do a dangerous firewalk, I would much rather be under the directive of a firewalking master in Sri Lanka than a skeptical scientist in California, because if you read their articles closely, they've been burned!" [56]

THE FIREWALKING DEBUNKERS

Just who are these scientists who would rain on the firewalking parade? Many of them are members of a national group called Concerned Scientists Investigating Claims of the Paranormal (CSICOP). Leaders of the group characterize themselves as "a small group of academics fighting an uphill battle against a huge, oozing mass of unverified mysticism that threatens to exploit or defraud its followers." [57] Current CSICOP members include science writers Isaac Asimov and Martin Gardner, famed debunker and magician Amazing Randi and, in the southern California affiliate, physicist Bernard Leikind and psychologist William McCarthy.

In their effort to investigate the firewalk as it was being taught in southern California, Leikind and McCarthy took a Tony Robbins firewalk. Then they staged several of their own, inviting a skeptical public to walk across hot coals through the grace of the natural laws of physics. And in the several papers they subsequently published, they described how it could be done.

Their papers focused on the difference between temperature and heat and on the varying conductivity of different substances. "For example, when we are baking a cake," they wrote, "the air in the oven, the cake, and the cake pan are all at about the same temperature. None of us would think for a moment about putting our hands into the hot oven air, but we know that we cannot touch the cake pan for more than an instant without being burned. Why is this?" [58]

The answer, they explained, is that air is a poor conductor of heat; the pan contains much more thermal or heat energy because of its higher conductivity. "It is for these reasons that we put a potholder, a poor conductor of heat, between our hands and the pan and don't worry about the [hot oven] air."

Firewalking, they explained, is based on the same idea:

> The embers are light, fluffy compounds. Although they may be at a fairly high temperature (1,000 degrees F. to 1,200 degrees F.), they do not contain as much energy as we might expect . . . Thus, so long as we do not spend too much time on the embers, our feet will probably not get hot enough to burn. In fact, because the heat capacity of the embers is low and that of our feet relatively high, the embers cool off when we step on them. How do I know this? Well, the color and the intensity of the light from the embers tells us their temperature; yellow embers are hotter than orange, orange hotter than red, etc. When I watched people walking across the beds of coals, I could clearly see darkened footprints where the coals had cooled because of contact with the feet. In a couple of seconds, the combustion reactions restored the embers' temperature and glow. [59]

If short contact with a poor thermal conductor is what allows us to safely walk on fire, then why do some people burn? With predictable scientific methodology, the skeptics say it is the variables: variable fires, variables temperatures, variable methods of walking, variable numbers of steps, variable walking speeds, variable toughness of the soles and variable amounts of protective "Leidenfrost" sweat.

Leikind in particular is annoyed at what he perceives as most firewalking leaders' misappropriation of the laws of thermodynamics, but he is even angrier at what he perceives as their deceptive use of it. Says the physicist, "I'm highly in favor of people expanding their strengths and expanding their world and increasing the possibilities of what they can do. But I object to the firewalking psychological gurus because they use deception in order to achieve that end." [60]

Leikind intimates that the firewalkers' conquest of fear is very real, but that the firewalk leaders are dishonest in suggesting that one must achieve a special mental state in order to do it.

As for those who burn, he says, "They believe they have to look the right way and breathe the right way and chant the mantra and all this other stuff. And for some reason that day — maybe they walked slower, or maybe they got an ember stuck between their toes — so two-thirds of the way across, their feet got hot enough so that they were burning. The temperature was just going up the whole time. It had nothing to do with them losing their concentration at all. Because pain's in your head, it's a perception; and whether your foot is burned is a matter of physics." [61]

Not entirely, it would seem. For scientists have induced blistering in hypnotic subjects who have been told they're being touched by a red-hot object, an object which is in reality quite cold. Hypnosis can also *eliminate* blistering in patients who have been burned. That is not conventional physics; it is mind over matter!

So dramatic were Leikind and McCarthy's demonstrations, however, that for many years following — and during the later 80's in particular — the instructors of some of UCLA's physics classes held firewalks to demonstrate the laws of thermodynamics. Students could walk the coalbeds barefoot, if they chose, or they could just watch.

One instructor who regularly staged these events, but who did not walk himself, was Dr. Art Huffman. I spoke with Huffman, who described this unusual class demonstration. "We've done it six or eight times," he said, "but the fad died out and no one's requested it recently."

I asked him whether low thermal conductivity was the secret to firewalking. "I'm pretty convinced," he said. "And I'm totally convinced that the way you think can't protect you from getting burned if you're going to get burned." [62]

So is John Taylor, a physicist at the University of Colorado. Wrote Taylor:

> The ability to walk barefoot across a bed of red-hot embers has long been considered a sign of supernatural powers. . . . That thousands of middle-class Americans can be taught to walk on coals strongly suggests that the exercise does not require any mystical or supernatural powers, and that there is instead some straightforward physical explanation. This suggestion is correct, and the physical explanation of firewalking has been well described in a recent article by Leikind and McCarthy. [63]

Taylor built a small firebed himself and walked barefoot across it. He, too, blistered, feeling nonetheless that he had proved his point. In particular, he noted the significance of tolerance for pain in the firewalk:

> It seems certain that the ability to withstand some pain is an important part of the firewalking phenomenon. My own experience bears this out. After my first session, I developed two blisters on my

> feet, even though I was quite unaware of any damage at the time. Tolerance for pain is presumably even more important at firewalk classes, where excitement has been built with inspirational speeches and chanting, and there is a clear implication that to be burned is a sign of failure. Under these conditions, many participants would presumably not admit to being hurt even if they were. [64]

I spoke with Dr. McCarthy, and he reframed his and Leikind's investigation into the firewalk. They had heard claims on a radio talk show, claims that new powers could be developed in a one night seminar. So, said McCarthy, "We set out to investigate these claims, and to use the scientific method to establish if there are any consequences [of the seminar], what they are and what the mechanism is. The breathing techniques and all the distractions effectively serve to reduce the pain of those who burn at firewalk. I'm convinced, at least with the evidence in so far, that psychology plays absolutely no role in whether tissue will burn or tolerate higher levels of heat without burning. It's all physics." [65]

For McCarthy, there is deception not only in the firewalking seminars, but in the very word itself. "Although we call it firewalking," he said, "in fact, it's not firewalking; it's *ember*walking. If we converted the study of the phenomenon from firewalking to emberwalking, all of a sudden there's less interest, it's a less fascinating subject, because it's easier to explain how people can walk on hot embers and not get burned than how they can walk on fire." [66]

McCarthy has firewalked three times. He has also burned his feet three times, blistering on each occasion. "Tender feet" is his explanation. He may have injured himself slightly in his investigation, he says, but he is serious about wanting to help others avoid injury — including the psychological injury that he believes can result from contact with the firewalking movement.

"Why are people attracted to these seminars?" he asks. "There aren't data of a hard nature to support this contention, but my impression is that these people are looking for what I might call 'fast-food therapy.' What they're looking for is an answer to life problems that can be encapsulated in a six-hour seminar, and then from that point on, they'll be forever changed. It's a nice, clean, rapid transformation that they're looking for." [67]

The firewalk has engendered a similar controversy in England. There, "coal strolls" have become almost a popular pastime, with the mystically-inclined believing in the power of faith, and skeptics maintaining it is all possible because of established laws of physics. In 1990, *New Scientist* reporter Susan Blackmore joined the Wessex Skeptics and more than a hundred others as they walked a 12-foot bed of glowing embers in a back garden at Southampton University. Their intention: to "confirm the laws of physics!" They certainly confirmed something, as there were no reported injuries. [68]

REVIEWING THE EVIDENCE

What has science shown us about the firewalk? Do we know any more about it now than when Samuel Langley investigated it in 1901? Is it completely explainable by physics, or is there a psychological or perhaps even a spiritual component? Can we really alter our immunity to the burning effects of fire at will? These questions, posed at the outset of my inquiry, still seem to me unsatisfactorily answered by science.

Clearly, the firewalk is a tremendously variable event. It is not amenable to scientific measurement and totally unsuitable for laboratory scrutiny. Furthermore, evidence indicates that there may well be *two* kinds of firewalks: short, relatively cool ones that are completely explainable by conventional physics; and longer, relatively hot ones that require subtle yet substantial self-modification in order to create immunity.

Our overview of the scientific research into the firewalk starts with Samuel Langley, whose investigation first pointed to the low thermal capacity and low thermal conductivity of the materials on which many firewalkers walked. James Purves-Stewart's examination introduced the possibility of an altered response to high heat, induced through suggestion. Harry Price and his associates established exact contact times for any given spot on a firewalker's walking foot. More recently, Christos Xenakis and his fellow Greek researchers produced laboratory simulations of the firewalk, concluding that momentary contact with noxious thermal stimulation without burning was within normal human limits. Also in Greece, Vittoria Manganas introduced high-tech Kirlian photography into the firewalk investigation, uncovering dramatic evidence that a firewalker may be creating a supercharged protective force field.

From the wide variety of evidence examined so far, it seems clear that the psychological state of firewalkers the world over so varies that if some common mental-emotional factor connects them all, that factor must be profoundly simple. People have successfully walked over red-hot coals after months of intensive praying, fasting and abstinence; and they have successfully walked over red-hot coals after hours of casual listening. Some have even walked over fire spontaneously, without any prior thought or preparation. Perhaps, as McClenon suggests, the firewalk is really accomplished through a variety of physical and psychological factors. Perhaps any of us can touch red-hot coals without burning, simply by relaxing instead of tensing.

There is significant data to support the hypothesis that our tensing in response to harmful stimuli only worsens the pain, and often the injury. All of the martial arts are centered in this concept: *using* the energy of the assault rather than resisting it. Perhaps if we brought a heightened relaxation to fire along with a mood of reverence and awe, we could establish a new rapport with this burning power.

There is still much to learn about the firewalk. In my conversations with researchers, and in particular in my discussions with one of the most reasonable investigators, William McCarthy, I felt I had reached a surreal summit concerning our abilities to contact red-hot coals. This is something I explore every winter, as I carefully examine my own abilities to safely handle glowing coals from my woodstove. I notice generally that my immunity to burning under these circumstances is extremely limited. But Dr. McCarthy, as he attempts to explain the firewalk with conventional physics and physiology, says it is within our normal capability to be able to handle red-hot coals for "a couple of seconds" without injury! [69]

Obviously, Dr. McCarthy and I are living in different worlds. He is not describing my experience at all, and I wonder if he is even truly speaking for himself. Here is a man who has firewalked three times and, even from his fleeting contact with red-hot coals, blistered each time. I have been plagued with the question of our "normal" response to contact with red-hot coals ever since I first set foot on them.

Can we normally cozy up to red-hot coals and not get burned, as Dr. McCarthy implies, even for a second or two? What about people who accidentally step on a campfire? My instincts say red-hot coals burn. I have received just such burns on several occasions, and yet I have also walked over a bed of red-hot coals without injury. What was the difference? Possibly my contact with the coals was shorter on the firewalk, and possibly those coals were cooler. But my next intentional contact was with a glowing orange coalbed, which I stood in for at least three seconds. And though I received a small blister, I have received worse damage in the past from far more fleeting contact with fire.

Similarly, firewalking instructor Michael Sky writes that he has had six campfire burn victims come to his firewalks, each of whom asserted that the coals which had badly burned them were much cooler and their contact with them much shorter than with the firewalk coals. [70] Sky has walked over hundreds of coalbeds and one night stood unmoving for seconds on glowing coals; yet, he reports being badly burned by a fleeting and accidental contact with a single errant coal the very next night. [71]

What could possibly account for the difference here, a difference that has also spared Tolly Burkan from injury on about a thousand walks over glowing coals, and yet left him prone to a burn accident nearly identical to Michael Sky's? [72]

THE NATURE OF BURNS

What is a burn, this injury we so dread? Surely it is the consequence of some too-close acquaintance with the force that has traditionally cooked our food and heated our homes. For fire is at once our friend and our enemy: It keeps us warm, it transforms our foods and it is soothing to watch when under control. But loosed of its constraints, it becomes a monster; and when it catches us accidentally, we usually get burned.

The pathology of a burn is complex. Burn damage to the skin causes cellular death, capillary damage and coagulation of protein. According to burn specialists John Burke and Conrado Bondoc, "First-degree burn implies thermal damage to the superficial cells of the epidermis." [73] Such burns are without blisters but are often accompanied by mild pain and discomfort, and heal in a few days without scarring.

"Second-degree burns may be superficial or deep," the doctors say. Superficial second-degree burns — those involving the epidermis and the upper layer of the dermis — are characterized by blisters and seepage of fluids. The burn surface is uniformly pink, very painful to the touch and heals within three weeks with very little or no scarring. Deep dermal burns appear pale at the surface and feel somewhat "boggy" and insensitive. These burns may take more than a month to heal and usually leave severe scars. [74]

By contrast, third-degree burns destroy the whole thickness of the skin and all of the nerves and capillaries within it. If such burns are small, they can heal from the edges by scar formation; otherwise, they require skin grafting. [75]

Burns also vary according to the magnitude of the heat source and the length of contact time. The classic study in this area was done by Harvard researchers A.R. Moritz and F.C. Henriques, Jr. Surprisingly, these two found that rapid burning of the skin begins at about 140 degrees F. "At surface temperatures of 70 degrees C [158 degrees F] and higher, the rate of injury so far exceeds that of recovery that less than 1 second is required to cause trans-epidermal necrosis." [76]

If rapid tissue burning begins around 140 degrees F, how can we account for James McClenon's 325-degree reading on a temperature-sensitive pad on his foot after a successful firewalk? If his foot really was subjected to such heat, how did he go unburned? Could it be the material's low thermal capacity and thermal conductivity?

Certainly this is a critical element that Moritz and Henriques did not factor into their study. Their work, much of which employed guinea pigs, exposed the subjects to thermal stimulus supplied by hot water passed through a thin-walled glass chamber, the base of which was in contact with the skin. Thus, the thermal capacity and conductivity of their heat source was very close to that of humans themselves, and far greater than that of wood coals.

We must bear this in mind as we hear testimony from the medical community: their standard for burning temperatures is generally based on the Moritz-Henriques study, which implies a noxious thermal stimulus of considerably greater thermal capacity and conductivity than the one over which firewalkers pass. [77]

THE BURN SPECIALISTS SPEAK

Still, the burn specialists know what burns and what doesn't. Dr. Ron

Sato, a Stanford University Medical School professor and director of a nearby burn unit, says that live human skin momentarily exposed to temperatures in the neighborhood of 1,200 degrees F (the temperatures most often recorded by pyrometers at Burkan's and Robbins' regular firewalks) would sustain third-degree burns to the epidermis and dermis, charring the entirety to a black, carbonized residue. [78] As evidence to support his statement, Sato cites his treatment of patients who had accidentally stepped on campfire coals, some of whom were so badly burned they required skin grafts.

How, then, do some people walk over beds of red-hot coals unharmed? Says burn specialist Sato, "There's no logical explanation." [79]

Further testimony about the normally fragile nature of skin comes from the chief of plastic surgery at Koto Hospital in Tokyo, Japan. Dr. Mashahiko Muramatsu has said that even split-second contact with solid objects at temperatures over 140 degrees F is enough for the protein in the skin to begin breaking down. Contact with a solid, hot mass at a temperature of 167 degrees F, he says, will cause blistering in one second. [80] These are temperatures far below those encountered by firewalkers, even considering the fact that porosity and contact times are greatly variable.

Perhaps, different people have different sensitivities to fire. Perhaps some are more susceptible to burns than others. Burn researcher Florence Jacoby points to just such a possibility. "Some people appear to be relatively burn resistant," she reports. "Others have serious problems with what appears to be superficial injury. There appear to be physical, biochemical, and genetic differences among people that affect the outcome of burn injury." [81]

Jacoby's observations point to factors both in experiencing injury and responding to that injury, and it seems likely there are variables among human beings. But the essential question remains: can any of us, or all of us, change our susceptibility to burning through an act of will?

In the early 1970s, psychophysiologist Elmer Green conducted a series of illuminating experiments at the Menninger Foundation's Voluntary Controls Project, experiments which shed light on that very question. The subject was Jack Schwarz, a man widely known for his abilities to control heart rate, bleeding and a variety of other normally autonomic functions. A burning cigarette was held against Schwarz's forearm for as long as 10 seconds, and in most of the trials, he remained uninjured in any way. Moreover, a careful monitoring of his physiology indicated he was undergoing very little stress before, during or after the normally injurious thermal stimulation. [82]

In the final account, each of us is a burn specialist of sorts. Each of us carries a catalogue of personal disasters with fire that we will always refer to whenever we are near flame or something hot. In particular, our individual experience with incandescent hot objects is unmistakable. Most of us can't even hold a finger over a lighted match for more than a second or two without burning. We can't even touch a 100-watt bulb that's been on for awhile without pulling our finger away in pain. Yet under the right circumstances, many of us — perhaps all of us — can walk over red-hot coals without injury. To my mind, physical science has yet to satisfactorily explain why. Psychology seems no less certain, and medicine appears to be at a loss. This is my estimation after evaluating the relevant research.

For me, the firewalkers themselves are at least as insightful as the scientists who studied them. Listen to Michael Sky explain how he could stand on glowing coals without burning one night, then be burned by only slight contact with a single coal the next night while transporting a hot rock into a sweatlodge:

> It is quite apparent that a major factor in this experience was my personal intention. The first night, I knew exactly what I was doing, where I was going, why I was doing it, etc. My intention was clear, very focused, and contained not a trace of conflict. The second night, my intention was to carry a hot stone from the fire to the lodge, to do it as quickly as possible, and then to lead the group through a wonderful experience that had nothing at all to do with firewalking. Thus, when I stepped on the coal, I did so without intention, accidentally, and my body reacted with a nasty little burn. [83]

If research within the field of the firewalk has yet to offer conclusive evidence, perhaps we should look slightly afield, to related phenomena. Perhaps there we can discover other experimenters who can demonstrate such long-term, injury-free contact with high heat that we can come to a clear conclusion.

6

A Christian Faith, Tested in Fire

. . . and the fire will test what sort of work each one has done. If the work which any man has built on the foundation survives, he will receive a reward. If any man's work is burned up, he will suffer loss, though he himself will be saved, but only as through fire.

1 Corinthians 3:12-15

Because the firewalk has so many facets, it proves useful to examine related phenomena to see if we can glean any further insight. Surprisingly, there is a long tradition of direct contact with fire right here in the United States. Besides the Native American firewalks and the Indian secret societies that practiced firehandling, many Southern Christians handled fire earlier in this century, and many continue to do so today.

Sometime around 1913, in the tiny hamlet of Cleveland in the hills of eastern Tennessee, members of the Church of God began to handle fire as a ritual test of faith. With the biblical figures Shadrach, Meshach and Abednego as their models, these parishioners used music, song and dance to affect an altered state in which they could enjoy varying degrees of immunity. The faithful were not burned, and many men, women and even children found they could handle fire with relative impunity. Firehandling grew in popularity among Church of God parishioners, and by the early 1920s, ecstatic reports of safe and energizing direct contact with fire began to flow in from a number of states, including Alabama, Georgia, Tennessee, Illinois, Texas, Oklahoma, Florida, Mississippi, Arkansas, Missouri, Virginia, West Virginia, Kentucky and North and South Carolina.

By the late 1920s, a schism developed in the Church of God, with most worshippers abandoning the firehandling practices. The small sects that held onto the rites were mostly those in the mountainous, rural regions of eastern Kentucky, Tennessee, and parts of Virginia and North Carolina. Today, in these remote areas, members of the Free Pentecostal Holiness Church, as it is called, still practice their Christianity with a fervor that includes frequent trials by fire.

The men are mill and factory workers, coal miners, construction and railway workers, and subsistence farmers. The women are homemakers, tending the garden and the needs of a generally large family. Many adults have not completed their elementary education, and some are illiterate. Most members don't go to the movies, and most don't drink alcohol, tea, coffee or even soda. These people appear to live for church, and they worship at least two nights a week, sometimes *every* night. The service may be held in a private home; more often it is held in a simple cinder-block church. Attendance varies from small meetings of about a dozen to about 200. Parishioners generally range in age from 12 to 80, with men and women equally represented, though separated during the service. [1]

Services start around 7:30 in the evening, often lasting as long as four hours. Besides firehandling, activities include snake handling, prophesying and speaking in tongues. Although there is a great sense of unity and cohesion within the church, there is also a hierarchy, with the "brothers" and "sisters" given respect because of their demonstrated faith and the "saints" given utmost honor because of their remarkable feats of faith.

Upon arrival, the brothers and sisters mingle with the other worshippers, while the uniformly male saints hug and kiss each other with the greeting, "How are you, honey?" The service commences with a rousing hilltown hymn, frequently original, as the entire congregation sings at full volume to the accompaniment of guitars, clashing cymbals and tambourines.

Following this stirring start, the gathering quiets, then soon erupts into a cacophony of prayer, with individuals crying out to God in their own conversational idiom, thanking the Lord for His mercy and favors, and beseeching his help for healing and for the trials to come. Then the congregation quiets once more, and individuals preach or testify. They confess or vow a public repentance; and they witness and relate their own stories to those of other people and to biblical figures.

Gradually, or quite suddenly in some cases, individuals go into frenetic states. Writes Berthold Schwarz, a psychiatrist who studied these Church of God members in the late '50s and early '60s:

> Their exaltation superficially resembles mania. At these times, they shout, scream, cry, sing, jerk, jump, twitch, whistle, hoot, gesture, sway, swoon, tremble, strut, goosestep, stamp, and incoherently "speak in new tongues." The glossolalia sounds like: "ma-ma-ma-ma-ma." When in deep, dissociated trances, the members appear as if they were intoxicated, and their faces are very similar to those seen with reactions induced by mescaline and LSD 25. They describe the depersonalization phenomena as: "I feel high in the spirits" . . . "happiness in the bones" . . . "a shield has come down over me" . . . "I've got conviction" . . . "I lose sight of the whole world" and . . . "I can't tell if my head and face are all together." [2]

When the spirit moves them, impulsively, many of the churchgoers test their faith, interpreting various biblical passages literally. They may at first turn to screened, flat, wooden boxes, and from them carefully extract poisonous snakes, often rattlesnakes or copperheads. After the snake handling, and sometimes continuing with a snake entwined on one arm, worshippers light up crude "coal oil" torches or carbide lamps. The torches are made from soda pop bottles, milk bottles, slightly larger juice bottles or brake fluid cans filled at least halfway with kerosene and topped by tightly twisted, cotton rag wicks. They give off a very sooty, orange-yellow flame six to 24 inches high. Amidst the singing, shouting, guitar playing, and cymbal and tambourine clashing, the brothers and sisters apply the flaming torches to various parts of their bodies. Reports Dr. Schwarz:

> The worshippers slowly move their outstretched open hands and fingers over the midpoint of the flames from three to five seconds or even longer. Frequently, one turns the burning torch horizontally and puts the proximal flame to the palm of his hand for five seconds or longer. On three occasions, two of the saints put their exposed toes and the soles of their feet directly in the flames for five to 15 seconds. [3]

On one occasion, Schwarz reports, a man known as the most faithful of the saints, "picked up a flaming 'stone coal' the size of a hen's egg and held it in the palms of his hands for 65 seconds while he walked among the congregation. As a control, the author could not touch a piece of burning charcoal for less than one second without developing a painful blister." [4]

Controls are important in any scientific investigation, especially in situations that involve as many variables as firewalking and firehandling. Nevertheless, no control in these phenomena could possibly lay any claim to objectivity. Here we are dealing with the possible impact of suggestion on physiology. Certainly the researcher himself is a poor candidate to act as a control, since his psychology is already laden with speculation and suggestion. Nevertheless, Dr. Schwarz acting as his own control is not without meaning. And given the disorienting context of the Church of God firehandling, his physiological responses seem like the last link to normalcy.

Later, Schwarz describes other efforts at scientific control:

> As a control, the author could not keep his own hand closer than 3 cms. to the coal oil torch flame at its base for longer than one or two seconds without pain or the danger of getting burned. Other control attempts, under ordinary circumstances and simulating the ordeal, were impossible to complete, because of almost instantaneous pain and the risk of incurring severe burns. [5]

Beyond his observations of the ritual and his controlled attempts at firehandling himself, Schwarz carefully examined the brothers, sisters and saints who had handled fire. "In all these fire ordeals, except one," he reports, "there were, apparently, no evidences of painful reactions; and there was no erythema, blistering, charring, singeing, suggestive odor of a burn or gross change in sweat production. . . . In no instance . . . was there ever any evidence that clothes had been either scorched or burned." [6]

Dr. Schwarz also psychiatrically examined six of the saints. In doing so, not only did he discover much about the psychology of their displayed physical immunity, but he also heard other amazing stories about firehandling in the Church of God:

> For instance, "the most faithful saint" inaugurated his gift 26 years ago by rushing to the hearth, balancing — with his hand — red-hot logs on his shoulders, and walking around the congregation without any ill effects to his person or clothes. Another minister is alleged to have jumped up on a red-hot iron stove, to have sat on it, and to have put his exposed feet and legs among the glowing coals while he delivered his sermon. A third saint has a reputation for putting his head and neck in a red-hot stove for "many seconds or a few minutes." . . . The same man is reported to have had a welder's acetylene torch applied to his outstretched upper arm for many seconds, and also later to his forehead, against which was placed a piece of paper which instantaneously disintegrated. In neither case was there any burn to his skin or shirt. [7]

The fire ordeal has been undertaken by Church of God members from seven to 80 years of age. In winter, red-hot coals are sometimes passed among the congregation, from hand to hand. At times, some of the witnessing includes accounts of how "sinner people," skeptics, scoffers or disbelievers attempted to duplicate the firehandling, only to suffer bad burns. Reports Schwarz:

> Some of these people were ministers, of other sects than the fire-handlers, who tried to prove the trials fraudulent. They apparently considered them to be superstition or heresy, or perhaps felt the need to expose as hoaxes something that differs from, or threatened, their own convictions. However, it can be surmised that there was a close connection between their not being in receptive, dissociative states (their lack of "faith") and their suffering serious burns. [8]

But apparently even the faithful might burn should they contact fire outside the particular state of consciousness in which they enjoy immunity. Schwarz noted two incidents of worshippers who had safely handled fire many times during church services, but who burned when they were distracted from their trance states:

> An interesting story was provided by one brother who reported applying the "coal tar" torch flame to the palm of his hand with complete immunity until he noticed that a piece of wick was breaking off. This trivial incident was enough to cause him to awaken from his trance and engender anxiety. At this point, he suffered a very discrete and localized blistering burn. The surrounding area that had previously been in contact with the flames during the trance, and had been of no apparent concern to him, showed no burn.
>
> In a like manner, a sister who had, during previous ordeals, frequently handled a hot glass chimney [from a kerosene lamp], developed blistering burns when one evening while at church, the electric power failed, and she, in a reflex action, grabbed the brightly burning kerosene lantern that was hanging on the wall. She was not entranced at that particular moment. The fact can, therefore, be noted that when Holiness members are not entranced, they, like everyone else, suffer burns . . . [9]

These accounts seemed remarkably similar to those of firewalkers who suddenly burned when they found themselves distracted or doubtful.

Given the astonishing demonstrations Dr. Schwarz observed, it is not surprising he should draw some startling conclusions. "It appears to be fact," he writes, "that some people in a state of religious ecstasy and faith can have varying degrees of immunity to burns on their body and their clothing." [10]

Before continuing the discussion of his conclusions, Schwarz duly notes the limitations of his "scientific" observations, including the problems of uncontrolled subjects and inaccurate measurements. "Despite the many drawbacks of the present field-trip observations," he states, "there still exists the fact of varying degrees of fire immunity and no satisfactory explanation." [11]

In seeking to explain how such fire immunity might be physiologically possible, Dr. Schwarz runs through every hypothesis his seasoned mind can synthesize, including circulatory cooling mechanisms, some "recipe" that might have been applied to the skin, and possible ingestion of drugs, among others. In the end, he is forced to discount all of them.

Another researcher who studied the Church of God firehandlers is psychotherapist-anthropologist Steven Kane, whose field research was supported by the National Science Foundation. Kane spent a total of 18 months in six southern states between 1972 and 1979. His observations confirmed those of Schwarz. In assessing what he had seen, Kane formulated a new aim: to suggest specific psychophysiological factors and mechanisms that might account for devotees' general immunity to the injurious effects of torch flames. [12] Here is some of what he saw:

> On two separate occasions, an elderly Kentucky preacher seized a burning torch with his right hand and slowly rotated his outstretched open left hand in the flame for about 10 seconds. In two different services, a West Virginia man, said by his fellow communicants to have "good victory over fire," alternately held each hand stationary in the mid-point of a flame for 10 to 15 seconds. Once, he grasped the torch with both hands, held it at chest level, and permitted the flame to touch his neck and chin for five seconds or more. He handed the torch to another man, aged 19, the youngest fire handler I saw, who . . . held both hands in the middle of the flame for approximately 10 seconds . . .
>
> At the conclusion of the services, the fire handlers cleaned the soot from their hands and permitted me to inspect them carefully. They claimed the flames had not caused them the slightest degree of pain or discomfort, and in no case did I detect blistering, tactile hypersensitivity, erythema, edema, or other indications of thermal injury. [13]

Kane also attempted what controls he could: "Once, after a meeting, I myself attempted to handle a torch in order to have some basis for assessing the risk of physical injury involved. Painful singeing of the hand occurred almost instantaneously, and I involuntarily jerked it away from the flame before I had even reached the midpoint or hottest part." [14]

Like Dr. Schwarz before him, Kane interviewed the firehandlers, who revealed other luminaries in an unusual galaxy of stars.

> Some persons were able to sit on hot stoves and even to place their heads inside. This last feat was the specialty of the late Raymond "Buck" Hayes, the preeminent Kentucky fire handler until his death from snakebite in 1968. On numerous occasions, he thrust his head into a scathingly hot stove, "talked in tongues while he was in there," and withdrew unharmed. Another man, a West Virginian, once put his bare feet into a hot stove. Although he held them in there for "about five minutes — long enough to burn them off," he experienced no ill effects. [15]

For the communicants of the Church of God, firehandling is a test and confirmation of their faith, but it is also a demonstration to "lost souls" of the power of the Lord and of the literal truth of the scriptures. As such, religious firehandling aims to help the community at large, motivating individuals to renounce evil and "get right with God." There are two ways to successfully handle fire, say these church members: by faith and by anointing. Writes Dr. Kane:

> *Faith* is confidence in God. If a worshipper's faith is absolute, believers aver, he can take a torch and no harm will come to him. A burn would indicate that an individual had less faith than he thought he had, or that his faith "failed" him after the start of his demonstration. *Anointing* denotes the communication of spiritual power from God to the individual. . . . Individuals must believe God has power over fire, or the Holy Ghost will never anoint them to handle a torch.
>
> In naturalistic terms, the crucial difference between the two modes of handling fire is this: an anointed worshipper is in an altered state of consciousness commonly designated "trance" in the literature, whereas one who proceeds by faith is not. The trance is regarded as the supreme religious experience, a "foretaste of heaven" vouchsafed believers with whom God is pleased. Communicants are unanimous in asserting its utter ineffability. [16]

Kane notes a wide variety of descriptions of the trance state. "It makes a different person out of you," said one. "I about lose sight of the world for a while," said another. "You feel queer all over, like you stick your finger in electricity," reported a third. Others described it as getting drunk in the spirit, getting struck by a bolt of lightning, feeling numbness or sleepiness in the limbs, or as though they were safeguarded by a protective shield. [17]

According to Kane, feeling no pain during the rite is not in itself remarkable, since the scientific literature is full of studies indicating that pain does not necessarily result from noxious stimulation. On the other hand, he provides evidence for a conclusion that is far more startling: namely, that the absence of pain may also be directly linked to the absence of tissue damage.

Kane recounts the work of British physician J. Arthur Hadfield, who more than half a century ago "burned a hypnotized subject with the end of a steel pencil-case heated in a Bunsen flame, suggesting that there would be 'no pain' in consequence of the burns." As suggested, the result was no pain. More remarkably, however, there was no inflammation, either: "Round each of the two spots, which themselves presented the ordinary appearance of blisters," writes Kane, "there was a thin red line and nothing more." Later, when Hadfield repeated the experiment, suggesting to the same subject that he *would* feel pain, the subject experienced both pain and inflammation — and the burn took longer to heal. Reports Kane, "These and other experiments led Hadfield to venture the provocative hypothesis 'that it is not the inflammation primarily that produces the pain or sensation, but the pain that produces the inflammation.'" [18]

If it is the pain that produces the inflammation, and pain has clearly been shown to be subject to erasure through hypnosis, then by logical implication, it would seem that inflammation or burning might also be subject to erasure through hypnosis. In this vein, Kane goes on to cite the even more striking studies of Chapman, Goodman and Wolff (1959), in which the investigators hypnotized 13 adult men and women and suggested to them that one arm would be vulnerable while the other would be anesthetized. Eighteen hours after the application of the burning probe, the doctors reported "no visible damage" in the "anesthetic" arm, but "a readily detectable lesion" in the other. [19]

Even more spectacular, says Kane, are Hadfield's studies showing that tissue damage can be caused in some subjects in the complete absence of applied heat:

> Hadfield (1917) produced a blister "full of fluid and surrounded with hyperaemia," in a hypnotized patient by touching his finger to the subject's arm, suggesting that the finger was a "red-hot iron" and would cause pain. He repeated the experiment with this subject on two other occasions, each time under stricter conditions. The results were the same. . . . Subsequent to these experiments, Hadfield (1920) produced suggestion blisters in another subject that were actually more painful and inflamed than those caused by a heated thermometer case. [20]

Dr. Kane believes that such studies explain the fire immunity displayed by members of the Holiness Church:

> . . . I think it not unreasonable to suggest that the entranced fire handlers' belief in their own invulnerability mobilizes the same protective nervous system process. In fact, there is good evidence that this is precisely what happens. Recall the believers' reports of numbness, coldness, and deadness in the hands, arms and other parts of their bodies. These are symptoms of peripheral vasoconstriction, cited by Chapman, Goodell, and Wolff as one of the factors inhibiting inflammation and damage in arms suggested to be "anesthetic." Furthermore, worshippers apply the torch flames only to those body parts that become numb and cold, believing that the spirit has rendered these areas burn-proof.
>
> Of course, there is a limit to the central nervous system's capacity to prevent tissue damage. The fact that I observed no worshipper apply the flame to a portion of his body for longer than 10 to 15 seconds would seem to indicate that this duration of exposure marks the extent of that capacity. Continued exposure would certainly overwhelm the protective neural mechanism and cause injury.
>
> Scientists tend to dismiss native explanations of unusual abilities displayed by worshippers in religious ceremonies. In this case, however, there appears to be more than a little objective truth in the communicants' assertion that 'it takes faith' to handle fire. [21]

In essence, Kane asserts that when entranced, humans have the possibility of affecting a substantial-but-limited immunity to the burning effects of fire. He also suggests that internal bodily mechanisms enable this immunity, and that its duration is strictly limited. While Dr. Schwarz agrees that faith may indeed render one relatively immune to burns, he points to some other possible mechanism of protection. In closing his report, Schwarz runs through all possible explanations of fire immunity, concluding:

> The suggested explanations of immunity from burns are, therefore, all inadequate, because in the literature, in histories given by the Holiness members, and in some instances that were confirmed by direct observations by the author, the apparent immunity to burning is even extended to other people watching the service and to clothing. . . . The question of why these people are not burned on their bodies and their projected body images, when in their exalted states remains a mystery for future probing. [22]

Notice that Dr. Schwarz observed a phenomenon of inexplicable bodily immunity, as well as an immunity of "projected body images" extending outward from the body. Dr. Kane noticed the same thing: "Nor was there any sign that clothing that appeared to have been in direct contact with the flames had received damage." [23] What could account for such projected immunity? Could it be the "L-field," the same force field detected and studied by Harold Burr and others? Neither Kane nor Schwarz speculate on this.

After years of observation, research and personal experimentation, Dr. Kane has come to the conviction that a limited fire immunity is every person's birthright, that each of us through minimal psychological self-manipulation can develop a dramatic new rapport with fire. This astounding transformation Kane ascribes to belief in the broadest sense. "It doesn't have to be a religiously grounded belief system," he says. "The person's conviction of immunity — whether he believes it is a spirit conferring that immunity is not relevant — the conviction that you can emerge unscathed seems to be the critical factor. The psychology really does influence the physiology." [24] Once again, mind over matter.

In a telephone conversation, I asked Dr. Kane what he thought about the possibility of the paranormal operating in fire immunity. "That definitely gets into the kind of psi phenomenon that I don't feel comfortable with," he replied. I don't say that it's not happening, I just don't know. And some people tend to get a little mystical when they venture forth into those areas." [25]

On the other hand, Kane confirmed that we do give off an "electrical field," and he had much to say about untapped human powers. "I think we have all kinds of incredible powers that we're not utilizing," he said. "Whether it's being relatively impervious to the thermal stimuli . . . or [an increase in] memory, or perception, or whatever . . . most of us are content to let our abilities lie fallow, and that's too bad. . . . It's conceivable that there are powers we don't even know we have." [26]

7

Taking a Stand — In the Fire

I had the feeling that I had pushed to the brink of the world; what was of burning interest to me was null and void for others, and even a cause for dread. . . . After all, there was nothing preposterous or world-shaking in the idea that there might be events which overstepped the limited categories of space, time, and causality.

Carl Jung

To assess further the phenomenon of firewalking, we should carefully examine any evidence that brings into question conventional physical explanations. Without resorting to a whole battery of new experiments, we might scrutinize the claims of scientists that short contact with the coals is the reason why most of us can safely walk across a glowing firebed. Besides the low thermal capacity and conductivity of wood coals — a fact which is not open to question but whose effects seem in some dispute — the short contact theory is the most popular scientific explanation of how the firewalk is possible. Yet repeatedly, both my own experience and that of others strongly suggests there is something else going on.

If there were any reliable reports of long contact, they might at once dispel both the short contact and the low thermal capacity and conductivity theories. For few would deny that if a firewalker simply stood on glowing, red-hot coals, he or she should normally suffer serious burns within a matter of seconds at most.

Zusne and Warren emphasize this in their exploration of anomalistic psychophysiology: "One of the factors not stressed in reports on fire walking is that fire walking is *walking*, not standing still on embers or stones. There is no recorded instance of anyone's ever having attempted to just stand on red hot stones or glowing embers for any length of time." [1]

JOE NUZUM AND THE *CHI*

Herewith, let us record several such instances. We already have my own account of standing on a bed of glowing coals for several seconds, though I did receive a small blister. We also have Michael Sky's report about his standing in the fire — and his witnessing others not only standing in fire but lying down on the coals without singeing skin, hair or clothes. Equally impressive is the experience of Joe Nuzum, a former foundry worker from western Pennsylvania who spent years working around incredibly hot fires and molten metals. Now he spends his time giving demonstrations of what he calls "Ninja Magick" and teaching martial arts. Among the rituals he teaches his students is the firewalk.

Nuzum says he first firewalked in 1975, when he was 16. Before he firewalked, though, he experimented extensively. Having heard about firewalking Tibetan monks, he began by holding his hand over a candle flame. "Once I realized the different states of mind I could enter into," he told me, "I found a way where I wouldn't get burned. I went from getting burned almost instantly to being able to hold my hand in the flame for close to 45 seconds." [2]

Nuzum says he also practiced holding his hands in the flames of burning papers, then eventually progressed to firewalking and from there to standing on red-hot coals. "And that I've done for maybe 45 seconds," he said. [3]

I have not witnessed this, but I *have* seen videotapes of Nuzum holding flaming coals in his hands for a period of 40 seconds. I have also read reports about him and discussed him with a psychiatrist who has both examined him and written about him. [4] In conventional physical terms, Nuzum's performances are amazing and inexplicable. Nuzum attributes his fire immunity to "the protective qualities of the *chi*," the field of bioenergy around the body that Eastern mystics tell us can be controlled by the mind. "There's been a lot of fascinating things done with the *chi*," says Nuzum. "It's mind blowing." [5]

THE WORLD'S LONGEST AND HOTTEST FIREWALKS

Perhaps it is also time science confronted the activities of another amazing firewalker, a Washington state resident named Steve Bisyak. Bisyak is a Tolly Burkan-trained firewalking instructor who runs his own human potential seminars, Challenges Unlimited. And he is undoubtedly one of the most experienced firewalkers in the world. "I've firewalked over a thousand times now," he said when I spoke with him in early 1991. "I've walked on a red-hot metal plate, red-hot coals and red-hot briquettes. . . . In Kansas City, in front of 300 people, I pretty much gave my whole lecture from the center of the fire. I was on a red-hot fire for minutes." [6]

Bisyak first saw firewalking on the "You Asked For It" TV show when he was nine. Fifteen years later, in 1984, he learned firewalking from Tolly Burkan. Even since then, he says, he has continued to "push the limits." Today he holds the record for the world's longest firewalk (120 feet) and is listed in the *Guinness Book of World Records* for the hottest firebed ever walked on.

For the longest walk, he used 10 cords of wood with the highest BTU factors he could find (cherry, madrono and oak) stacked in a pile 126 feet long. For the hottest fire, he and 10 other walkers braved a coalbed 15 feet long, 12 inches deep, with three inches of flame on top. Its average temperature was measured at 1,546 degrees F. After his walk, not even the hairs on Bisyak's toes were singed.

Bisyak has also done some tests with the firewalk — tests that lead him to conclude that the ability to walk safely over hot coals is all a state of mind. For example, in August 1990, he and three other volunteers were fitted with EEGs, blindfolded and, one by one, paraded around a grassy area. Then, unannounced, each was led onto a bed of red-hot coals. All four were badly burned.

"If you take the mind away from the situation, it's guaranteed burn," Bisyak said. "If you step on fire by accident, you get cooked. Other people who were there and in the right state of mind walked across that fire with no problem." [7]

Moreover, the EEG, said Bisyak, indicated a common brain wave pattern for those who burned and another pattern for those who did not burn. "Alpha and beta [brain waves] are extremely wide; theta is fairly narrow; the very bottom of delta is pegged out wide. And without delta being pegged out wide, it was *hot* — meaning that if you were very peaceful and calm and relaxed, you got burned! [8]

After all his semi-scientific investigation, Bisyak has come up with a folksy formula for figuring a person's burn possibilities prior to any firewalk. "One hundred, minus the percentage of attention," he says, "equals the number of blisters — meaning if you're 98 percent, you probably got two blisters; if you're 75 percent, you got 25 blisters; if you're 50 percent, you got cooked!"

Bisyak has also done what he calls the "nylon stocking test," walking across a glowing coalbed wearing nylon stockings. "They don't burn," he says. "You can put the nylon on the coalbed, and it doesn't last; it disintegrates — you can't put it out! That's what brings me to the conclusion that it's a bioelectric field that protects us, something like the human aura." [9]

Bisyak says he's convinced that this field is activated by a combination of fear and faith. He's also convinced that if it could be isolated, the same energy or chemical that prevents burns could also be used to treat serious burn victims. "Two out the three serious burns that I've had — and I mean where the whole bottom of the foot comes off — healed almost spontaneously. I was able to go out and play tennis the next day. There was no sign of damage at all." [10]

Bisyak's testimony is also revealing in regard to the skeptics' argument that a firewalker's immunity can be attributed to the way in which the feet are placed on the coals. If we examine Bisyak's experience and that of many other firewalkers, we must admit that coals are not only underfoot but also to the sides of the foot and on top of it as well. Bisyak at one point described his feet as "submerged" in glowing coals. Similarly, when I stood in the fire myself, my feet were buried in orange coals, and the surface coals covering the tops of my feet were in no way less radiant than when I entered the fire.

It seems equally clear that short contact with the fire cannot explain many firewalks in which the participants stand, dance or linger on the coals. "You have to be committed," says Bisyak. "That's the difference between what the physicists are saying and what the firewalkers are saying. If you're not committed, you get burned." [11]

JACK SCHWARZ: TOTAL BODY CONTROL

Another committed man who is equally adept with fire is Dutch-born American Jack Schwarz. In his early teens in Holland, Schwarz began increasingly to realize voluntary controls over many of his normally automatic physiological functions. He concentrated on the control of pain, frequently pushing an unsterilized knitting needle through his arm to test himself, but soon he could also control bleeding and burning. By the time he arrived for testing at the laboratory of Drs. Elmer and Alyce Green of the Menninger Institute in Topeka, Kansas in 1971, Schwarz was regularly sleeping only two or three hours a night, eating only several small meals a week and had demonstrated fire immunity to himself and to his friends. [12]

In the late 1970s, Schwarz got an opportunity to demonstrate his controlled fire immunity to a convocation of 55 doctors. At a meeting of the Los Angeles County Medical Association, psychiatrist Kurt Fantl introduced Schwarz, announcing that he would demonstrate a variety of astonishing, self-regulatory controls. The most startling among these was immunity to fire. First, Schwarz allowed the physicians to examine his hands, which they found to be normal and untreated in any way. Next, two medical students wearing asbestos gloves carried a burning brazier into the conference, and from the container Schwarz scooped out a double handful of red-hot coals. Walking calmly among the doctors, Schwarz showed them the fire in his hands, allowing them to feel the heat and observe his immunity to burning. Finally, he laid the coals to rest on a newspaper, which immediately burst into flames. When his hands were examined once more, they again appeared to be perfectly normal, with no signs of their lengthy contact with red-hot coals. [13]

When tested in the Green's laboratory at Menninger in 1971, Schwarz again demonstrated his immunity to fire, as well as his control of bleeding and pain. Fire immunity, Schwarz found, was not automatic; in certain states, he could still be burned. In other states, his immunity seemed complete and absolute. To him, the critical factors appeared to be intention and need. And when intention and need are strong enough, he says, they activate "the power of the radiance of our body," which he says can protect us not only from fire but also from other noxious stimuli. Schwarz also maintains that this body radiance creates "a living Faraday cage — a high voltage, low amperage energy field" that can even prevent one's hair and clothes from burning. [14]

Jack Schwarz believes that his remarkable abilities are not so remarkable, and he repeats over and over again that his performances are potentials we all have. "At a laboratory once," he said, "they told me, 'Now we are going to test some normal people.' I said: 'I beg your pardon; I am the only one whom you have ever tested who was normal. I follow the principles which are normal principles; the other ones have not bothered to, so they are still operating in a subnormal way.'" Schwarz seemed especially adamant about this last point. "I make that statement not just to you," he said, "but in every lecture I give: 'Now, look, people, don't sit there in admiration, and don't tell me, "Yeah, but you were born that way." You forgot: you were born that way, too.'" [15]

8

Of Faith and Flesh, Mind and Matter

If the sun and moon should doubt, they would immediately go out.

William Blake

From all I've read and experienced so far, my conclusion seems inescapable: firewalking and firehandling seem to be the nexus of fear and faith, of flesh and fire, a crossing point where varying blends of these elements yield astounding results. From the mouths of firewalkers, firehandlers and fire researchers, I've repeatedly heard that the common denominator is faith. But what exactly *is* this ethereal concept, faith, and how could it have such profound physiological impacts?

"Faith is the substance of things hoped for, the evidence of things not seen," says an early passage in Hebrews. As such, it is the fundament of nearly every established religion, connecting the practitioner to the invisible Creator. The life of Jesus, in particular, is eloquent testimony to the power of faith. Jesus was always questing faith — in himself, in his followers, in the common man. Faith is a state of mind that undermines all our worldly beliefs. It can be confirmed neither by science nor by the human senses, but only through inner knowing. Yet with faith, we are elevated, connected to a vast potential where the forces of this world are robbed of their ordinary power and all things become possible.

Firewalking, then, appears to be an expression of faith. From another perspective, it is an expression of mind over matter, an alteration of the properties of the human body through the action of psychology alone. Often mind over matter is considered to be an expression of the paranormal; however, there are countless examples of it in our daily lives. Every time we move our body, we use mind to direct matter. If we stop to examine it, the simple lifting of an arm is a miracle in itself. Foodstuffs have supplied the fuel for thought as well as the energy for work, and mind has directed matter.

Yet when we think of mind over matter, we are usually looking for something considerably more out of the ordinary than bodily movement. What would qualify? How about voluntary control of the autonomic functions in the body? That would be a start. If we find out that humans have the possibility of controlling their autonomic functions, maybe there is scientifically-validated evidence that humans can control much more. And maybe we can begin to understand the limits and possibilities of this species, of its range for psychologically-induced physiological control. Maybe we can begin to get a glimpse of the psychology of physical immunity.

MEDITATION AND THE FAITH FACTOR

In the late 1960's, Robert Keith Wallace was completing his Ph.D. in physiology at UCLA, researching the effects of Transcendental Meditation (TM) on the human body. Monitoring his subjects' brain waves, blood pressure, heart rate and other physiological functions, Wallace soon discovered that TM did indeed affect the body, in a host of remarkable ways. Minutes after beginning their practice, his meditating subjects entered a state of deep relaxation whose hallmarks were slower breathing and heartbeat, decreased oxygen consumption and marked increase in alpha brain wave activity. Wallace noted emphatically that his subjects were neither asleep nor in a trance. And most of them reported heightened awareness in a state the researcher subsequently called "hypometabolic wakefulness." [1]

It was clear to Wallace and those who studied his data that some aspects of mind over matter had been demonstrated by his subjects: psychological alterations directly influenced physiology. It has since been shown that TM offers significant relief from headaches, angina pains and stress, and that regular practice can even retard the aging process. Wallace discovered that a typical 60-year-old meditating for five years or more would have the body of a 48-year-old. A backup study in England later calculated that for every year a person meditates, he or she reduces biological aging by approximately one year. Altogether, the data strongly suggests that aging is controlled by consciousness — matter is controlled by mind. [2]

Master meditators have exhibited even more astounding powers. Tibetan yogis, for example, are known to spend the entire winter in caves between 11,000 and 18,000 feet, warming themselves without fire in an attempt to increase their *tumo*, or inner fire. Researcher Alexandra David-Neel has reported that the training of *tumo* students is sometimes concluded with a remarkable examination:

> Upon a frosty winter night, those who think themselves capable of victoriously enduring the test are led to the shore of a river or lake. If all the streams are frozen . . . a hole is made in the ice. A moonlit night, with a hard wind blowing, is chosen . . . The neophytes sit on the ground, cross-legged and naked. Sheets are dipped in the icy water,

> each man wraps himself in one of them and must dry it on his body. As soon as the sheet has become dry, it is again dipped in the water and placed on the novice's body to be dried as before. The operation goes on in that way until daybreak. . . .
>
> It is said that some dry as many as forty sheets in one night. One should perhaps make large allowances for exaggeration, or perhaps for the size of the sheets which in some cases may become so small as to be almost symbolical. Yet I have seen some *repas* dry a number of pieces of cloth the size of a large shawl . . . [3]

Another scientist who has explored the realm of mind over matter is Harvard-educated physician Dr. Herbert Benson, author of *The Relaxation Response*. In this popular 1975 book, Benson confirmed Wallace's findings that even the simplest form of meditation brings about astounding physiological benefits. Eventually, Benson added to his purely mental "relaxation response" a concept he calls the "faith factor," the spiritual connection. These two elements in combination, Benson says, can empower a person to achieve astounding feats of mind over matter. "If you truly believe in your personal philosophy or religious faith," he writes, "if you are committed mind and soul to your world view — you may well be capable of achieving remarkable feats of mind and body that many only speculate about." [4]

HEALING WITH THE MIND

Empowered by faith, individuals can alter their physiology to perform in otherwise-impossible ways. This concept must surely be at the core of faith healing and most spontaneous remissions. Despite a fatal prognosis, a patient becomes catalyzed to perform a seemingly miraculous self-healing, through an act of faith. Research on such spontaneous cures — especially among cancer patients — shows that just before the cure, nearly every patient experiences a dramatic shift in consciousness. Suddenly the patient expresses a deep confidence that healing is in process, expanding into a view of their body that includes the whole universe. [5]

But meditation and faith are apparently not the only avenues for dramatic physiological empowerment. The power of suggestion, self-initiated or otherwise, has been shown to offer an individual radical new pathways into and through the body. Decades of data have shown that nearly half the population has the capacity to spontaneously rid themselves of warts. The details of the methods people use are as variable as is humanity, with one very young successful wart remover being told that if he could sneak something out the refrigerator at night and not get caught, then his wart would fall off. It did. [6]

Faith healing may operate in very similar ways. Though medical science is extremely skeptical of the laying on of hands and faith cures in general, there are enough documented healings in the literature that the phenomenon cannot be ignored.

Of particular note are the relatively recent efforts of a German physician, a Dr. H. Rehdér. The subjects of his benign experiment were three severely ill, hospitalized women. The first had gallstones accompanied by chronic gallbladder inflammation; the second hadn't recovered from major abdominal surgery and was "practically a skeleton"; and the third was dying of metastatic cancer. Reports Andrew Weil, M.D.:

> The physician in charge first authorized a well-known local faith healer to attempt to cure the patients from a distance without their knowledge. Nothing happened. He then told then patients about the faith healer and, over several days, built up their expectations of his ability to help them. He told the women that the healer would attempt to cure them from a distance at a particular time. In fact, the healer was not working then. At the stated time, all three patients improved dramatically. The second was permanently cured. The cancer patient, whose body was swollen with retained fluid, quickly eliminated it and recovered sufficiently from severe anemia and general weakness to go home and take over her household duties; she had no further symptoms until her death. The gall bladder patient also lost her symptoms, went home, and remained free of problems for several years. [7]

Psychic healer Lawrence LeShan relates a similar case, in which a man phoned to ask for a long-distance healing, to alleviate a very painful condition that would otherwise require immediate surgery. Recalls LeShan:

> I promised to do the healing that night, and the next morning when he awoke, a "miraculous cure" had occurred. The medical specialist was astounded, and offered to send me pre- and post-healing X-rays and to sponsor publication in a scientific journal. It would have been the psychic healing case of the century except for one small detail. In the press of overwork, I had forgotten to do the healing! [8]

Again, a case in which the patient cured himself, simply through his belief in the suggestion that he would be cured.

Suggestion has also been powerfully employed in surgery, in a variety of ways. Dr. Berne Siegel reports two intriguing personal successes:

> Recently I was operating on a very husky young man, built like a football player. His size led to some minor technical problems, and while solving them, I looked up at the monitor and saw his pulse was 130. I knew that he had been anxious about the operation, so I said to him, "Victor, I'm having some mechanical difficulties because

> you're a big guy, but there's no problem with the surgery. This part is just a little difficult to do. You're doing well. Don't be nervous. I'd like your pulse to be 83." During the next few minutes, without any other medication, his pulse came down to 83 and remained there. [9]

An even more astonishing suggestion-mediated response was gained from a patient who was clinically already dead. Reports Siegel:

> Once, as I finished a difficult emergency abdominal operation on a young, very obese man, his heart stopped just as we were about to move him to the recovery room. He didn't respond to resuscitation. The anesthesiologist had given up and was walking out the door when I spoke out loud into the room, "Harry, it's not your time. Come on back." At once the cardiogram began to show electrical activity, and the man ultimately fully recovered. I can't prove it, of course, but I am sure the verbal message made the difference. I know the experience made believers out of the other staff members who were present." [10]

THE PLACEBO RESPONSE

Something similar is at work in the well-known placebo effect. In a typical case, a sick patient is secretly given a sugar tablet instead of real medication, yet the body responds as though the medication were real. In many patients, their symptoms often disappear rather rapidly. Here, the curative suggestion seems to appeal to the body's already highly intelligent healing mechanisms which are capable of creating the essential pharmacopoeia of modern medicine. Reports writer George Leonard:

> Placebos have been shown to be 77 percent as effective as morphine in relieving postoperative pain; the more severe the pain, the more effective the placebo. A test with 88 arthritic patients revealed that a placebo is equally effective with aspirin and cortisone in the relief of symptoms. What's more, the benefit from the placebo in these cases included improvement in sleeping, eating, elimination and reduction of swelling. . . . The placebo effect, as previously suggested, can be extremely precise. The patient who is told what to expect from a certain drug can produce that exact effect when given a sugar pill, down to creating a surplus of specialized blood cells called eosinophils. Just as a placebo can produce healing conditions in the body, it can also produce the side effects of the drug it mimics. [11]

Some say laughter is the best medicine. Through the curative powers of laughter, the late Norman Cousins was able to spend the last decade of his life exploring the mind-body connection. Most remarkably, he managed to cure himself from a supposedly incurable, degenerative nerve disease, ankylosing spondylitis, by viewing comedy videotapes, especially "The Candid Camera" and the Marx Brothers. This "laughter therapy" suggested to him that all healing processes might be mind mediated. Subsequently, he, too, studied the placebo effect, noting a variety of startling results.

With a placebo, expectation is everything, and the greater the authority with which the expectation is delivered, the better the results. Cousins cites an instance in which patients with bleeding ulcers were divided into two groups:

> Members of the first group were informed by the doctor that a new drug had just been developed that would undoubtedly produce relief. The second group was told by nurses that a new experimental drug would be administered, but that very little was known about its effects. Seventy percent of the people in the first group received significant relief from the ulcers. Only 25 percent of the patients in the second group experienced similar benefits. Both groups had been given the identical "drug" — a placebo. [12]

Modern medicine is just beginning to make use of the placebo effect. Some of the most remarkable recent results have shown that through the use of the placebo, the human immune system can be trained, conditioned to produce the healing effects of the appropriate therapeutic drugs. Robert Adler and Anthony Schulman, of the University of Rochester, demonstrated that by alternating real medication with placebos, side effects, dependence and cost can be dramatically reduced until the conditioned body can be trained to produce the healing chemicals internally. [13]

THE FEAR-PAIN-INJURY CIRCUIT

In the early 1970s, medical science was abuzz with the discovery of "communicator molecules," a class of chemicals called "neurotransmitters" that chemically link the brain with the entire body. By the mid-'80s, over 50 neurotransmitters and neuropeptides had been discovered, speedy chemical messengers that link cell to cell and the brain to the entire body. [14]

What sorts of messages might these chemical messengers be carrying? Among the most significant, for this investigation, are messages blocking pain, through the chemical called endorphin. This naturally-produced painkiller is sometimes spontaneously brought into play when the body's own pain-alarm system has become dysfunctional. But pain blocking has also been demonstrated in many laboratory and field tests, where the endorphins are brought into play through psychological self-manipulation. That's the good news — that pain, and quite possibly some of the injury associated with it — are potentially under our control. The bad news is that if we're controlled by fear, we won't be producing many pain blockers, so our likelihood for pain and injury go way up.

We seem to be tapping into another human circuit here, a circuit that starts with fear, proceeds through pain and then to injury. From my investigation, I am beginning to develop a radical but physiologically supportable hypothesis: that if you can experience but transform fear, you can completely control pain; *and if you can completely control pain, you can completely control injury*.

Conventional science and medicine have a hard time swallowing this last clause. For if this fear-pain-injury circuit exists, the transformation of it would yield a body with near miraculous properties: an essentially fearless, pain-free, immune creature empowered through its own consciousness. This is precisely the view of the Hindu scripture called the Vedas, one of whose foundations is that *consciousness creates the body*. Physician and best-selling medical writer Deepak Chopra concurs. In his popular 1989 book, *Quantum Healing*, he writes:

> Consciousness is nothing but awareness. You can be aware that your hand is hot, which is passive awareness, but as the hypnosis research shows, you can also make your hand hot, which is active awareness, or attention. When you "pay attention" to something, you shift from passive to active awareness. Attention exerts far more control than people ordinarily realize. That is because we are victims of passive awareness. A person in pain is aware of the pain, but not that he can make it increase, diminish, appear, or disappear. Yet all this is true. (People can walk on fire, for example, because they can control their level of pain; more remarkably, they can control whether their feet actually get burned — that too is under the control of attention.) [15]

THE POWER OF HYPNOSIS

For a respected professional to make such a radical statement, there must be a good deal of supporting evidence. Hypnosis alone offers quite a bit. First, and least reliably, there are the anecdotal accounts of hypnotic immunity, such as those referred to by English researcher Brian Inglis in his report on the firewalk: "To prove to audiences that hypnotized subjects really are entranced, the hypnotist holds a lighted match under their extended forefingers. When they come out of their trances, they neither feel pain nor show any signs of a burn." [16]

In his 1988 book *The Hidden Power*, Inglis elaborates:

> Not merely do the volunteers feel no pain, they show no sign of a burn afterwards, no reddening, no blisters. The implications for medical science ought to be obvious. In the trance state, the mind can switch off not merely the mechanism by which we feel pain, but also the process by which the body ordinarily reacts to a burn.

> Hypnotists, in other words, have been practicing the same craft as the shamans and the gurus who lead fire-walks. [17]

In his 1961 report entitled "The Physiological Effects of Hypnosis," Dr. Theodore Barber, indicates that the effects of hypnosis take many forms. Given the appropriate suggestion, he says, some subjects have been rendered temporarily color blind, and even completely blind and deaf. Other subjects have been able to raise or lower local skin temperatures, alter heart rates and even stop their hearts altogether. Most significant for this investigation, Barber also notes many instances of hypnotically induced blisters — burns that were initiated through contact with room-temperature objects said to be red-hot. [18]

Among the most intriguing reports cited by Barber is the previously mentioned J. Arthur Hadfield research, entitled "The Influence of Hypnotic Suggestion on Inflammatory Conditions." In a series of experiments during World War I at the Royal Naval Hospital in Chatham, England, Hadfield hypnotized a sailor being treated for "shell shock" and suggested that a red-hot iron was being touched to his arm. In fact, the doctor only touched the patient with his finger. Wrote Hadfield:

> When I touched him with my finger, he withdrew his arm with such evident pain that I proceeded to suggest that a blister would form. I then wakened him and thought little more about the matter. But half an hour later, the patient returned and asked if I had done anything to his arm when he was hypnotized, as it was painful and burning, and he pointed to a blister which was indeed forming and ultimately became full of fluid and surrounded with hyperaemia. [19]

Excited by this turn of events but unsatisfied with the conditions of the experiment, Hadfield repeated it many times. On every occasion, the subject formed the suggested blister, and the "burns" from the touch of Hadfield's finger were indistinguishable from those that might have been caused by a red-hot iron.

In the fourth experiment, Hadfield hypnotized the seaman, gave the usual suggestion that he was being touched by a red-hot iron and again touched him with a finger. At another site on the subject's arm, Hadfield repeated the suggestion but this time suggested that there would be no pain, even though the site would blister. The first site blistered as usual; but at the second site, where the patient was instructed not to feel pain, no blister formed, even though the patient had been "instructed" to blister there as well.

Though Hadfield did not spell it out in his report, the course of his actions indicates he thought that his subject *not* blistering was in some ways as remarkable as the hypnotic blisters he produced. For him, it seemed to suggest that inflammation and blistering are produced *as a result of pain*, rather than pain being produced from the injury.

Hadfield's experiments are somewhat isolated and by no means conclusive. They surely raise as many questions as they answer. In the instance where no blister was formed when the suggestion was made that one should, it seems the body found it impossible to hypnotically manufacture a burn without subjectively experiencing some pain. Hence the suggestions of "no pain" and "blistering" are contradictory when a hypnotized subject is touched with a room-temperature object that is said to be red-hot. Apparently, the body cannot manufacture injury of this type without first experiencing pain.

Remarkably, hypnosis is a state with almost no physiological hallmarks. In summarizing his comprehensive overview, Barber notes, "The studies reviewed above suggest the general conclusion that many if not all of the physiological effects which can be induced in some subjects during 'hypnosis' can also be induced in some persons without hypnosis." [20]

Barber also cites several pioneering studies in which powerful suggestion without hypnotic trance induced remarkable behavior. For example, in the early 1920s, he says, Dr. W.R. Wells demonstrated that direct commands repeated emphatically for a few seconds — for example, "Your arm is insensitive to pain!" or "You cannot speak your name!" — were sufficient to elicit anesthesia, amnesia, limb rigidity, hallucinatory pain, automatic writing and posthypnotic behavior in a large proportion of male college students. Wells said his subjects were not drowsy, and he reported quicker results through such direct methods than by a "hypnotic induction" designed to induce trance. [21]

Writes Barber in another paper:

> When the subject is concerned only with the words of the hypnotist and when he literally believes that the hypnotist's words are true statements, he experiences many or all of the hypnotic phenomena. When he "believes" he is insensitive to pain, he does not experience the expected pain response to noxious stimuli. . . . The psychology of hypnosis is therefore one aspect of the psychology of "belief" and "perception." [22]

In modern hypnosis, the hypnotic trance is close to a sleep-like state, where healing can be induced through suggestion. It was this model that Dr. James Esdaile used to introduce hypnotism in a government hospital in India, around 1845. This was before the introduction of chloroform, ether or other anesthetics, when surgery was an agonizing process for both patient and practitioner alike. Using simple hypnotic techniques, Dr. Esdaile hypnotically anesthetized his patients, performing a total of 261 surgical operations, including numerous amputations. The resultant mortality — 6 percent — was very low for those days, and most of the wounds healed with unusual rapidity. [23]

Apparently, remarkable cures have also been initiated through hypnosis. One such case, initiated by a friend of Drs. Elmer and Alyce Green, is detailed in their book *Beyond Biofeedback*, published in 1977. Suffering acute pain from a cancerous tumor in the pelvis, the patient was hypnotized and asked to find the room in his brain that housed the valves supplying the blood to his body. When he found the valves, he was asked to turn off the blood supply to the tumor. The patient complied, and during two months of sessions, the tumor shrank to a quarter of its original size. The pain disappeared, and the man walked away from the hospital. [24]

Hypnosis, it seems course, is only one of a variety of "altered states" that afford remarkable physiological effects. The powers of self-hypnosis or autohypnosis are also well documented. Autosuggestion has traditionally been found in yogic disciplines, where it is seen in the mantra and other repetitive combinations of sound and meaning. In the West, it found vogue in Emile Coue's upbeat mantra, "Every day in every way I'm feeling better and better." More modern American groups may have updated the words, but the tune is still the same: repeat a good, and beautiful, and empowering thought enough and you'll hypnotize yourself into believing it's true.

RITUAL, MODELING AND IMAGINATION

Most psychologists see self-hypnosis as a process of the conscious mind controlling and influencing the unconscious mind. If you can tap into your healing power and the mastermind that orchestrates your bodily functions, you can empower yourself in many extraordinary ways. This is the aim of healers, medicine men and shamans the world over who employ altered states of consciousness in order to bring about healing and empowerment.

The methods of altering consciousness are as numerous and varied as the world's cuisine. Healers and evolutionary adventurers choose from a mind-boggling menu that includes dancing, chanting, drumming, music, candlelight, firelight, mandala gazing, rhythmic breathing, sex and consciousness-altering drugs of all types. Together with a vast array of dramatic rituals, we human beings have an awesome selection of evolutionary devices at our disposal, most of which yield precise and extraordinary physiological control.

In most consciousness-altering rituals, the aim is to control the powers of the unconscious mind. When the psychoactive power of the ritual is combined with group fervor and some form of consciousness alteration, the effects can be astounding. This is one reason why it seems safest for most people to firewalk within the context of a guided ritual, including lots of group fervor. There are hundreds of firewalking rituals alone. And in each, apparently, lies the power to catalyze the unconscious to produce an immunity to fire.

Much of ritual and ceremony is based on modeling, in which the veterans of a tribe or group perform ecstatic acts, sometimes surpassing their normal abilities. The Zuni Fire Fraternity is an example of this, and through it, empowerment is passed on by demonstration. The firewalking ritual is a similar empowerment-by-modeling, a sight so startling it literally convinces many of those who view it that they have the ability to perform it themselves.

We're good at modeling — it's how we learned to walk, no doubt — and a whole industry of sports-modeling videotapes has recently emerged, with both supportive scientific data and thousands of satisfied sportspeople all attesting to the superior performance of complicated physical tasks though watching excellence in action. *Imagined* visual modeling seems to work nearly as well. Top athletes use this technique extensively these days, and even more remarkable results have been achieved with cancer patients, some of whom have been able to visualize the disappearance of their terminal diseases.

Drs. Carl and Stephanie Simonton developed such techniques in the early 1970s, working at first with a patient in the advanced stages of throat cancer. Specialists had given the patient little chance for survival, but he visualized the treatment as the Simontons suggested, focusing on powerful healing through his white blood cells, and quite quickly, he recovered completely. Continuing to use the imagery technique, he went on to cure his arthritis and a 20-year case of impotence, all within four months of his self-induced cancer cure. [25]

This at first seemed exceptional, but many of the Simontons' other patients, it seemed, could do something similar. The results of guided visualization were little short of miraculous: with the first 159 patients, all of whom had been diagnosed as terminal and none of whom had been given longer than a year to live, 30 cured their cancer completely and another 35 pushed it into a state of remission. [26]

Dr. Bernie Siegel explains this awesome power:

> Visualization takes advantage of what might almost be called a "weakness" of the body; it cannot distinguish between a vivid mental experience and an actual physical experience. Psychologist Charles Garfield studied cancer survivors at the University of California Medical Center in San Francisco and concluded that most of them had the ability to enter states of mind that enabled their bodies to perform, like those of athletes, at levels beyond the ordinary. Garfield found remarkable similarities between what the cancer survivors often did and the methods used by the Soviet and Eastern European competitors who have enjoyed success in the Olympics during recent decades. These techniques, mainly developed in Bulgaria, have recently been described in detail by Sheila Ostrander and Lynn Schroeder in

> their book *Superlearning*.
>
> Eastern European trainers often have their students and athletes lie down and listen to calming music, especially the largo movements of baroque instrumental music, with their strong, regular bass-line rhythms of about sixty beats per minute. After a few minutes, the listener's heartbeat becomes synchronized with the beat of the music, producing deep relaxation. Then the athlete visualizes, in full color and complete detail, the winning performance. This is repeated until the physical act becomes merely a duplication of the mental act that has already been successfully visualized. Soviet research indicates that athletes who spend as much as three-fourths of their time on mental training do better than those who place more emphasis on physical preparation. [27]

The message is coming in loud and clear: when you want peak performance, dramatic healing, freedom from pain and/or radical immunity, imagine yourself enjoying these things, relish the picture of yourself at the height of your powers . . . and soon you actually will be!

TRANSCENDING THE FLESH

The altered states/altered physiology connection can be seen clearly through the use of psychoactive drugs, and there is good evidence that a psychedelic drug, much like the firewalk, only catalyzes what is already waiting inside a person's psyche. Dr. Andrew Weil, , who has experimented on himself with psychedelics, reports a variety of physiological empowerments while under the influence. These include: "(1) the ability to handle rough or sharp objects, such as spiny cactuses, without being scratched or hurt; (2) the ability to receive repeated and forceful blows without sustaining injury or even marks on the skin; (3) the ability to tolerate cold water or cold air without clothing, yet remain warm and feel warm to the touch of other people; (4) the ability to touch and walk upon surfaces so hot they are intolerable to others and quickly cause burns." This last ability sounds remarkably close to the firewalk. Significantly, Weil reports that he experienced these physiological empowerments at first only under the influence of psychedelics, but later *without* them as well. [28]

Our senses of pain and temperature, it seems, actually share neural pathways, so it is not surprising that the ability to alter the degree of sensitivity to either one dramatically affects sensitivity to the other. "It's interesting to note," writes George Leonard, "that the pathways for pain and temperature in the spinal column appear to be inseparable, and that there is close relationship and some sort of interplay between the sites of pain and warmth, suffering and pleasure, in the brain." [29]

Most modern firewalkers report sensations of "no temperature" or even "coolness" when their walks prove successful. Conversely, the fire reportedly feels "hot" when their walks cause pain and burns. Here, then, we are uncovering another close correlation, yet another apparent circuit of the human being, the temperature-sensation-pain-injury circuit. If we can transform the feeling of a fire's heat into some merely extreme sensation, something beyond our capacity to distinguish it, might we not short-circuit certain of our own neural pathways, averting both pain and injury?

A fakir spends his whole life in just such explorations, repeatedly and continuously mortifying the flesh so that he can transcend it. This is a way of living and thinking that seems diametrically opposed to Western ways. In the West, it seems, we spend our whole lives — and a great deal of our time and energy — avoiding pain. No wonder, when it comes up, we're so unprepared and frightened. No wonder we generally tense up and contract at the pain's onslaught, further exacerbating the hurt. By contrast, the fakir wants to become comfortable with pain, make it his friend and ally, and through it ascend to the level of the gods.

A fakir concentrates on pain control, often skewering his flesh or performing some other intentional self-mutilation to test and develop his powers, but his practice is not simply one of dissociation or non-attachment. For a fakir also attains other forms of bodily control. A highly adept fakir can regulate the blinking of his eyelids; display dexterity in the toes equal to that of his fingers; relax or tense any muscle at will; swallow his tongue; and control his heartbeat and blood circulation. [30]

Still, control of pain is at the heart of a fakir's practice. Not the eradication or elimination of pain; a fakir has the highest regard for pain, knows that it is his protector, his empowering angel. A fakir meets his pain, and utilizes its innate power as a springboard to higher consciousness.

The first fakirs were Moslem Sufis, who emerged among the Shiite sect in Persia in the late 10th and 11th centuries. But gradually, the significance of their bodily obsession became understood, and fakirs began to develop all through the Middle East and into North Africa. They were ascetic men, known as miracle workers and generally living off what people gave them. *Fakir* literally means "humble man," and even the great sultan Omar Kyayyam humbled himself with the fakir's ways, working as a tentmaker to keep his position in perspective. [31]

For Roland Loomis, it is much the same. Loomis is a Silicon valley businessman. He is also a modern-day fakir of sorts, one of few individuals who still perform the tortuous Native American Sun Dance. This ritual is an awesome meeting of mind and matter in which the practitioner is almost sure to die, either physically or psychologically. Through the transmutation of his pain, the Sun Dancer systematically crosses the threshold of individual consciousness into the world of pure primal energy. This intended ego eradication is not undertaken as an individual quest; rather, it is intended to work some group magic for the benefit of the entire tribe. [32]

In performing the Sun Dance, a man's flesh is pierced with large hooks at various sites, lines are strung from the hooks to a tree, and the man hangs in the sun, dangling by his own impaled flesh. "There's a moment," says Loomis, "as great weight is gradually transferred to the piercings, when 80 or 90 percent of the body weight is on those piercings, that you flicker back and forth between having to stop and being able to surrender." [33]

Loomis didn't just decide to become a fakir. Through a troubled childhood, he says, he was plagued with memories of past lives, one of which was that of the 11th-century ascetic, Fakir Musafar. Also astounded by strange psychic powers that vanished with puberty, Loomis was alienated from friends and family. Eventually, he found sanctuary among a local tribe of Native Americans. Through them, he found his way to the Sun Dance, and through the Sun Dance, he found a way out of all his incarnations. Here is how he describes the experience:

> During a ceremony like the Sun Dance, I am not Roland; I am not the Fakir; I am no particular known identity. I am the wind that is blowing. I am the earth under my feet. I become, in consciousness, everything around me. I become a part of everything in nature. I lose all touch with my personality and memory. I lose it all. It's all totally wiped out, at least for the moment when I slip into the primal state.
>
> The piercing of the body becomes a means in which you enter the primal state. You don't feel any pain because you are in a state of alert self-hypnosis, and you've already started releasing all those neat little internally generated endorphins. [34]

Without this primal state, says Loomis, the pain would be too intense to bear and the practitioner might be unable to transmute it. Playing with pain, then, is much like playing with fire: if we cannot achieve some electrified ecstasy while meeting these powerful strangers, they will surely hurt us. It is handy to have pain as an alarm, useful to have it as a health check to monitor certain conditions. But it seems equally important to gain control of it, and to know how and when to transform it.

THE CIRCUIT OF PAIN AND INJURY

Pain has traditionally been thought of as a one-way street, with hurtful stimuli ascending along neural pathways to the brain. Recently, however, *descending* responses have been discovered to be just as critical. On contact with a noxious stimulus — a pinprick, flame or red-hot coal, for example — our skin sets off a process of rapid electrochemical communications. First the nerve endings do their job, sending an electrical jolt up the neural pathways. Then, instantaneously, the mind and body respond. To a great degree, the specific electrochemical response to the initial signal determines the amount of pain and injury the person will suffer. [35]

In 1965, the actual pain gate and its workings were described for the first time. The key gate is the *substantia gelatinosa*. When this gate is closed, pain messages cannot reach the brain. The gate is closed by comforting messages that descend from brain and body. Ascending messages of pain open the gelatinosa, allowing messages of hurt to reach the brain. [36] Pain, then, is a dynamic tension between messages of hurt and messages of response, and in this communication lies both our suffering and salvation.

Pain is a marvelous, body-protecting autonomic mechanism, but it can also be a chronic irritant that substantially increases the likelihood of physiological damage. Pain is automatic; but as science and the fakirs have shown us, and as hypnotically anesthetized patients have shown us, pain is also subject to our control. We must first, however, control our own attention, for if pain captures it, we are lost to suffering. If we can focus attention elsewhere, it seems — especially on empowering ideas or images — we may not only be able to eliminate pain, but also much of the injury normally associated with it.

AUTOGENIC TRAINING AND BIOFEEDBACK

The tantalizing possibility of such voluntary control of normally autonomic systems was raised by Autogenic Training (AT) in the early 1900s. At about that time, Dr. Johannes Schultz, a Berlin psychiatrist and neurologist, started assembling the factors he felt might encourage a stress-relieving, self-induced hypnotic state. He found that a heavy feeling, first in the extremities and then in the whole body, together with an associated feeling of warmth, were the hallmarks of the hypnotic state. Remarkably, in order to produce this self-induced hypnotic state, a person need only passively concentrate on certain verbal formulas implying heaviness and warmth in the extremities.

The results achieved by AT were startling, and they were backed up by clinical studies showing that it helped in the treatment of disorders of the respiratory, cardiovascular, gastrointestinal and endocrine systems. AT also has been effective in the treatment of 60-90 percent of patients with long-standing disturbances such as insomnia, headache and bronchial asthma. [37]

To summarize Luthe's overview of autogenic training: passively concentrate on certain easily effected physiological responses (warmth or heaviness, for example) and you will be able to influence your brain chemistry; influence your brain chemistry and you mobilize powerful regulators in your body that will help to harmonize both body and mind. [38]

Biofeedback training is another related psychophysiological discipline. From earliest times, yogis have attempted to regulate their basal metabolic rate through breathing regimens with a biofeedback loop, using their diaphragm as a monitor. Essentially, they slowed their breathing to about one breath per minute, inducing the body to come a high state of optimum hormonal balance. [39]

Similarly, Schultz developed a form of non-instrumental biofeedback training when he taught patients to use the feedback of their own heart to control their heart rates. In this third standard AT exercise, patients are instructed to lay the hand over the heart until the heartbeat is detected. They then tell the heart what to do, to speed up or slow down, using the vibratory beat as an indicator of progress. This feat is normally associated with yogic adepts. In fact, AT practitioners assert, it is something most of us are capable of doing without great effort. [40]

In the mid-'60s, before they met and studied Jack Schwarz, Drs. Elmer and Alyce Green established a laboratory for autogenic feedback training and voluntary control. The site was the Menninger Hospital in Topeka, Kansas. One of the Greens' first successes involved the experimental treatment of a variety of subjects who suffered from migraine headaches. The Greens devised an exquisitely sensitive temperature monitor, then asked the migraine sufferers to raise the temperature of their hands. Watching a temperature gauge whose needle fluctuated with every hundredth of a degree F, most subjects were able to raise their hand temperature markedly, some up to 10 degrees. More significantly, the biofeedback-facilitated ability to raise hand temperature was also found to eliminate migraine headache. Writes Alyce Green:

> Practice with the meter can usually be discontinued within a month, but daily practice without the meter continues, with the aim of learning to initiate relaxation and warmth in a few seconds to prevent or abort headaches. About 80 percent of the migraine-headache patients have obtained relief, ranging from slight to excellent. A few have reported a migraine-free life since completing the program. [41]

The implications of this go far beyond hand-warming and headache relief. The Greens strongly suggest that such ability can be transferred to almost any area of life. As Elmer Green puts it:

> The person visualizes and feels the desired change that will influence the meter and allows the body to carry out the instruction. The feeling seems to be the instruction. This feeling has been reported by many successful performers to be, at least in the early stages of learning, a composite of imagery, emotion, and body sensation, but after a skill is thoroughly learned, the body sensation can be "turned on" at will, often with no need for any particular mental image or emotion. [42]

The Greens' research seems to indicate that our unconscious is the source of psychosomatic illness. And since the unconscious is open to our control, they infer, psychosomatic illness is also completely under our control.

Recalling the near miraculous self-regulating and healing capacities of the unconscious, it seems that we've entered a magic kingdom. As we survey this vast and splendid territory, hitherto unknown to us, we began to glimpse astounding connections, together with equally astounding possibilities for new connections. We have entered the realm whose topography includes the psychology of physical immunity.

OUR "THINKING" IMMUNE SYSTEM

The human immune system has been much in the news the last decade, with acquired immune deficiency syndrome (AIDS) reaching epidemic proportions. While trying to understand and find better treatments for AIDS, science has also been uncovering the marvels of the immune system and how it normally protects us from a variety of devastating intrusions. The science of modern immunology is very different from the one we lived by only a decade ago. Now, we understand that the immune system can learn, memorize, reason and be conditioned, just like the brain — that it is in fact an *extension* of the brain and works within the same chemical network. [43]

While investigating the rapidly growing literature that directly links attitude with immune system, former *Saturday Review* editor Norman Cousins undertook a number of experiments on himself. Among them was a very short immune-system test. First, he had a blood sample drawn from his arm. Then, after putting himself in the most positive frame of mind he could manage, he had another sample taken. Wrote Cousins in his 1989 book, *Head First, the Biology of Hope*:

> After taking the first blood sample, I tried to imagine the very best thing that could happen to our world — and then tried to make it seem as real as possible. I tried to imagine what a wonderful planet we might have if the Soviet Union and the United States had rational foreign policies. I tried to visualize all the benefits that might accrue to the human race if the madness at the top subsided and the leaders of major nations broke away from the accumulation of weapons that, if used, could change the basic conditions of life itself. I tried to imagine the changes for the better that might flow out of the realization that true security depended on the creation of a workable world order.
>
> I confess I found this train of thought both energizing and stimulating; after about five minutes, we took the second blood sample. The results couldn't have been more gratifying. In just five minutes, there was an average increase of 53 percent in the various components of my immune system — from a low of 30 percent in the precursor NK (natural killer) cells to a high of about 200 percent in the antibody-coated T cells. [44]

THE DIALOGUE OF IMMUNITY

Apparently, our conscious attitudes dramatically affect our immunity to everything, from disease to fire, from insult to injury. Similarly, our unconscious attitudes, though little known to us, also profoundly affect our immunity. Our conscious and unconscious minds converse all the time, but it is a conversation that we rarely are privy to — and even more rarely do we initiate the conversation ourselves. Yet a substantial aim of many of the consciousness-altering methods is to commence such an open, intentional, internal dialogue.

Besides their substantial success in training ordinary citizens how to gain control of normally-unconscious processes, Elmer and Alyce Green brought a number of exceptionally talented subjects to their laboratory, including Jack Schwarz and Swami Rama, an Indian yogi. These were men who had trained their unconscious to extraordinary degrees, men in whom the inner dialogue, conscious to unconscious, was clear, free and lively. Accordingly, a great many physical powers came to them, including an astounding control of their own physiology.

In particular, the Greens witnessed and documented Swami Rama's ability to control his brain waves; raise and lower skin temperature; stop his heart without muscular clenching; slow his heart to 20 beats, then immediately speed up to 250; and have his skin pierced without bleeding or damage. Schwarz also demonstrated his ability to be pierced without suffering pain, and to completely control bleeding and injury. In one test in which a puncture wound did bleed on Schwarz' arm, Elmer Green reported: "Bleeding was continuous for about ten seconds, and then I heard Jack say very softly, 'Now it stops.' Much to my surprise, the hole in the skin that I was dabbing closed up as if drawn by purse strings. It took about one second to close, and not another drop of blood appeared." [45]

Not only can Schwarz completely control pain and bleeding, but he can control infection as well. This is probably even more substantial a feat, considering some of the germs, toxins and diseases with which he has intentionally contaminated himself in order to test his own immune power. In this regard, Schwarz' experiments are akin to the Church of God members imbibing strychnine and other poisons in order to test their faith. In Schwarz' case, this has taken the form of puncturing of his arm and other parts of his body with a knitting needle or sailmaker's needle that he has first rolled under his shoe in order to "sterilize." Says Schwarz, "In 36 years of doing this, sometimes with a rusty nail, sometimes contaminating the needle with bacteria, cancerous tissues, or viruses, I have never gotten a single infection." [46]

For Jack Schwarz, such immunity is directly correlated to a person's attitude, the totality of which appears as his or her "body radiance." Apparently, it is this radiance, this biophysically generated force field that is our protective shield from insult, injury, infection, and burns. As Schwarz himself puts it, ". . . if we are in high state of radiant excitement, then we are not going to be affected by anything of a polluting nature, or by disease or by negative thought processes." [47]

It seems clear that within our own unconscious physiology, at least, mind over matter is an ongoing phenomenon. This is not some mystical, showman's stunt, nor is it some godly power that we can wield to impress our friends; mind over matter happens in all of us — with our conscious cooperation or without it. Whatever we think and feel shows up in our physiology.

Mind, then, utterly controls and suffuses matter. And, as Jack Schwarz and others have proven, in embodying enlightening attitudes, we can reach uncommon states of health, immunity and personal power. Elmer Green noted this when he reported on the core of Swami Rama's personal power:

> The most potent of the various ideas of the Swami is that all the body is in the mind but not all the mind is in the body. This simple phrase has vast theoretical implications. The control of every cell of the body is possible, according to the Swami, because every cell has a representation in the unconscious. Not only that, each cell exists, not only symbolically in mind, but also as a section of a real energy structure called mind. When we manipulate the representation of the unconscious [as in visualization], we literally manipulate the cell itself, because the cell is part of the mind.
>
> The second half of the phrase "but not all the mind is in the body" is related to the extension of mind into nature in general and accounts for parapsychological events, psychokinesis, psychic healing and all such scientifically impossible phenomena. The reason scientists felt these phenomena are impossible is because scientists, at least the majority, have not been able to conceive of the mind as an energy structure which interlocks with energy structures both in the body and in "external" nature. [48]

MIND OVER DISTANT MATTER

Mind over matter most commonly refers to using the mind to initiate actions outside the body. Such feats are harder to document than the influence of psychology over physiology, yet they do happen. Generally referred to as psychokinesis, or PK, the process consists of exerting a physical force at a distance with the mind alone. This is not of evident significance to our well-being, nor does it seem to enter into the firewalking equation; however, it is interesting to note that at least one prominent firewalker has such abilities. Joe Nuzum, for example, has demonstrated his ability to extinguish flame and to move lightweight objects with his mind alone. I have personally seen videotapes of such feats and confirmed them with psychiatrist Dr. Berthold Schwarz, who has observed them firsthand. [49]

One of the most scientifically observed demonstrations of PK is that of Soviet psychic Nina Kalugina, who has been repeatedly filmed levitating a 30-gram ball. She has also demonstrated her ability to separate the yolk of an egg from its white as the egg floated in a saline solution in a distant glass chamber. [50]

Lest you think these odd but intriguing feats are for special sensitives only, in 1958, firewalking chemist Mayne Reid Coe demonstrated that we may all have these capabilities, should we wish to develop them. Coe studied yoga, fasted and practiced breathing exercises. Eventually, by getting himself into a state of heightened relaxation, he was able to move a suspended, heavy cardboard box with the power of his mind alone. Doctoral psychology researcher Jan Merta did much the same thing in the '60s, spending hours each day before a pair of chicken feathers suspended from a cord within a large, airtight Pyrex jar. Eventually, he could move them at will from across the room, without even looking. [51]

MIND IN MATTER

In firewalking and firehandling, of course, no one is making the claim that we are moving or altering the fire; rather, the usual explanation is that we have altered *ourselves*. Carrying this concept a bit further, many who have studied the mind-over-matter phenomenon feel that the phrase itself is a misnomer, that a more precise description for it would be "the demonstration of mind *in* matter." The concept of mind in matter posits a world of pure energy — energy in various forms, some denser and less lively, others lighter and much more easily transformed.

Someday, perhaps sooner rather than later, we will come to know and control matter more directly with our minds, even as we now fashion it with our hands and technology. Once we more fully recognize the mind in matter — especially the mind in our *own* matter — perhaps then we can begin the dialogue between energies, and the finer and faster can begin to influence the slower and denser.

We are all yogis, fakirs, meditators, medicine takers, and hypnotics; we are all shamans, medicine men, healers and mediums. Whether we choose to enter these potential forms is up to us, and how we manifest the finest and densest forms of our energy is also up to us. Being an amalgam of our unconscious and conscious feelings, our attitudes affect everything, both within and without. Our attitude not only affects our immunity, more accurately, it *is* our immunity. In a very direct and tactile drama, the firewalk serves to demonstrate this unity of attitude and immunity. Faith can live in flesh, mind in matter. Faith can protect flesh, mind can protect matter.

9

Beings Brighter Than Fire

The light of the body is the eye; therefore, when your eye is single, your whole body also is full of light.

Luke 11:34

From all my research and personal experiments, I can draw a number of conclusions. Most significantly, I am convinced that the firewalk provides a pathway to an altered state, a state in which almost any of us can increase our immunity to the burning effects of fire.

For me, there are far too many well-documented instances of people standing in fire, dancing on it or comfortably handling glowing coals for the short contact/low thermal conductivity theory to seem valid. Furthermore, many of these accounts contain descriptions of the burn immunity extending outward to include clothing and hair — even the hair on feet covered with glowing coals for several seconds or more.

Explanations that point to some increased sweat exudation or vapor barrier also seem unrealistic to me. Generally speaking, human skin burns almost immediately on contact with red-hot coals. Furthermore from Harry Price in England during the 1930s to Vittoria Manganas in Greece during the 1980s, scientific studies repeatedly report the physical state of a firewalker's foot after the walk as cold and clammy, never hot and sweaty.

Likewise, I am convinced that explanations pointing to previously unknown physiological responses can only be partial at best. None of these could explain the immunity to burning that is apparent in many firewalkers' clothing and hair. Besides, the skin of successful firewalkers and firehandlers rarely shows any signs of exposure to burning temperatures or of an effort to disguise injury.

Instead, all evidence points to a human force field, a protective, self-generated "shield" that might profoundly affect our immunity to fire, and quite possibly our immunity to many diseases. This field has often been postulated by many firewalkers themselves. During my research, I came across it time and again, both in relation to traditional and modern American firewalking: the "bioenergy field" or "extended body image," that band of potential immunity that must surround us and provide a variably safe cocoon in which to walk over hot coals.

Most of us, it seems, have far too limited a view of ourselves. For most of us, *we* stop where our body ends. That's us, marrow to skin. The idea of an energy field surrounding us may sound mystical. On the other hand, we are all familiar with some components of our multifaceted, invisible force field. At the crudest level, we are all familiar with the subtle, invisible body heat we produce, the heat that creates radiant bands around us, made visible through infrared photography. That we are radiant beings, warm blooded creatures surrounded by a narrow band of electromagnetic heat energy, no one would deny.

But we also apparently produce many other forms of normally invisible radiant energy. And though they may be harder for science to detect, their effects are far more profound than heat radiation. Our own "bioluminescence," I am convinced, affords us immunity from all the noxious substances and stimuli we encounter in life, and it can be brightened or dimmed according to our consciousness.

For thousands of years, ancient traditions have asserted this. The Chinese call this energy *chi*. In the martial arts, despite the attention to muscle movement, it is the movement and control of the *chi* that is at the heart of the practice. In India, this energy is called *prana*; and there too, special exercises and disciplines are performed to control and enhance it. For the *kahunas* of Hawaii and for most other spiritually oriented Pacific Islanders, this energy is called *mana*. For the Native American Iroquois, it is *orenda*. In Africa, it is the boiling energy called the *!num*. The Sufis call it *baraka*. To Jewish cabalists, it is *yesod*; to Christian ecstatics, the Holy Spirit.

This inner electricity and corresponding radiance can be seen iconographically in the early images of holy figures with halos around their heads or entire bodies. Conceptualizations of the human energy field have been around since the Middle Ages, when the controversial, 16th-century alchemist and physician Paracelsus spoke of a "fiery globe" that radiated around the entire body of every human being and which could be used in healing.

A few centuries later, Franz Anton Mesmer developed a similar view, perceiving what he called "animal magnetism" radiating from every human being. In his *Maxims on Animal Magnetism*, Mesmer wrote that "everything in the universe is contagious by means of a universal fluid in which all bodies are immersed." He, too, believed this force field could be used in healing; and though his methods were largely discredited, he did effect many cures.

In the mid-19th century, German industrialist and scientist Baron Karl von Reichenbach began the quest for a universal force field. In researching scores of sensitives who claimed to be able to see such an energy field, Reichenbach more clearly defined its appearance and properties. But because he could offer no visual method of confirming his findings, and because of his unfavorable association with the ideas of Mesmer, Reichenbach's universal energy, his "Od," failed to set the world aglow. [1]

At the dawn of the 20th century, the inventor of alternating current, Nicola Tesla, displayed photographs of himself with a radiant, sparking aura around his body, taken while he stood in an electric field. Not long afterwards, in 1908, a physician at London's St. Thomas Hospital, Dr. Walter J. Kilner, was appointed head of the hospital's just-founded X-ray department and began his investigations into human emanations. Kilner soon discovered he could detect three forces emanating from the body, including heat. Experimenting with filters through which he might directly view other radiations, he concluded that he could indeed see a three-part luminous force field surrounding the human body.

Excited but cautious, Kilner studied 60 patients before making any conclusive statements about his findings. As a result, when he published his first paper, he was not only able to mechanically reproduce visual proof of his claims, but he was also able to correlate a substantial portion of what he saw with human health.

Naming these luminous energy emananations the "etheric double," the "inner aura" and the "outer aura," Kilner showed that in times of disease, the aura dimmed, seemed to disappear or was marked by a dark patch. Intense behavior of any kind expanded the aura, Kilner found, while depression shrank it. And affection between two people brought about an energy transfer, the auras mingling and blending. An egg-shaped, luminous ball was the ideal, healthy aura, Kilner concluded; however, in trance states, it dimmed almost to invisibility, and at death it disappeared altogether.

Kilner wrote up his research in a book called *The Human Atmosphere*, stirring even further controversy. Soon, his work was picked up by Oscar Bagnall, a Cambridge biologist who was able to confirm most of Kilner's findings. Furthermore, Bagnall found a better dye to use in the filters and developed additional insights into the successful viewing of auras. The aura could be best seen, he stated, not through the cones of the retina, which we use for day vision and color perception, but through the rods of the retina, which we use for night or low-light vision.

Accordingly, in the book he wrote crowning his career, *The Origins and Properties of the Human Aura*, Bagnall offered these instructions on aura viewing: "Since the rods lie to the side of the center part of the retina, which is lined solely by cones and which receives the direct image of the object being viewed, it would . . . clearly be an advantage to look at the object, if not out of the corner of one's eye, at least by not peering hard and directly at it." [2]

Bagnall says the aura cannot be dispersed with an air current but that it is attracted to a magnet held near the body. He has discerned two distinct layers, the outer one hazy and more diffuse, the inner one brighter and more sharply defined. Sparks, or flares similar to solar flares, arc out from the body periodically, he says, as might be expected from any intensely radiant object. [3]

Biologist Harold Saxon Burr was next to enter this controversial arena, during the mid-1930s. But his work at Yale was so solid, and subsequently repeated so often by other researchers, that it amounted to a breakthrough in energy-field research. Burr wasn't particularly interested in *seeing* the energy field, only in detecting it and noting as many correspondences as he could.

Using a volt-meter that was able to detect differences as small as a millionth of a volt, Burr conclusively demonstrated that every living entity is surrounded by an "electrodynamic field." At first, he monitored trees on the Yale campus, demonstrating that this field fluctuated according to environmental electromagnetic variances such as thunderstorms, phases of the moon and sunspot activity.

Even more amazingly, he concluded that this field has an intimate relationship with the physical body, in one sense creating it and in another being created *by* it. "The pattern of organization of any biological system," he wrote, "is established by a complex electrodynamic field, which is in part determined by its atomic physico-chemical components and which in part determines the behavior and orientation of those components. [4]

To begin his studies on the electric fields produced by animals, Burr created one of science's more elegant experiments. Starting with the principle of a generator, he created possibly the world's first and only salamander generator. With a live salamander floating in a dish of salt water, Burr immersed two electrodes at opposite sides and spun the dish slowly. The equipment indicated that the lizard-like amphibian was indeed radiating the predicted field. As Burr slowly spun the dish, the field was repeatedly interrupted, producing a weak alternating current. Without the salamander, the slowly spinning dish produced no current. [5]

Next, the scientist went to work on humans, measuring their energy-field fluctuations over a long period and under a wide variety of circumstances. Burr was able to show that abnormal voltage patterns could be detected *before* disease symptoms appeared in the physical body. For Burr, the L-field was the mediator of incoming cosmic energy; rather than its merely being an emanation of physiology, he claimed the physical body depended on it. And like many researchers before and after him, Burr was able to see not only the present and near-future health of the entity disclosed in his or her force field, but also a clear record of *health history*, complete with internal scars. [6]

Burr's work was carried forward by his student and colleague, Leonard Ravitz, who focused on human emotional and mental states and how they affected the L-field. While Burr had discovered that trees respond to a 24-

hour solar rhythm and a 25-hour lunar rhythm, Ravitz found that the human L-field reaches a maximum positive value at full moon and a maximum negative value at new moon. Ravitz was also able to measure the depth of hypnotic trance by detecting the voltage change in a person's L-field. His startling conclusion: "Both emotional activity and stimuli of any sort involve mobilization of electrical energy, as indicated on the galvanometer; hence both emotions and stimuli evoke the same energy. Emotions can be equated with energy." [7]

At about the same time, psychoanalyst Wilhelm Reich was developing a similar understanding of the human energy field. He called the vital energy "orgone," and he went to great lengths to amplify it. Reich's early work on character analysis and the muscular rigidities of neurosis set the stage for a variety of today's body therapies. Unfortunately, like Mesmer, his research and methods were suspect, and his promotion of his "orgone box," a purported energy accumulator, led to his decline.

The whole field of aura research brightened in 1939, when a Soviet electrician, Semyon Kirlian, was summoned for a routine repair job at a research laboratory in the town of Krasnodar. Kirlian made the repair. On his way out, however, he chanced to see a demonstration of electrotherapy treatment in which a patient was about to be hooked up to a high-frequency generator. As he watched, Kirlian noticed a flash of light arc between the patient's body and the glass electrodes nearing the skin. Intrigued, he wondered if the effect could be photographed. He began experimenting, first trying to create an image of his own hand.

The results were painful. He burned his hand under the high-frequency current, but produced an interesting, rather impressionistic photograph. Said Kirlian later, "I studied the picture with pain, excitement and hope all combined. Had I made a discovery? Had I invented something? It wasn't clear yet what I'd done." [8]

He set to work refining his equipment and methods, building a high-frequency generator that could deliver an oscillation of 200,000 sparks per second between a pair of electrodes. Together with his wife, Valentina, he began to photograph a variety of objects without using any camera. Instead, he recorded their images and auras strictly by inserting them in the high-frequency field.

The first refined Kirlian photographs were those of a leaf, which Kirlian described as "a world of myriad dots of energy." Around the edges of the leaf, turquoise and reddish-yellow flares emanated in specific channels. A human finger looked like a complex topographic map. A human hand produced light effects that were blurred and disorganized if the subject was worried or ill, while the same hand produced a bright, sharp luminescent field when the subject was happy and healthy. [9]

Unsatisfied with mere photographic evidence, Kirlian wanted to observe these energy fields in action. The result was his optical aura viewer, which is now the subject of 14 Soviet patents. Once again, with his prototype viewer, Kirlian's first subject was his hand. According to one report:

> ... a fantastic world of the unseen opened before the husband and wife team. The hand itself looked like the Milky Way in a starry sky. Against a background of blue and gold, something was taking place in the hand that looked like a fireworks display. Multicolored flares lit up, then sparks, twinkles, flashes. Some lights glowed steadily like Roman candles, others flashed out, then dimmed. Still others sparked at intervals. In parts of his hand there were little dim clouds. Certain glittering flares meandered along sparkling labyrinths like space ships travelling to other galaxies. [10]

The Kirlians continued their investigations, placing a half-withered leaf within the electromagnetic field. "It looked like a great metropolis turning out its lights for the night," reported researchers Lynn Shroeder and Sheila Ostrander. "The Kirlians tried an almost completely withered leaf. There were almost no flames and sparks, and the 'clouds' scarcely moved. As they watched, the leaf seemed to be dying before their eyes, and its death was reflected in the picture of energy impulses." [11]

"In living things," the Kirlians reported, "we see the signals of the inner state of the organism reflected in the brightness, dimness and colors of the flares. . . . The inner life-activities of the human being are written in these luminescent hieroglyphs. We created an apparatus to write these hieroglyphs. But to read them we're going to need help." [12]

Help was spotty. From the international scientific community, there were some glimmers of recognition; however, there were also legions of skeptics who sincerely believed that the Kirlians' hieroglyphs were actually created by the subject's moisture interacting with the high-frequency field.

Soon, though, researchers who supported the Kirlians' work began to make some astounding photographs of their own. The first series was a "before-and-after" photo of a healthy leaf, a section of which was then torn away. In the "after" photo of the torn leaf, half the leaf appeared to be gone, yet its energy pattern remained intact. The phantom aura itself showed subtle changes, "the sparkling outline and veins seemed airier, the background fluffier," but the energy body was still there. After a while, the phantom field faded and disappeared. Researchers liken this to the phantom pain amputees often feel in the limbs they no longer have. [13]

Though most of the modern world has yet to accept the Kirlians' findings, in 1968 their work was officially accepted into the Soviet canon of science. Reported a panel of Soviet physicians and scientists, "All living things — plants, animals and humans — not only have a physical body made of atoms and molecules, *but also a counterpart body of energy*." The panel called this energy field the "biological plasma body," concluding that "the bio-luminescence visible in the Kirlian pictures is caused by bioplasma, not by the electrical state of the organism." [14]

Here, then, is at least one modern scientific assertion that the human energy field not only exists, but exists independent of the body's electrical activity. Another comes from UCLA psychologist Thelma Moss, who has even recorded the Kirlian images of seeds, reporting 100 percent success in using Kirlian photography to predict the ability of soybeans to germinate. Says the outspoken scientist, "I wouldn't see any purpose in mucking about in this field if I thought it were entirely an electrical phenomenon." [15]

Neuropsychiatrist Shafica Karagulla emphatically agrees. In her book *Breakthrough to Creativity*, published in 1978, she reports that the sensitives she was testing were able to perceive a number of interconnected energy streams around the human body. This suggested to her that the so-called "solid" material body was in fact a by-product of these energies. Like Burr before her, she concluded that humans have an energy field that is "the exact blueprint of the dense physical body." In her view, that field is created by the chakras, the "seven vortices of energy related to the glands of the body and interconnected with the spine through the nervous system." [16]

A more down-to-earth approach to the body electric was taken by orthopedic surgeon and researcher Robert Becker, of the Veterans Administration Hospital in Syracuse, New York. Questing for the mechanism that heals bones, Becker studied the regenerative capacities of salamanders and other primitive animals, noting a "current of injury," a mild electrical current that flowed to the site of injury. Theorizing that such electrical energy could stimulate regeneration, Becker found that he was able to regenerate amputated forelimbs in frogs and rats by administering a weak electrical current. Furthermore, he found that hypnotized human patients can produce voltage changes in specific areas of their bodies on command.

In Becker's view, we are electronic beings, and our health can be beneficially influenced by carefully manipulating magnetic and electrical fields. His work has led to the development of a variety of injury-healing electronic stimulators that seem to work by enhancing the body's own electronic healing. [17]

We are, it seems, electrical beings, coursed by electricity, healed by electricity. As Jack Schwarz has said, "The main aim of all therapeutic methods, including nutrition, should be directed to restoring, preserving and regenerating electrical potentials, because it is the electrical potential of the body that holds the key to the miracles and mysteries of health and healing." Considering our needs for elements such as copper, zinc, and iron, and the dielectric saline solution in which they operate, says Schwarz "our bodies are wet batteries! Every cell is like a minibattery, with each holding positive and negative charges." [18]

Schwarz sees the human energy field with his own unaided eyes, and he has trained others to see it. He has also made countless correct diagnoses of physical ailments merely by observing the aura. Explains Jack Schwarz, "Radiance is emitted by activity — the activity of the mind, the body, nutrients, expressions, emotions — all the energy in motion. Full involvement of the body, mind, heart, and soul, without concern for the outcome of the activity, brings the processes of transformation to their most radiant state." [19]

In the early 1970s, the Energy Research Group of New York's Institute for Bioenergetic Analysis was able to confirm with scientific equipment much of what Schwarz and others have been saying all along. As their energy detector, they used a modified photomultiplier tube. Photomultipliers respond to extremely small quantities of light by producing a measurable electrical charge. However, the investigators' tube was specially modified and monitored so that it would not respond to the infrared rays produced by the body's radiant heat. Instead, their tube responded only to light in the visible and ultraviolet ranges. By placing their human subject in a light-tight room, the researchers were able to electronically "see" the aura quite clearly, conclusively demonstrating that some portion of the human energy field lies in the visible and ultraviolet spectrum. [20]

This is most likely the portion of the aura that sensitives report seeing. Jack Schwarz, for example, has been tested in a laboratory, demonstrating that his sight extends from 335-1,700 nanometers, 1,000 nanometers beyond the "visible" spectrum. Physiologist John Adams of the University of Washington in Seattle, could scarcely believe his eyes. But after suddenly revising his own thinking about what might be visible, he, too, found that he could see well up into the "normally" invisible infrared range. [21]

Jack Schwarz delineates seven distinct layers of the human energy field, the first two being the most prominent. The first one he calls the "physical aura" (others call it the "human corona" or "etheric body"). This, he says, appears as a smoky blue field extending from four to 12 inches away from the body. According to Schwarz, in this layer a person's physical state is most clearly perceivable. And surrounding this corona, he reports, is a luminous, egg-shaped field which he calls the "ovum." This golden-ivory field, an extension of the physical aura, radiates out from between 12 to 24 inches from the body. The remaining five layers, variously colored, extend successively even farther from the body. [22]

This description is very close to the one given by the Yaqui man of knowledge, don Juan, to Carlos Castaneda in his instructions preliminary to the task of *seeing*. "A man looks like an egg of circulating fibers," don Juan tells Castaneda, "and his arms and legs are like luminous bristles, bursting out in all directions."

"Is that the way everyone looks?" Carlos asks.

"Everyone," replies don Juan. "Besides, every man is in touch with everything else, not through his hands, though, but through a bunch of long fibers that shoot out from the center of his abdomen. Those fibers join a man to his surroundings; they keep his balance; they give him stability. So, as you may *see* some day, a man is a luminous egg whether he's a beggar or a king, and there's no way to change anything." [23]

For Soviet physicist Victor Inyushin and his associates, this "luminous egg" is the "biological plasma body." These researchers maintain that bioplasma is a previously overlooked state of matter consisting of electrons and other subatomic particles that are associated with living objects. They also maintain that it may have far more importance than we yet know — that it may, in fact, be tantamount to an undiscovered system of the body. Writes psychologist Stanley Krippner:

> Dr. Inyushin speculated that the "biological plasma body" is some kind of counterpart of the body composed of solids, liquids, and gases. However, the highly ionized particles of the bioplasmic body behave differently from the atoms, molecules, and compounds that make up the other body. Indeed, the body's bioplasmic system may some day take its place as an important component of the organism along with the circulatory, lymphatic, and nervous systems. [24]

American writer-researcher George Leonard has been teaching this concept for years, in what he calls "Energy Body Workshops." He also goes much farther in speculating about the energy body's importance, not only to our health and welfare but to our overall understanding of who we are and our ultimate connection to the rest of the universe. Writes Leonard in *The Ultimate Athlete*:

> Energy Body workshops begin with the assumption that a field of energy exists in and around each human body. . . . The individual is viewed as an energy being, a center of vibrancy, emanating waves that radiate out through space and time, waves that respond to and interact with myriad other waves. The physical body is seen as one manifestation of the total being, coexisting with the Energy Body. Its reality and importance is in no way denied. It provides us with the most reliable information as to the condition of the total being. The Energy Body, on the other hand, is less reliable and more difficult for us to perceive at this stage of our development. But it is far less limiting than the physical body. It can change shape, size, density, intensity, and other qualities. Each of these changes influences the physical body to some extent. In some mysterious way that we can't yet fully understand, the Energy Body also seems to transcend space and time, connecting each human consciousness to all of existence. [25]

Visible or not, our energy field is an integral part of us and a reflection of the radiance with which we are living. More significantly for this investigation, I am convinced that it acts as our vital shield, our immunity. Science has confirmed that lower energy fields cannot penetrate higher ones. Whether we come into contact with contagious diseases, inadvertently ingest chemically tainted foods, unavoidably breathe polluted air, unknowingly live and work in proximity to offensive radiations, or intentionally walk across red-hot embers, we need to be radiant, aglow with the possibilities of our full humanity.

And how can we create that radiance? How can we activate our energy bodies to their full glow? Through focus, attention, concentration and faith. As Luke says, "When your eye is single, your whole body also is full of light." The single eye is the mystical third eye, the center of consciousness depicted on the American one-dollar bill. This is the focused attention that amplifies the aura of light, making possible not only firewalking but myriad other "impossible" feats that have astounded the world of science. Writes aikido master Koichi Tohei:

> The things one can do when he is sincere and when his spirit and body are one are astonishing. The cornered rat has been known to turn on the cat and down him. People often display powers in time of fire that they would never dream of in ordinary life. Women have been known to lift automobiles to drag children out from under them. In desperate situations of life or death, people come up with unheard-of wisdom. All of these cases involve manifestations of power made possible by the unification of the spirit and the body. [26]

So, too, with firewalking. When we are focused, one-pointed and singleminded, we become transcendent, radiant creatures of light, beings brighter than fire. Engaging our radiance, the firewalk lightens and enlightens us, stretching our perceived limits toward potentials unimagined.

10

The Craze for Hot Coals

To be an American is precisely to imagine a destiny rather than inherit one. We have always been inhabitants of myth rather than history.

Leslie Fiedler

Now that we've examined the firewalk in considerable detail and finally drawn some tentative conclusions, it might be useful to take a closer look at the phenomenon in the United States. What attitudes and philosophies fuel the firewalk here? Who is participating and why? Is the movement growing or shrinking? And what are people getting out of it?

"Just when Americans thought their psyches were safe from anymore California crazes," wrote a *Life* magazine reporter in 1985, "here comes a doozy: walking on fire." [1] And the doozy came on hot, with thousands of new firewalkers swelling the ranks every year. By now, Tolly Burkan asserts, some 500,000 Americans have walked across glowing coals. [2] At one 1990 California firewalk alone, Tony Robbins ushered 2,700 people over beds of hot coals. [3] Who are these people? And how have their lives evolved to the point where this irrational act was the next supposedly sane and logical step?

Over centuries, firewalking has traditionally been found in Third World countries, because these cultures are more aligned with intuition and less wedded to causality than we in the industrial world. Ritual magic and belief in the supernatural are the very foundations of many of these societies. This is hardly the case in America, where society is founded on strictly logical constructs. Until recently, for a "normal" American even to consider the relativity of such constructs — for example, the fact that fire does not have to burn — would send the mind swirling. Except perhaps in California.

EMBERS OF THE HUMAN POTENTIAL

It is no surprise that *Life* identifies California as the source of the firewalking craze, or that America's two leading firewalk instructors operate out of that state. "Sooner or later, we are going to have to understand California," observed Jacob Needleman in his 1973 study, *The New Religions*, "and not simply from the motive of predicting the future for the rest of the country. Something is struggling to be born here." [4]

One of the things that was born in California was the human potential movement, in which millions of Americans eventually discovered that there is more to life than a good job and early retirement. Another California offspring was the New Age movement, whose prophets and proponents now suggest that we create our own reality and that we are on the verge of a global spiritual awakening. Though it burns with a life of its own, the firewalking movement in America is the philosophical child of these two movements.

All three movements share the radically new paradigm of a co-creative universe, a world in which we have significant freedoms to exercise our untapped personal resources. These movements say it is not our parents, not our bosses, not our governments that ought to shape the essential stuff of our lives; we alone ought to have that power. And, all three movements assert, we can tap into personal powers undreamed of by our parents if we can adopt the mentality of explorers on a great adventure of discovery.

The renewed zest for this sort of psychic venturing itself came about through a crisis, a period of alienation and disaffection by predominantly white, upper-middle-class youths who came of age in the '60s. Sensing a spiritual emptiness in the midst of the American bounty, these disillusioned idealists set out to create a new world, at least for themselves and their friends. They are now in their forties, and have struggled finally to reconcile the world as it is with the world they would like to see.

Though the firewalking movement tends to attract a significantly broader age group, including those from the teen years through their sixties, all three of these movements seem to share members. In a small scientific study, California psychologist Julianne Blake established the American firewalking movement's first demographic data, a sampling of some 100 first-time walkers about equally divided between a Tony Robbins firewalk and one led by Tolly Burkan. The participants ranged in age from 14 to 73, with a mean age of 37. Significantly, over 75 percent of the new firewalkers were unmarried. They were a highly educated group, with well over half holding college degrees and nearly a quarter with graduate degrees. [5]

Regardless of how they are classified, these well-educated, independent new American firewalkers have found yet another of life's transformative offerings, a short walk down a high-energy path. Writes anthropologist Loring Danforth in his perceptive study, *Firewalking and Religious Healing*:

> It is not only fire, however, that acquires new meaning for those who attend firewalking workshops. Because fire is a symbol for the self and for the lives people lead, the firewalk also enables people to

> experience themselves and their lives in a new way. They acquire a new sense of identity, a more powerful self that cannot be burned . . . The American Firewalking movement . . . provides people with an opportunity to experience fire as a symbol of transformation and healing and in this way develop a more positive self-image and greater sense of self confidence. [6]

This phenomenon is by no means unique to the United States. Even cultures with well-established firewalking traditions have recently seen young, disaffected, disillusioned professionals and artists return to their roots by participating in the ancient ritual. By 1986, for example, a group of veteran firedancing Anastenarides in Ayia Eleni, Greece had been joined by Keti, a young artist from Athens; Dimitris, an architect educated at an American university; Kiriakos, a physics student; and, most astoundingly, their new leader, Tasos, a young doctor.

Like their American counterparts, these Greeks were also young, middle class, well-educated, and in the midst of a spiritual quest. Conventional society had been unable to offer them significant answers or satisfactions, so they had gone searching and found . . . the firewalk.

According to Danforth, the firewalk "allows these young people to experience something that is both old and traditional, on the one hand, and new and exotic on the other. Kiriakos . . . can enter an altered state of consciousness for the first time surrounded by the symbols of the Orthodox Church he grew up with. He can be possessed by the same spirit that possessed his grandmother." [7]

But these rituals are no longer the clandestine, esoteric rites they once were. Though still frowned upon by the Orthodox Church, the Greek firewalk is currently touted by tourist boards. And most years, says Danforth, it is attended by university professors, government officials, dignitaries, and newspaper, television and radio reporters. [8]

BURNING THROUGH THE SKEPTICISM

In America, the media is even more voracious, and the firewalk has accordingly had its day. Originally, when the story started breaking in the mid-'80s, most reporters were wide-eyed and a bit incredulous. It was hard to believe what they were reporting on, yet it was hard not to report on it. Few facts were available, and the claims of the instructors seemed almost as preposterous as the act of walking on fire itself. The networks covered it cautiously. The talk shows hosted it, warming themselves by the controversial fires and reaping hot ratings. The print media wrote it up, at first in a tone of neutral amazement, and then, increasingly, with negativity.

Participants in firewalking workshops began to be characterized by some mainstream reporters as gullible, naive and emotionally needy — desperate for a quick fix. One writer called the firewalk a "self-improvement scam" and characterized Tolly Burkan as "just another in a long line of human-potential hucksters cashing in on the enormous gullibility of baby boomers." [9] *Rolling Stone's* always cynical reportage called the new American firewalk "the hottest new theosophy among those with upwardly mobile consciousness," dubbing Burkan "the grand pooh-bah and founding guru of American firewalking." [10]

Even before the American firewalking movement was challenged by a group of skeptical scientists, skeptical citizens in the land cried foul. The promises made by firewalking promoters seemed too grandiose, too revolutionary, too disturbing to the tenets of established psychology and physiology. If everybody (with a few, not-too-disastrous exceptions) could perform this seemingly impossible feat after a few hours of instruction, very likely anybody could do it, probably without instruction.

This, of course, was the persuasive tack taken by UCLA researchers Leikind and McCarthy in their well-publicized and far-reaching attempts to debunk the firewalk beginning in 1984. In spite of their efforts, however, Tony Robbins' firewalks keep getting bigger (though less frequent), with thousands trodding the coals in a single night. In a particularly American twist, Robbins has also registered a trademark for "The Firewalk Experience."

Regardless of his ability to control the "product," Robbins' stocks have soared, and it is hard to clearly differentiate between his own attraction and that of the firewalk. In 1991, Robbins was more of a phenomenon than ever, with half-hour advertisement specials airing regularly on regional TV, reportedly reaching up to 50 million viewers.

Narrated by former pro quarterback Fran Tarkington, the programs do not mention the firewalk, but concentrate instead on Robbins' positive-programming tapes. Star-studded endorsements are sprinkled throughout the lengthy ad, featuring the likes of basketball coach Pat Riley, actor LeVar Burton, pro golfer Sally Little, wealth expert Charles Givens, author Harvey McKay and U.S. Representative Claudine Schneider. [11]

Tolly Burkan seems to be prospering as well. In Twain Harte, California, his Firewalking Institute for Research and Education is well established and has become the nexus for the firewalking circuit. Where once a firewalk was a rare and exceptional event in America, by 1991, through Burkan's network alone, there were 30 firewalks given nationally in the month of March. And on a single Saturday, in locales as distant as Lynchburg, Virginia and Bellingham, Washington, FIRE-sponsored firewalks were held in at least eight different places across the country. [12]

Burkan has also begun giving "Firewalking Instructor's Certification" courses at the prestigious Esalen institute in Big Sur, California. With his recently stated goal of training 200 new firewalking instructors a year, he may indeed reach the millions of Americans he believes might benefit from it.

Like his fellow firewalking leader Tony Robbins, Burkan's promotion of the rite has given it some distinctly American twists. Stated a recent

FIRE newsletter: "By 1990, firewalking had evolved into a multi-million-dollar industry." But the pitch went further: "We invite you to become a Firewalking Instructor and give yourself a new career for the 1990s. The Firewalking Institute of Research and Education offers the only certification course anywhere in the world. A profitable, new vocation can be yours in just seven days. One of our recent graduates made over $8,000 teaching his first firewalk seminar!" [13]

This is what Herbert Marcuse calls capitalism's "commodity fetish," the transforming of ineffable experience into marketable goods and services. For businessman/firewalking teacher Tony Robbins, it even evolved into a "Multi-Level Marketing Plan," in which books of cut-rate firewalking tickets were sold to students who would then resell them for a profit.

THE CORPORATE FIREWALKERS

Tony Robbins seems to attract some of the same types as Tolly Burkan; however, principally because of his style and no-nonsense salesmanship, Robbins' firewalks appeal more to the business executive. Strutting across the glowing coals barefoot in his suit and tie, he seems to embody the New Age Yuppie vision of do-what-it-takes to maximize personal dynamism. Not surprisingly, a variety of business leaders have employed him to pass on to their sales forces the surety and faith they might glean through firewalking.

In September 1985, Robbins traveled to Hilton Head, South Carolina, to give just such a corporate firewalk. His fee: $75,000. The corporation: Record Bar, Inc., the second largest retailer of tapes, records and CDs in America. For their annual convention, they hired Robbins as part of their "human systems" program, to maximize worker potential. Explained the Record Bar chairman at the time, "If you can walk on hot coals, it's fairly easy to sell a record." [14]

But what if you *can't* walk on hot coals? The president of Record Bar who hired Robbins suffered second-degree burns during his walk. But with Robbins' guidance in reframing the event, the ultimate outcome became a different matter altogether. Said the corporate president, "I decided, 'Hey, get over it; I got burned, and so what?' It became a positive experience." [15]

Another corporate executive who is keen on Robbins and the firewalk is Englishman Ken Weller, vice president of the California-based Good Guys audio-video chain. Like so many others, Weller first investigated the firewalk out of "intrigue, to see whether this was really true or hokey." After his first walk, he decided to take his store managers to Robbins firewalks as exercises in exposing them to new belief systems. Weller has the Good Guys pick up the tab for the firewalk. The seminar is required for all managers, though walking on the coals remains optional. Explains Weller:

> What I want to do is to expose them to this whole aspect of state [of mind] management. I think that football coaches and moti-

> vational experts like the army understand that, but I don't think the average professional business person really understands that. Yet there are some things you can do to bring it back to an everyday application in the work process. There's a camaraderie, where they've all shared the same experience, a genuine enthusiasm that's brought out in different ways. Quite honestly, other people in my organization think I'm nuts for sending them all through it. Luckily, I'm VP of sales, and I have free rein. [16]

Not every business person I spoke with shared Weller's enthusiasm for Robbins and the firewalk. Some, for example, objected to the peer pressure, the clapping, the music and the unstated company mandate to walk on the coals.

THE LESSONS OF THE COALS

Regardless of the commercialization of this ancient religious rite, and regardless of the accuracy of the claims made by those teaching it, firewalking continues to have significant impacts on the walkers themselves. Notes Loring Danforth: "As a form of symbolic healing, as a vehicle for promoting personal and spiritual growth, . . . walking on fire is a metaphor for performing miracles and accomplishing the impossible . . . [17]

Psychologist Joan Steffy concurs. Summarizing a thesis she wrote for San Francisco's Saybrook Institute, she says,

> I looked at how people felt it had affected them . . . And about two-thirds of the people felt they'd had a significant long-term change. People who had more personal transformational experiences seemed to have been less affected than people who were sort of first time out. . . . Just about everybody said it was a positive experience. About four people out my sample of 80 said it wasn't a negative experience, but it was not a positive experience, either — but they also recommended it to other people. So there was a kind of contradiction: "Well it didn't help me, but you should do it. [18]

Few who participate or hear of it go unaffected by the firewalk. Even those who are disturbed by it admit that it has the ability to awaken powerful energies and feelings. Sometimes the energies are too powerful. In the mid-'80s, psychiatrist Norma Baretta of San Pedro, California treated several dozen Tony Robbins students who had firewalked without getting physically burned but who had been overwhelmed by the energies released by it. The firewalk, she said, "stirs up a tremendous amount that some people are not equipped to handle. That can be devastating." [19]

A CHORUS OF FIREWALKERS

Firewalkers almost universally seem to obtain a transformational, empowering experience. A significant percentage of the new American firewalkers and the traditional firewalkers burn, and it appears that even veteran firewalkers burn on occasion. But even most who burn consider their passage through fire to have been highly beneficial. So here in America, we have a subculture of people who will line up and pay a substantial fee to risk being seriously burned on a fire they could have built in their own backyards. And even when they get burned, they seem to be happy. Some magic's afoot here.

Tolly Burkan surely helped spread the magic, because in many respects, it was the firewalk that transformed his life. After his first firewalk, Burkan wrote, "What I was left with was my own experience of it — an experience that I knew, from the moment I had walked across the coals, would change my entire life." [20]

Apparently it has — so profoundly that hundreds of thousands of Americans have followed in his footsteps. Legions of Burkan's students exclaim their enthusiasm for the firewalk, as do those of Tony Robbins and others.

Says poet Pat Schirrmacher of Tucson, Arizona, "I am still in awe of the total transformation I am experiencing. For the first time in my life, I am at a loss for words to adequately describe my feelings." A Virginia Beach mother of three is convinced that her three young firewalking sons will never be the same. An 83-year-old Oakland, California woman says, "It may be the most important thing I've ever done." [21] And Peggy Dylan, Tolly Burkan's former wife, speaks of the "deep communion and healing" that comes from firewalking. [22]

Actor Orson Bean firewalked with Burkan and devoted an entire chapter to it in his autobiography, *Too Much is Not Enough*. For Bean, the little walk turned out to be a remarkable journey that ended in elation. "People are pumping my hand and congratulating me," he wrote. "I feel such pride. It's a pride that doesn't seem to be connected to my poor miserable ego." [23]

Besides the tens of thousands Burkan has personally guided across the coals, he has guided scores of others through much more rigorous instructor's training, including a 40-foot firewalk. Those newly empowered firewalking instructors weave various forms around their hot-coal crossings, but it always seems uplifting. They speak of the joy of overcoming perceived limitations; of love and connectedness; of higher levels of awareness.

For Michael Sky, who has firewalked scores of times and written about it at great length, businesses and individuals are interested in firewalking because it has so much to teach in so many areas:

> The act of walking on fire imparts lessons in walking through all of life — lessons in biology and psychology, lessons in ecology and

> theology, lessons in taking risks, lessons in group dynamics, lessons in singing, dancing and breathing, lessons in the conscious co-creation of reality. Most urgently, I believe, firewalking is a model for the positive experience and expression of the energies of fear . . . a metaphor for living with spontaneity, joy and creative excitement. [24]

Steve Bisyak would agree. Like Tolly Burkan and Tony Robbins, he and his Challenges Unlimited associates have helped thousands of people overcome their fears and walk safely through fire — individuals as young as three and as old as 96.

One of those who spoke on a Challenges Unlimited firewalk video was Richard Reynolds of Redmond, Washington. Reynolds, in his late forties, is a U.S. West Communications employee and also teaches ballroom dancing. His feet are important to him. But the firewalk dramatically changed his step, he said, from being an "angry man" to a very patient one. "You have to be totally free of anger, frustration and arrogance to make it through the fire," he said. "And once you go through the fire, all the pettiness you felt in your life is an extreme waste of time. After walking, you're aware of more, you feel things more." [25]

In her early fifties, Marie Kenney has firewalked five times, and her teenage daughter Meegan has done it three times. "The first time I walked, it changed my entire life," said the teenager. "I can do more things now than I ever thought I could. And, since it changed so much the first time, I figured I could change more the second and third times — and it did. I'm more outgoing — I used to be really shy and inward, but I'm not anymore. I recommend it to all my friends." [26]

Said first-time firewalker Kathleen Stewart: "I'm not saying that I'm never afraid anymore . . . I'm afraid. I was afraid tonight of the fire, because I recognize I could get burned. But I know how to step through that membrane of fear and overcome it." [27]

One veteran firewalker was interviewed just before he stepped onto the glowing runway. Why did he do it? "It reinforces your concentration," he replied. "You have pay attention, and this is just continuous reinforcement. If you can overcome your primordial fear of fire and the basic laws of physics, there's not too much you can't do. And doing it again and again is just a reminder, a memo pad to let me know that I can do it and that nothing can stop me. Just the way you'd go jogging every day to stay in shape, I do this to stay in shape mentally." [28]

Asked if the firewalk had helped him overcome specific fears, the veteran replied, "It's not a grand revelation. The sky doesn't open up. But it's basic: you feel more confident, you step forward. The basic state of mind you need to get into for this, which is a lot of concentration, I've applied to business, sales, martial arts — it's very, very applicable." [29]

Two middle-aged Northwestern women felt demonstrably empowered by their firewalks. When asked how she felt afterwards, one replied, "I really feel a calmness, a kind of peacefulness and at the same time a sort of excitement at having accomplished something that part of me thought wasn't possible." [30]

The changes for the other woman were even more noticeable. "All I know is I walked on fire," she said. "And it's a seemingly impossible thing to walk on fire and not be burned. And I've done it. So there are other things that are seemingly impossible in my life that I can do . . . and I'm doing them. It's changed my life dramatically!" [31]

For a bearded, 55-year-old Washington State man, the firewalk was so hot it was the one thing that finally captured his attention. "One of the reasons I initially started this," he said, "is to really learn how to pay 100 percent attention to what I'm doing right now, in the moment, rather than thinking about what I'm going to do tomorrow or later today or what I did yesterday." [32]

"We need to understand the element of fire in our lives," said Ken Cadigan at one of his firewalk seminars. "We need to bring the fire home. The fire within us is a fire of transformation. We're afraid we're going to change, so we sit separately in fear and doubt. We have to try to use the fire as a mirror for the fire within ourselves. It's an open door. You can walk through the fire, and you can heal your relationships." [33]

In the 1980's, the firewalk emerged as a psychoactive fad in the United States. From a fad, it developed into a phenomenon. The firewalk continues to thrive in America because it empowers and because it heals.

11

Fear into Power, Sickness into Health

You gain strength, confidence and courage by the experience in which you really stop to look fear in the face, and you must do the thing you think you cannot do.

Eleanor Roosevelt

However the firewalk is accomplished, and whatever its ultimate secrets might be, the rite itself is unquestionably one of psychological empowerment. In walking on fire, a human being faces one of his or her greatest fears. We approach fire, swinging wildly from fascination to dread. The flames dance before our eyes, entrancing, mesmerizing, hypnotizing. We are relaxed and excited simultaneously. We are not only afraid of too close an acquaintance with this magic, gaseous light, we have a whole history of unfortunate contact with it, of painful injuries that often took a long time to heal.

In their laboratories, the alchemists used fire to attempt to transmute lead into gold; for most alchemists however, their laboratory work was a metaphor, and they used this psychologically fiery situation to heat themselves internally, transforming base emotions into finer ones. Similarly, a firewalker takes his walking laboratory out onto fire, heating his fear to transmute it into power. This is verifiably the case, no matter how short the walk or how hot the temperature of the fire. People are empowered by firewalks. In facing their primal fears, even most firewalkers who are burned feel empowered. Even the skeptics, who believe that anybody, anytime can safely walk on fire — even those who decry the entire firewalking movement — admit that empowerment takes place.

But how can a 10-foot stroll transform deep-seated fears into newly found powers? Part of the answer lies in the reality that a glowing firebed is not just any path: 10 feet down this sort of walkway can be quite a distance. In contacting this one acute fear, all others seem to be contacted as well, and a new vision of fear is attained. Our fear of fire is quite reasonable. The history of mankind confirms that fire burns. And fire kills, and fire destroys. Everyone, from the toddling child to the doddering old person, has this fact of life ingrained at what may very well be a cellular level. We do not have to think about avoiding contact with red-hot objects; we do not have to remember not to touch fire. The old adage, "Once burned, twice shy," accurately sums up our personal history with fire, and it is conventionally a history added to only by accident.

Except in the case of a firewalker. A firewalker is that eccentric creature who is willing and even eager to invite usually distant fears to a celebratory barbeque, where in the spirit of the moment, the fears themselves are barbequed. Through spiritual challenge, then, a firewalker generates sufficient inner heat to transform his fears into near-magical power.

"You must do better than that," said the sorcerer don Juan to his student, Carlos Castenada. "You must push yourself beyond your limits, all the time."

"But that would be insane, don Juan. No one can do that."

"There are lots of things that you now do which would have seemed insane to you ten years ago," replies the sorcerer. "Those things themselves did not change, but your idea of yourself changed; what was impossible before is perfectly possible now . . ." [1]

This is good reason for *tapas*, for the inner heat of spiritual challenge. It empowers us, enlarges us, dramatically increases our possibilities. At its polar opposite is apathy, a kind of spiritual protectionism, and the continuous lack of challenge and lack of discovery it generates.

For don Juan, the true art of a warrior is balancing terror with wonder. [2] This is the firewalker's balance as well, standing before a radiant path that can lead either to great pain, or to great empowerment. A balance of power, seesawing terror and wonder. "From wonder into wonder," wrote Lao Tzu, "existence opens." It is quite understandable then, that firewalking fits into a modern human potential thrust that aims to challenge and confront fear, and in so doing, to empower.

In the broadest sense, courses like Outward Bound accomplish this, teaching practical physical skills in order to catalyze self-generated psychological ones. Sports, and indeed any performance art, also lift the practitioner to a certain level of competence and then demand that he or she go beyond it.

Accordingly, any performance art can engender performance anxiety, a personal insecurity and tightening that makes optimal performance impossible. It is this fear that we face in public speaking, in new meetings, sometimes in sex, and certainly in critical moments in sports. When fear and performance anxiety grip, an athlete or performer is said to be "choking." At the other extreme, when performance reaches its peak, an athlete is said to be "in the zone" or "playing out of his mind."

We intentionally put ourselves into fearful situations — rafting down rapids, racing motorcycles, skydiving, skiing, mountain climbing, scuba diving and firewalking, to name a few — because we feel more alive when we challenge ourselves. We feel an exhilaration in our fear, especially when we conquer it. And undeniably, every contact with our fears, every meeting we arrange and to a great degree control, empowers us. Not only are we empowered for our next meeting with that same fear, but we also walk taller, talk firmer and behave with more confidence in most every other stressful situation.

In studying the risk factor in sports, psychologist Sol Rosenthal argues convincingly for the healthful effects of danger. He divides the sports world into two categories: "RE" (risk exercise), such as skiing and skydiving, and "non-RE" sports, such as tennis and golf. Foremost among his observations is that non-RE sports tend to exhaust or bore, whereas RE sports tend to exhilarate. "All forms of exercise are excellent," says Rosenthal, "but risk exercise is essential." [3]

Stress researchers have described a pleasurable form of stress that invigorates, called "eustress." "Eustress is associated with excitement, adventure, and thrilling experiences," notes researcher Dorothy Harris. "This stress is fun, it enhances vital sensations, it 'turns on' individuals, and in the process of turning on, it releases energy." Harris also suggests that eustress may not only consume energy but mobilize it as well. "Most people have far more energy resources than they are aware of," she says, "and do not realize they have the capacity to generate energy for other activities." [4]

This was similar to the conclusion reached by Harvard physiologist Walter Cannon in the 1920's. Under the heading "The Feeling of Power," in his classic study *Bodily Changes in Pain, Hunger, Fear and Rage*, Cannon wrote:

> . . . in times of strong excitement there is not infrequent testimony to a sense of overwhelming power that sweeps in like a sudden tide and lifts the person to a new high level of ability. There is intense satisfaction in these moments of supreme elation, when the body is at the acme of its powers. And it is altogether probable that the critical dangers of adventure have a fascination because fear is thrilling, and extrication from a predicament, by calling forth all the bodily resources and setting them to meet the challenge of the difficulty, yields many of the joys of conquest. For these reasons, vigorous men go forth to seek dangers and to run large chances of serious injury. . . . And thus, in the hazardous sports, in mountain climbing, in the hunting of big game, and in the tremendous adventure of war, risks and excitement and the sense of power surge up together, setting free unsuspected energies, and bring vividly to consciousness memorable fresh revelations of the possibilities of achievement. [5]

It would seem that to successfully firewalk, handle fire, perform risk exercise or even non-risk exercise in highly competitive situations, one would need to become acquainted with the mechanism of transforming fear into power. This is the central, operative metaphor of the American firewalking movement, and it is both accurate in concept and effective in implementation. Firewalking in particular provides an element of danger that elevates the practice to the level of shock therapy.

Notes Loring Danforth:

> The power that lies at the heart of the healing experiences firewalk workshops provide is the power to transform people in such a way that they are more fulfilled in their personal lives and more successful in their professional lives. This rhetoric of transformation, therefore, encompasses both the expressive goals of the counterculture and the utilitarian goals of the mainstream American culture. [6]

What a topsy-turvy world this is, where a burn can be healing, where an injury can be empowering. But that is precisely the upside down logic of shock therapy, that whole range of controversial psychological, pharmacological, and/or electrical assaults on the mind/body that are intended ultimately to heal. As a species, we have found that there are times when some of us are so stuck, so caught in restrictive, obsessive psychological jails of our own making that we need an explosive release. And even though that fiery release is usually dangerous itself, for many people, the possible benefits outweigh the risks.

To perform at our best, we need continuously to transform our fear into power. In every endeavor, we are repetitively met by obstacles that threaten the project's outcome, and in some manner, may threaten our own well-being. Such crises engender fear — fear of failure, fear of loss of control, fear of suffering the psychological and/or physical consequences. Optimal performance requires that we — instantaneously and without breaking stride — transform this nervous anxiety into effective action. Great performers know this circuit by heart. They get anxious before a big performance just like the rest of us. But through the mastery of their skills, and mastery of themselves, they take the pre-performance butterflies and fly with them into peak performance.

Psychologist Mihaly Csikszentmihaly has studied the dynamic state of optimal performance, a state he calls "flow." The hallmarks of this heightened state are: the merging of action and awareness into a sustained, highly focused concentration on the task at hand; self-forgetfulness with heightened awareness of physiology; and clarity regarding situation clues and appropriate responses. [7]

For Csikszentmihaly, life offers the possibility of three basic paths: one is through boredom; another is through anxiety; and the third is through the "flow" channel. By continuously perfecting one's skills, one is ever challenged, and even relishes outside tests as a further challenge, all in the meta-game of life. [8]

If fear into power is both a central transformation in peak performance life and in firewalking, it stands to reason that the perfected skills are mutually applicable. And if indeed it is this marvelous transformation that accounts for various degrees of immunity to fire, the fear-faith-power circuit has profound resonance throughout our inner and outer lives, even to a cellular level.

A central notion involved in any spiritual trial or test of faith is the observed empowerment that naturally comes to a human in time of crisis. This is sometimes called "hysterical strength," when a threatening moment instantly transforms a person's terror into uncommon physical strength, speed, agility, or whatever attribute the body needs to escape injury or save another. No doubt such displays are in great measure triggered by adrenalin, a chemical whose principal purpose is to initiate high-powered "fight or flight" activity. Responding to a threat, we are biodynamically designed to self-empower ourselves, creating the strength-enhancing chemicals in response to our own emotion, specifically fear.

Transforming fear into power, then is one of our most primal tasks, in every sense. Without such an ongoing transformation, we will be devoured by any stronger or quicker adversary; or possibly worse, be restrained to a life saturated with boredom or anxiety. We need the challenge of life, and challenges we invent for ourselves. Through both types of challenge, we create ourselves anew, reincarnating before our very own eyes.

Rites of passage are integral to most cultures, and often involve ordeals or trials. Young Native Americans were sent to the woods alone, essentially to suffer in solitude the ordeal of coming into adulthood and independence. But the time of suffering was also a time of breakthrough, discovery and empowerment; and through it all, there would indeed be the transformation of boy to man. Though most of these rites have vanished on the American continent — being replaced for American males by such ersatz rites as drinking, driving, and sexual conquests — the firewalk represents a renewal of such tradition, a rite of passage for people of both sexes and all ages. By providing a glowing walkway through which a person's fear can be transported and transformed into power, the firewalk serves as a high-energy path to a life beyond the ordinary.

RED-HOT HEALING

Medically, the firewalk is also a paradox. People marching barefoot onto a bed of red-hot coals in order to get well is not the sort of healing scenario that medical science normally embraces. Yet if the firewalk did not provide such restoration and renewal, people would have abandoned it long ago as a dangerous and foolish practice. And though here in America the firewalk seems most often to be performed as a rite of empowerment, traditionally it has been at least equally identified as rite of holistic healing.

How could something so obviously dangerous as direct contact with red-hot coals actually be good for your health? How could passage over a treacherous fire restore or strengthen vitality? The same questions have been asked of contemporary radiation therapy for cancer. Like fire, radiation involves energy that normally burns and is considered dangerous. But for some patients, the radiation burns selectively enough so that a specific region of mutant activity is checked and healthy cells are allowed to regenerate. Some firewalkers believe a similar phenomenon is at work in their passage across the radiant firebed.

Most early Native American firewalks were healing ceremonies, in which a truly sick individual was coaxed by a shaman or medicine man to cross barefoot over one or more fires. In this way, the illness or invading spirit could be driven off, leaving the person at peace. A similar theory is at work in the modern firewalks held annually outside Sao Paulo, Brazil, by the Japanese descendants of Buddhist monks. Psychologist Alberto Villoldo participated in such a firewalk and reported that, "The monks believe that if one is suffering from an illness, one will have a pin burn on the foot — on the acupuncture point that corresponds to the affected organ. The fire supposedly burns the illness out through the acupuncture point." [9]

The implication here is that not only might the act of firewalking be good for your health, but getting burned slightly might actually be therapeutic! Just as acupuncturists sometimes burn small pellets on a patient's skin right at an acupuncture point in a process called "moxibustion," the Buddhist firewalkers believe that the fire and body naturally conspire to give the walker just the response he or she needs.

Similarly, psychologist Richard Katz discovered that for the African !Kung, healing is an organic process in which a substance called sickness is transmuted by a substance called *n/um*. For the !Kung healers who participate in the firedance, the ritual is a balance between inner and outer fire, where supercharged men dance a fine line on the border of power and pain.

Healing through contact with fire is also at the heart of the Greek Anastenaria, a firewalking ceremony in which the curative stimulation is seen to come as much from the energy of the fire as from the psychological energy invested by the firedancer. The Anastenarides also believe they are guided and protected by Saint Constantine, who has the power to cure a wide variety of illnesses.

Writes Loring Danforth:

> The Anastenaria, like all rituals of religious healing, transforms people by moving them rhetorically from a negatively defined condition of illness to a positively defined condition of health. Central to this rhetorical movement of transformation is an elaborate set of

> metaphors of emergence, release, and opening up. During the therapeutic process, negative metaphors of obstruction and confinement are transformed into positive metaphors of freedom and openness. [10]

Here is a dramatic event, then, in which the created context causes psychological changes that in turn affect dramatic physiological changes. The demonstrated immunity to fire then deeply reinforces the original psychological changes in the form of healing and subsequent immunity. When we break through our limits, we are suspended in a state of limitlessness. Then we begin to test our possibilities. When we do, we discover that we are more than we thought we were — and as healthy as we truly want to be.

AMERICAN FIREWALKING HEALERS

Here in America, at the close of the 20th century, an eclectic, loosely interwoven tribe of evolutionary expeditionaries has found similar uses for fire. Among them are many healers. Physicians and chiropractors especially have been drawn to the fire. One of the most active of these is firewalking teacher Dr. Arthur Fagenholtz, a chiropractor from Santa Cruz, California.

Chiropractic is founded on the premise that once the body's alignment and joint movement are optimal, the innate life energy can flow, heal and energize. Says Dr. Fagenholtz, "My own experience of walking on fire, as well as teaching others to walk, continues to validate for me the intimate experience and healing powers innate within the body." [11]

Fagenholtz has found that walking on fire stimulates the nervous system in such a way that a personal shift in the body's own healing paradigm is set into motion. The fire facilitates a shift in consciousness, which in turn facilitates healing. "Walking on fire is a profound transformational tool," he says, "and I highly recommend it to my patients. It is a way to shift them to the next level of body awareness in their healing process." [12]

Firewalking, then, is one of the oldest and newest of healing rituals. It is also an instantaneous form of biofeedback training, and a significant dynamic in this process is what some people call "mirroring." In mirroring, it is not the biofeedback or the fire that transforms; the individual transforms *himself*, through the information that is reflected back to him. In sensing your pulse and experiencing the possibility of changing your heartbeat at will, you create a new biofeedback loop, expanding the possibilities of your mind/body combination. Similarly, in walking over red-hot coals, the mental state a firewalker brings to the fire is reflected in his relative physiological immunity. Every evidence indicates that once this loop has been securely established, it can be maintained without any further need for the biofeedback mirror.

Perhaps more than anything else, we are beings *becoming*. Whether we like it or not, we are evolving at every instant. If we foster our own evolution, speeding our spirits to support our bodies, we can come to a dynamic unity, one body/mind, healthy and essentially immune. Firewalking, I have come to believe, is one of a myriad of methods of transmutation, of rapidly speeding that evolution. Just as the ancient alchemists used fire to transmute lead into gold, so the modern firewalker uses fire to transmute fear into power and sickness into health.

But there is more to it than that. The supreme goal of alchemy is not turning a slab of lead into gold, or even transmuting sickness into health or fear into power. Alchemy aims high, seeking the very elixir of life. Such, I believe, is the real purpose of the firewalk. Perhaps it will teach us that we already have the elixir of life within us, and we need only use our precious share to make more.

12

The Path of Fire

Someday, after we have mastered the winds, the waves, the tides and gravity, we shall harness for God the energies of love. Then, for the second time in the history of the world, man will have discovered fire.

Teilhard de Chardin

When I first heard of firewalking, I was skeptical but intrigued. When I first walked on fire, it seemed to me a phenomenon made possible by some as-yet-unexplained capacity of human consciousness. Firewalking seemed such a dramatic expression of mind over matter that its implications might be staggering. Through all my research, that first impression has not changed; if anything, it has become even more profound.

I have spent years investigating the firewalk. I have been guided and educated by the findings of scientists, and by the testimony and performances of firewalkers of all ages. I have also been out on the fire a few times myself, and I am likely to return. I am not now, nor will I ever be, a firewalking advocate. I do not recommend that anyone rush out and walk over red-hot coals. Instead, I ask you to ponder the evidence and consider the possibilities inherent in the firewalk — especially the possibility that hidden within the shrouds of our undiscovered humanity may be potentials far greater than we have yet dared to dream.

Firewalking, I am convinced, is far more than a mystical stunt, far more than a religious ritual, a test of faith or a ceremony of empowerment. Firewalking, I have come to believe, is an *evolutionary stimulant*, a prod that we can consciously use to become more than we ever imagined ourselves to be. Even through word or picture, the prospect of walking on red-hot coals quickens us, kindling in us the light of untried possibility. By that light, we can begin to see our own nature more clearly and completely.

Apparently, we've barely begun to tap our potential. In the 1970s and '80s, as biological labs plumbed the depths of our DNA, scientists were stunned finally to get a glimpse of our genetic coding. "There is an air of bewilderment bordering on incredulity in molecular labs at the moment," wrote biologist John Rogers in a 1977 *New Scientist* article. They found our genetic blueprints, all right, but they also found that our cells are presently using only *one percent* of the information encoded in our DNA! [1] If indeed we have developed only one percent of our potential, we are truly incredible beyond our present imaginings. Moreover, it seems likely that our future evolution lies in nurturing a new relationship between our conscious minds, that familiar and comfortable tip of the human iceberg, and the enormous and mysterious ocean of unconsciousness that lies beneath it.

The path of fire seems to lead in this direction. A person who walks the path of fire continuously dances with danger in order to purify, expand and empower — in order to discover and develop the 99 percent of the human potential that in most of us lies fallow. As Jack Schwarz insists, most of us are subnormal; we need to open up to who we truly are, accept our birthright as beings brighter than fire. As evolutionary travelers, we can consciously practice self-challenging and self-catalyzing, propelling ourselves into hitherto unexplored states and into a full realization of our God-given, human abilities.

Human knowledge has been continuously updated to reflect the latest model of the universe. Even today, in the modern age of miracle drugs and quantum physics, no truly honest scientist would ever say he had devised an accurate description of the workings of the universe. Einstein put it aptly: "As far as the laws of mathematics refer to reality, they are not certain; as far as they are certain, they do not refer to reality." [2] Werner Heisenberg took that idea a step farther, stating that "every word or concept, clear as it may seem to be, has only a limited range of applicability." [3]

What we think of as reality is often just thought — a mental interpretation of the interaction of our five senses with a world of whirling energies. And often our thoughts are not even our own; they are the thoughts, opinions and constructs of others that we have willingly agreed to accept as our own reality. But reality does not always fit into our mental constructs. Just when we least expect it, some scientific anomaly or some earthshaking discovery explodes our comfortable assumptions, upsetting our mental applecarts.

The firewalk is just such an anomaly. To me, it is proof positive that although reality frequently obeys human logic and the so-called laws of cause and effect, occasionally it does not. As a result, it is an unsettling reminder that all our sciences are, at best, bodies of partial truth. As brave pioneers forge ahead onto the path of fire, science watches and is gradually molded into a broader construct. Those on the path of fire loosen their mental constraints, and eventually those on the path of science join them in their explorations, expanding science in the quest for higher consciousness.

Down through the ages, wise men and women have often said that we are all one in consciousness. Today, even the views of quantum physicists are finding accord with that thought. Consider the words of physicist David Bohm:

> The present state of theoretical physics implies that empty space has all this energy and that matter is a slight increase of that energy and therefore matter is like a small ripple on this tremendous ocean of energy . . . So we say deep down the consciousness of mankind is one. This is a virtual certainty, because even in the vacuum, matter is one; and if we don't see this, it is because we are blinding ourselves to it. [4]

So we're all one, all ripples of energy, all frozen light. The path of fire heats up that frozen light, brightening our radiance to new possibilities. The brighter we shine, the stronger our immunity and the more power we have, to be whoever we want to be. Firewalking brings us back to the here and now, demanding that we live in the present moment, the eternal now. The more we identify with personality, with that sophisticated creature we've created to deal with the world, the more we live *in* time, aging and suffering. The more we walk the path of fire, stepping out of time, out of mind and out of cause and effect, the more we free ourselves from the constraints of both mind and matter.

Where will we go once we've learned to step out of time and space, once we've learned to tap the awesome power of our unconscious minds? What will we do with our immunity to fire, disease and aging? The possibilities are mind-boggling. Writes Fred Allen Wolf in his 1980 book, *The Body Quantum*:

> I expect that we will be able to change our bodies at will. I expect that with the gain in sensitivity and consciousness, new messages will be received and our evolution will be speeded up so fast that it will make our heads spin. Perhaps we will be able to heal ourselves simply by thinking positively about ourselves. Perhaps we will be able to regenerate new limbs, increase our intelligence, and even live for 500 years or more. [5]

Writer George Leonard puts it more poetically. "For the atom's soul is nothing but energy," he says. "Spirit blazes in the dullest clay. The life of every woman or man — the heart of it — is pure and holy joy." [6]

Futurists Barbara Marx Hubbard and Ken Carey assert that this transformation was initiated when humans began to exercise their power to co-create their own reality. Mystics the world over have also spoken of the inevitability of this quantum leap, suggesting that it will happen when sufficient numbers of people feel that there is no other way, when the violence and destruction of our present reality is seen as an absurdity that cannot go on any longer. [7]

What we are talking about here, of course, amounts to a new species — or at least the realization that we are not limited by definitions of the old. How could such a wonderful thing come about? How could the most miraculous, most troubled creature on the face of the planet suddenly leap up to some unseen level on the evolutionary chain? Said the late mythologist Joseph Campbell, "Either by the trials themselves or by illuminating revelations. Trials and revelations are what it's all about." [8]

Revelations are best heard when we are quiet, and often they come in times of crisis. Trials, too, come in times of crisis, and we do not have to look far today to see the battery of trials that face us individually and collectively. Just as significant, though, are *intentional trials*, the challenges we seek out consciously in order to grow and expand. And it is here, I believe, that firewalking may serve as an evolutionary stimulant.

The path of fire is the way of *tapas*, consciously cultivating inner heat through spiritual discipline. It may take many forms, but almost invariably its influence spreads through the excitement and awareness of its practitioners. Spark begets spark, and soon there is a conflagration, a chain reaction. We often see this with social, psychological and spiritual phenomena; however, there is evidence that it may also exist in subtler, more pervasive ways — ways that could lead to a rather dramatic evolutionary leap.

Biochemist Rupert Sheldrake has devised an elegant theory that may explain how this is possible. In Sheldrake's view, every organism has an invisible "morphogenetic field," or "m-field" that guides form, growth, development and behavior. At conception, an organism tunes in to its m-field for complete instructions. For example, as an embryo develops, different cells take on different tasks and different structures. Immature heart-muscle cells, for instance, grown in a laboratory dish, will start beating by themselves. [9] As Sheldrake puts it, "The field of the hedgehog contains the memory of all past hedgehogs and is linked to them by a process I call morphic resonance, the influence of like upon like." [10]

Though we are guided by our morphogenetic fields, Sheldrake asserts, we can also change them. For when a sufficient number of creatures of a single species have altered their m-fields, the m-fields for all creatures of that species are altered. When a sufficient number of people have adopted a new way of being, the m-field of the entire species changes and the evolutionary leap has been made. [11]

Firewalking may well be a significant first step on the path to that evolutionary leap. Already, from ancient and traditional rituals the world over, the fever has spread, quickening, exciting, stimulating hundreds of thousands more to think beyond the possible, to imagine new limits (or no limits), to step through the boundaries of the known. Against all logic, a tiny but significant portion of Western humanity has taken a step into the unknown, demonstrated its trust in mind over matter and begun a dialogue within the great ocean of consciousness.

The Path of Fire is apparently one entry to the psychology of physical immunity. And through the firewalk, many are finding their way.

Notes

CHAPTER 2

1. Yatri, *Unknown Man, the Mysterious Birth of a New Species* (New York: Simon and Shuster, 1978), 18.
2. Tolly Burkan, *Dying to Live* (Twain Harte, CA: Reunion Press, 1984), 21-2.
3. Ibid., 3.
4. Ibid., 136-7.
5. Ibid., 204.
6. Tolly Burkan, "How to Walk on Fire" (Twain Harte, CA: Firewalking Institute), 2-3.
7. Tolly Burkan, *Walking on Fire*, a videotape (Twain Harte, CA: Sundoor, 1983).
8. Tolly Burkan, Promotional Literature, 4.
9. *FIRE Newsletter*, 1, Autumn 1989, 1.
10. *FIRE Newsletter*, 2, Winter 1990, 3.

CHAPTER 4

1. Sir James Frazer, *The Golden Bough* (New York: MacMillan and Company, 1955), 6:14.
2. Joseph Chilton Pearce, *The Crack in the Cosmic Egg* (New York: Pocket Books, 1974), 105.
3. Jim Doherty, "Hot Feat - Firewalkers of the World," *Science Digest*, August 1982, 71.
4. Herbert Thurston, *The Physical Phenomena of Mysticism* (Chicago: Henry Regnery, 1952), 171, 222-23.
5. Ernst Benz, "Ordeal By Fire," in Joseph Kitagawa et al, *Myths and Symbols: Studies in Honor of Mircea Eliade* (Chicago, University of Chicago Press), 242.
6. Ibid., 252.
7. Ibid.
8. Ibid., 256.
9. Ibid.
10. Ibid., 261-3.
11. Op. Cit. Thurston, 172.
12. Ibid., 173.
13. Gino Simi and Mario Segreti, *Saint Francis of Paolo* (Rockford,IL: Tan Books, 1977), 128.
14. Vincent Gaddis, *Mysterious Fires and Lights* (New York: David McKay, 1967), 117.
15. Op. Cit. Frazer, 6:3-4.

16. Ibid., 6:9-10.
17. Milbourne Christopher, *ESP, Seers and Psychics* (New York: Thomas Y. Crowell, 1970), 236-7.
18. L. Elizabeth Lewis, "The Firewalking Hindus of Singapore," *National Geographic*, LIX, 4, April 1931, 513-22.
19. Mayne Reid Coe, Jr., "Firewalking and Related Behaviors," *Journal of the American Society for Psychical Research*, LII, 3, July 1958, 92.
20. James McClenon, "Firewalking in Japan, Sri Lanka, and the USA," *International Journal of Comparative Sociology*, XXIX, 3-4, 1988, 204.
21. Richard Leavitt, "To Walk on Fire You Must First Master Yourself," *The New York Times*, April 29, 1973, 10-1.
22. Nicholas Gage, "Greek Ritualists Invoking Saints Walk on Coals," *The New York Times*, June 1, 1980, 5-1.
23. Loring Danforth, *Firewalking and Religious Healing* (Princeton: Princeton University Press, 1989), 19, 126-7.
24. Svyatoslav Slavchev, "Fire Dancing," *Psi Research*, Dec 1983, 77-8.
25. Ibid.
26. Edmond Gibson, "The American Indian and the Firewalk," *Journal of the American Society for Psychic Research*, 1952, 46, 151.
27. Ibid., 151-2.
28. Ibid., 152.
29. Joseph Campbell, *The Way of the Animal Powers* (New York: Alfred Van der Mark Editions, 1983), I, 238.
30. Mircea Eliade, *Shamanism — Archaic Techniques of Ecstasy* (Princeton: Princeton University Press, 1974), 206.
31. Ibid., 54.
32. Ibid.
33. Ibid., 372-3.
34. Ibid., 112.
35. Ibid., 442.
36. Ibid., 456.
37. Ibid., 335.
38. Ibid.
39. Ibid., 316.
40. Matilda Coxe Stevenson, *The Zuni Indians* (Washington: The Smithsonian, 1904), 502-3.
41. Op. Cit. Christopher, 239-40.
42. Henry Beauchamp, "Fire-Walking Ceremonies in India," *Journal of the Society for Psychical Research*, 1900, 9, 313.
43. Op. Cit. Frazer, 6:2.
44. Ibid., 6:5-6.
45. Ibid., 6:6.
46. Op. Cit. Thurston, 188.

47. Ibid., 189.
48. Harry Price, *Confessions of A Ghost Hunter* (London: Putnam and Company, 1936), 358-9.
49. Richard Katz, *Boiling Energy* (Cambridge: Harvard University Press, 1982), 100.
50. Laurens van der Post, *The Lost World of the Kalahari* (New York: Harcourt Brace Javanovich, 1977), 242.
51. Richard Katz, "Accepting Boiling Energy," *Ethos*, 10:4, Winter 1982, 348.
52. Ibid.
53. Joseph Chilton Pearce, *Exploring the Crack in the Cosmic Egg* (New York: Pocket Books, 1976), 50-1.
54. Peter Van Der Walde, "Trance States and Ego Psychology," in Raymond Price (ed), *Trance and Possession States* (Montreal: R.M. Bucke Memorial Society: 1968), 62.
55. Ibid., 67.
56. - - , as quoted in Igor Guberman, "Way Beyond the Horizon," *Psi Research*, Dec 1983, 75-6.
57. Mr. Gorten, *Boston Evening Transcript*, March 20, 1891, as quoted in Andrew Lang, *Magic and Religion* (London: Longmans, Green and Company, 1901), 292.
58. Op. Cit. Christopher, 238.
59. Op. Cit. Frazer, 6:10-11.
60. Max Freedom Long, *The Secret Science Behind Miracles* (Marina Del Rey, CA: De Vorss & Co., 1954), 34-6.
61. Ibid., 38-9.
62. Op. Cit. Gaddis, 150-3.
63. Ibid., 146.
64. Clement Stone and Norma Lee Browning, *The Other Side of the Mind* (Englewood Cliffs, NJ: Prentice-Hall, 1964), 128.
65. G.M. Feigen, "Bucky Fuller and the Firewalk," *Saturday Review*, July 12, 1969, 22-3.
66. Joan Gould, "Some Like It Hot," *The New York Times*, "The Sophisticated Traveler," 2, Oct 1, 1989, 77.
67. A.W. Howitt, *Native Tribes in Southeast Australia* (New York: MacMillan, 1904), 575.
68. Ibid., 581.
69. James McClenon, "Firewalking in Sri Lanka," *Psi Research*. Dec 1983, 18.
70. Leonard Feinberg, "Firewalking in Ceylon," *Atlantic Monthly*, May 1959, 203, 73-6.
71. Donna and Gilbert Grosvenor, "Ceylon," *National Geographic*, April 1966, 129, 481-2, 485-6.
72. Victor Perara, "The Firewalkers of Udappawa," *Harper's*, May 1971, 18.
73. Op. Cit. Gaddis, 135.
74. Op. Cit. Lang, 285.

75. Lucile Armstrong, "Fire-Walking at San Pedro, Manrique, Spain," *Folk-Lore*, 1970, 81, 204-5.
76. Ricky Jay, *Learned Pigs and Fireproof Women* (New York: Villard Books, 1986), 266.
77. Lord Adare, "Experiences in Spiritualism with D.D. Home," *Proceedings of the Society for Psychical Research*, 1894.
78. Lord Lindsay, as quoted in *Proceedings of the Society for Psychical Research*, 1894.
79. Richard Cavendish (ed), *Encyclopedia of the Unexplained* (New York: Arkana, 1974), 470.
80. W. Stainton Moses, as quoted in *Proceedings of the Society for Psychical Research*, 1894.
81. Op. Cit. Cavendish, 470.
82. Ibid.
83. Ibid.
84. Nathan Coker, as quoted in *The New York Herald*, Sept. 7, 1871, 1.
85. Ibid.
86. Ibid.
87. Ibid.
88. John Godwin, *This Baffling World* (New York: Hart, 1968), 150; Op. Cit. Gaddis, 140.
89. Op. Cit. Danforth, 221,248.
90. Michael Sky, *Dancing With the Fire - Transforming Limitation Through Firewalking* (Santa Fe: Bear & Co, 1989), 37-8.
91. Ibid. 48.
92. Dick Gunther, as quoted in Adam Smith, "Walking on Fire," *Esquire*, Jan 1984, 11-12.

CHAPTER 5

1. Samuel P. Langley, The Firewalk Ceremony in Tahiti," *Journal of the Society for Psychical Research*, 1901, 10, 118.
2. Ibid. 120-1.
3. Ibid.
4. Vincent Gaddis, *Mysterious Fires and Lights* (New York: David McKay, 1967), 141-2.
5. Ibid., 151.
6. Sir James Purves-Stewart, as quoted Gaddis, 153-4.
7. Harry Price, *Confessions of a Ghost Hunter* (London: Putnam and Company, 1936), 364.
8. Ibid., 367-8.
9. Ibid.
10. Ibid., 369.
11. Ibid., 370-1.
12. Ibid.

13. Harry Price, *Fifty Years of Psychical Research* (London: Longmans, Green and Company, 1939), 251.
14. Op. Cit. Price, *Confessions*, 373.
15. Ibid., 377, 379.
16. Ibid., 377-8.
17. Ibid.
18. Op. Cit. Price, *Fifty Years*, 252.
19. Ibid., 258.
20. Ibid., 261.
21. Op. Cit. Gaddis, 141-2.
22. Albert Ingalls, "Fire-Walking," *Scientific American*, 1939, 160, 135.
23. Ibid., 178.
24. Ibid.
25. Mayne Reid Coe, as quoted in Gaddis, 137-8.
26. Ibid.
27. Ibid.
28. C. Fonseka, "Fire-Walking: A Scientific Investigation," *Ceylon Medical Journal*, June 1971, 104.
29. Ibid. 108.
30. Jim Doherty, "Hot Feat — Firewalkers of the World," *Science Digest*, August 1982, 68-9.
31. Jearl Walker, "Drops of Water Dance on a Hot Skillet and the Experimenter Walks on Hot Coals," *Scientific American*, 237, August 1977, 126.
32. Ibid.
33. Ibid., 131.
34. Larissa Vilenskaya, "Firewalking," *Psi Research*, June 1984, 106.
35. Marvine Rowe, "Rites of Fire on a Greek Isle," *The New York Times*, May 13, 1984, 10:24, 30.
36. Christos Xenakis, "Psychophysiological Processes in Pyrovasy (Fire Walking)" *Archiv fur Psychchiatrische und Nervenkrankheiten*, 1977, 223:309.
37. Ibid.
38. Ibid.
39. Leonard Zusne and Warren Jones, *Anomalistic Psychology: A Study in Extraordinary Phenomena of Behavior and Experience* (Hillsdale, NJ: Lawrence Erlbaum, 1982), 63.
40. Ibid.
41. Giovanni Iannuzzo, "Fire Immunity: Psi Ability or Psychophysiological Phenomenon," *Psi Research*, Dec 1983, 71.
42. Ibid., 72.
43. Igor Guberman, "Way Beyond the Horizon," *Psi Research*, Dec 1983, 77.
44. Vittoria Manganas, "Fire-Dancing in Greece," *Psi Research*, Dec 1983, 82.
45. Ibid.

46. Ibid.
47. Ibid.
48. Harold S. Burr, *Blueprint for Immortality* (Spearman, 1952).
49. Leonard Ravitz, as quoted in H.S. Burr, *The Fields of Life* (New York: Ballantine, 1972), 92.
50. Julianne Blake, "Attribution of Power and the Transformation of Fear: An Empirical Study of Firewalking," *Psi Research*, June 1985, 62-88.
51. Andrew Weil, *Health and Healing* (Boston: Houghton Mifflin Company, 1983), 249.
52. Ibid., 248.
53. James McClenon, "Firewalking and Psychic Surgery: Defining the Paranormal By Investigating its Boundaries," *Journal of Indian Psychology*, 4:2, 1985, 88.
54. James McClenon, personal communication.
55. Ibid.
56. Ibid.
57. Peter Gott, "Cold Water on Firewalking," *The Berkshire Eagle*, July 31, 1985, 22.
58. Bernard Leikind and William McCarthy, "An Investigation of Firewalking," *The Skeptical Inquirer*, Fall 1985, 7-8.
59. Ibid., 8.
60. Bernard Leikind, personal communication.
61. Ibid.
62. Art Huffman, personal communication.
63. John Taylor, "Firewalking: A Lesson in Physics," *The Physics Teacher*, March 1989, 166.
64. Ibid.
65. William McCarthy, personal communication.
66. Ibid.
67. Ibid.
68. Susan Blackmore, "Playing With Fire," *The New Scientist*, July 14, 1990, 127:64.
69. William McCarthy, personal communication.
70. Michael Sky, *Dancing With the Fire* (Santa Fe: Bear & Co., 1989), 47.
71. Ibid., 48.
72. Tolly Burkan, personal communication.
73. John Burke and Conrado Bondoc, "Burns: The Management and Evaluation of the Thermally Injured Patient," in Thomas Fitzpatrick, Arthur Eisen, Klaus Wolff, Irwin Freedberg and K. Frank Austen (eds.), *Dermatology in General Medicine* (New York: McGraw Hill, 1979), 931.
74. Ibid., 932-3.
75. Ibid.

76. A.R. Moritz and F.C. Henriques, "The Relative Importance of Time and Surface Temperature in the Causation of Cutaneous Burns," *The American Journal of Pathology*, 1947, 23:718-9.
77. Ibid.
78. Dr. Ron Sato, as quoted in Dio Urmilla Neff, "Walking on Fire," *New Age Journal*, Jan 1984, 64.
79. Ibid.
80. Nicholas Regush, with Jan Merta, *Exploring the Human Aura* (Englewood Cliffs, NJ: Prentice-Hall, 1975), 96-7.
81. Florence Jacoby, *Nursing Care of the Patient With Burns* (St. Louis: C.V. Mosby Company, 1976), 14.
82. Elmer and Alyce Green, *Beyond Biofeedback* (New York: Delacorte Press, 1977), 235; and Jack Schwarz, personal communication.
83. Op. Cit. Sky, 65.

CHAPTER 6

1. Steven M. Kane, "Holiness Ritual Fire Handling: Ethnographic and Psychophysiological Considerations," *Ethos*, 10:4, Winter 1982, 370-2.
2. Berthold E. Schwarz, "Ordeal by Serpents, Fire and Strychnine: A Study of Some Provocative Psychosomatic Phenomena," *Psychiatric Quarterly*, 1960, 34:407-09.
3. Ibid. 415-16.
4. Ibid.
5. Ibid.
6. Ibid.
7. Ibid. 416-17.
8. Ibid., 417-18.
9. Ibid.
10. Ibid., 419-21.
11. Ibid., 418.
12. Op. Cit. Kane, 370.
13. Ibid., 373.
14. Ibid.
15. Ibid., 374.
16. Ibid., 375.
17. Ibid., 376-7.
18. Ibid., 379-80.
19. Ibid.
20. Ibid., 381-2.
21. Ibid.
22. Op. Cit. Schwarz, 421-2.
23. Op. Cit. Kane, 382.
24. Steven Kane, personal communication.
25. Ibid.
26. Ibid.

CHAPTER 7

1. Leonard Zusne and Warren Jones, *Anomalistic Psychology: A Study of Extraordinary Phenomena of Behavior and Experience* (Hillsdale, NJ: Lawrence Erlbaum, 1982), 64.
2. Joe Nuzum, personal communication.
3. Ibid.
4. Joe Nuzum, "Joe Nuzum - Ninja Magick," a videotape; Dr. Berthold Schwarz, "K: A Presumed Case of Telekinesis," *International Journal of Psychosomatics*, 32:1, 1985, 3-21; Dr. Berthold Schwarz, personal communication.
5. Joe Nuzum, personal communication.
6. Steve Bisyak, personal communication.
7. Ibid.
8. Ibid.
9. Ibid.
10. Ibid.
11. Ibid.
12. Elmer and Alyce Green, *Beyond Biofeedback*, (New York: Delacorte Press, 1977), 235-6; Jack Schwarz, personal communication.
13. Ibid.
14. Ibid.
15. Jack Schwarz, personal communication.

CHAPTER 8

1. Deepak Chopra, *Quantum Healing* (New York: Bantam Books, 1989), 189-90.
2. Ibid., 193-4.
3. Alexandra David-Neel, *Magic and Mystery in Tibet* (New York: University Books, 1958), 216-29.
4. Herbert Benson, *The Relaxation Response* (New York: William Morrow, 1975); and Herbert Benson, *Beyond the Relaxation Response* (New York: Berkeley Books, 1984).
5. Op. Cit. Chopra, 17.
6. Andrew Weil, *Health and Healing* (Boston: Houghton Mifflin, 1983), 172.
7. Ibid., 201.
8. Lawrence LeShan, *The Medium, the Mystic and the Physicist* (New York: Viking, 1974), 125.
9. Bernie Siegel, *Love, Medicine and Miracles* (New York: Harper and Row, 1986), 47.
10. Ibid.
11. George Leonard, *The Silent Pulse* (New York: Dutton, 1978), 123.
12. Norman Cousins, "The Mysterious Placebo: How Mind Helps Medicine Work," *Saturday Review*, Oct 1, 1977, 31.
13. Op. Cit. Siegel, 183.

14. Op. Cit. Chopra, 237.
15. Ibid.
16. Brian Inglis, "The Fire Walk," *Speculations in Science and Technology*, 9:3, Jan 1986, 165.
17. Brian Inglis, *The Hidden Power* (London: Jonathan Cape, 1986), 209.
18. Theodore X. Barber, "The Physiological Effects of Hypnosis," *Psychological Bulletin*, 58:5, 1961, 390-419.
19. J. Arthur Hadfield, "The Influence of Hypnotic Suggestion on Inflammatory Conditions," *The Lancet*, Nov 3, 1917, 678.
20. Op. Cit. Barber, 410-11.
21. Ibid., 413.
22. Theodore X. Barber, "The Concept of Hypnosis," *The Journal of Psychology*, 45, 1958, 127-8.
23. D. H. Rawcliffe, *Occult and Supernatural Phenomena* (New York: Dover, 1959), 223-4.
24. Elmer and Alyce Green, *Beyond Biofeedback* (New York: Delacorte, 1977), 188.
25. Op. Cit. Siegel, 152-3.
26. Ibid., 19.
27. Ibid., 153-4.
28. Op. Cit. Weil, 223-4, 244.
29. Op. Cit. Leonard, 38.
30. John Godwin, *This Baffling World* (New York: Bantam, 1968), 158.
31. Jerry Snider and Richard Daab, "The Secrets of Fakir Musafar," *Magical Blend*, Dec 1988, 73.
32. Ibid., 74.
33. Ibid., 75.
34. Ibid.
35. John Brant, "The Pain Gates," *Outside*, August 1988, 33.
36. Ibid., 33-4.
37. Op. Cit. Green and Green, 26-7.
38. Wolfgang Luthe, "Autogenic Training," in Charles Tart (ed), *Altered States of Consciousness* (Garden City, NY: Doubleday Anchor, 1969), 195.
39. Op. Cit. Green and Green, 43.
40. Ibid.
41. Ibid., 37-8, 45-6.
42. Ibid., 48-9.
43. Op. Cit. Chopra, 93.
44. Norman Cousins, *Head First - the Biology of Hope* (New York: E.P. Dutton, 1989), 252-3.
45. Op. Cit. Green and Green, 231.

46. Ibid., 229; Jack Schwarz, *It's Not What You Eat, It's What Eats You* (Berkeley: Celestial Arts, 1989)), 60; and Jack Schwarz, personal communication.
47. Jack Schwarz, personal communication.
48. Op. Cit. Green and Green, 86; and Nicholas Regush with Jan Merta, *Exploring the Human Aura* (Englewood Cliffs, NJ: Prentice-Hall, 1975), 86.
49. Joe Nuzum, personal communication; Berthold Schwarz, personal communication; and Berthold Schwarz, "K: A Presumed Case of Telekinesis," *International Journal of Psychosomatics*, 32:1, 1985, 3-21.
50. Op. Cit. Regush with Merta, 30; Benjamin Wolman (ed) *Handbook of Parapsychology* (New York: Van Nostrand Reinhold, 1977), 891.
51. Op. Cit. Regush with Merta, 27-34.

CHAPTER 9

1. Nicholas Regush with Jan Merta, *Exploring the Human Aura* (Englewood Cliffs, NJ: Prentice-Hall, 1975), 37-8.
2. Oscar Bagnall, as quoted in Regush, 42-3.
3. Ibid.
4. Harold Burr and F.S.C. Northrup, as quoted in Regush, 52-3.
5. Lyall Watson, *Supernature* (New York: Bantam Books, 1973), 72-3.
6. Ibid., 75; Op. Cit. Regush, 52-3.
7. Leonard Ravitz, as quoted in H.S. Burr, *The Fields of Life* (New York: Ballantine, 1972), 92.
8. Semyon Kirlian, as quoted in Sheila Ostrander and Lynn Shroeder, *Psychic Discoveries Behind the Iron Curtain* (Englewood Cliffs, NJ: Prentice-Hall, 1971), 72.
9. Ibid.
10. Will Bradbury (ed), *Into the Unknown* (Pleasantville, NY: The Reader's Digest, 1981), 284-5.
11. Op. Cit. Ostrander and Shroeder, 78.
12. Ibid.
13. Ibid.
14. Michael Harrison, *Fire From Heaven* (London: Sedgewick and Jackson, 1976), 72-3; and V. Inyushin, V. Grishchenko, N. Vorobev, N. Shouiski, N. Federova and F. Gibadulin, "The Biological Essence of the Kirlian Effect," Kazakhstan State University, Alma-Ata, 1968.
15. Op. Cit. Bradbury, 285-6.
16. Shafica Karagula, *Breakthrough to Creativity* (Los Angeles: De Vorss, 1967), 91.
17. Bernie Siegel, *Love, Medicine and Miracles* (New York: Harper and Row, 1986), 69; and Michael Sky, *Dancing with the Fire* (Santa Fe: Bear & Co, 1989), 85; and Op. Cit. Regush, 84.

18. Jack Schwarz, *It's Not What You Eat, It's What Eats You* (Berkeley: Celestial Arts, 1988), 3.
19. Ibid. 25-6.
20. Richard Dobrin, Carl Kirsch, Sander Kirsch, John Pierrakos, Eric Schwartz, Theodore Wolff, and Yuval Zeira, "Experimental Measurements of the Human Energy Field," in Stanley Krippner and David Rubin (eds.), *The Energies of Consciousness* (New York: Interface, 1975), 167.
21. Op. Cit. Schwarz, 68-9.
22. Ibid.
23. Carlos Castaneda, *A Separate Reality* (New York: Simon and Shuster, 1971), 23.
24. Stanley Krippner, "International Developments in Biological Energy," in Op. Cit. Krippner and Rubin, 13.
25. George Leonard, *The Ultimate Athlete* (New York: Viking, 1975), 68.
26. Koichi Tohei, *Akido in Daily Life* (Tokyo: Rikugei Publishing, 1966), 23.

CHAPTER 10

1. Nancy Griffin, "The Charismatic Kid," *Life* , March 1985, 42.
2. *FIRE Newsletter*, Winter 1992, 2.
3. *Robbins Research Report*, Fall 1990, 4.
4. Jacob Needleman, as quoted in Marilyn Furgeson, *The Aquarian Conspiracy* (Los Angeles: J.P. Tarcher, 1980), 60-1.
5. Julianne Blake, "Attribution of Power and Transformation of Fear: An Empirical Study of Firewalking," *Psi Research*, June 1985, 7-1.
6. Loring Danforth, *Firewalking and Religious Healing* (Princeton: Princeton University Press, 1989), 275.
7. Ibid., 156.
8. Ibid., 100.
9. Paul Galloway, "Hot Feat," *Chicago Tribune*, Dec 1, 1986, 5:1.
10. Jon Krakauer, "Get It While It's Hot," *Rolling Stone*, Aug 30, 1984, 22.
11. Tony Robbins, for Robbins Research, a video advertisement.
12. *FIRE Newsletter*, Spring 1991, 7:3.
13. *FIRE Newsletter*, Winter 1990, 6:3.
14. David Handelman, "Tiptoe Through the Embers," *Rolling Stone*, Nov 21, 1985, 26.
15. Ibid.
16. Ken Weller, personal communication.
17. Op. Cit. Danforth, 287-8.
18. Joan Steffy, personal communication.
19. Op. Cit. Griffin, 48.
20. Tolly Burkan, with Mark Bruce Rosin, *Dying to Live* (Twain Harte, CA: Reunion Press, 1984), 138.
21. *FIRE Newsletter*, Summer 1990, 4:1.

22. S.W. Virato, "Beyond Firewalking," an interview with Tolly Burkan and Peggy Dylan, *New Frontier*, March 1989, 15.
23. Orson Bean, *Too Much Is Not Enough* (Secaucus, NJ: Lyle Stewart, 1988), 133.
24. Michael Sky, Dancing With the Fire (Santa Fe: Bear & Co, 1989), xvi.
25. Renee Ricketts, "Walking On Hot Coals A Burning Desire in Many," *Snoqualmie Valley Reporter* [WA], Feb 13, 1991, A-11.
26. Debra Nelson, "Firewalk," *Valley Daily News* [Renton, WA], Jan 22, 1988, C-1.
27. *Conquering Fear — the Ultimate Challenge*, a video, Challenges Unlimited, Renton, WA.
28. Ibid.
29. Ibid.
30. Ibid.
31. Ibid.
32. Ibid.
33. Loring Danforth, *Firewalking and Religious Healing* (Princeton: Princeton University Press, 1989), 217.

CHAPTER 11

1. Carlos Castaneda, *Tales of Power* (New York: Simon and Shuster, 1974), 16.
2. Ibid., 95.
3. Sol Roy Rosenthal, as quoted in George Leonard, *The Ultimate Athlete*, (New York: Avon, 1974), 22.
4. Dorothy Harris, as quoted in Michael Murphy and Rhea White, *The Psychic Side of Sports* (Reading, MA: Addison-Wesley, 1978), 78.
5. Walter Cannon, *Bodily Changes in Pain, Hunger, Fear and Rage* (College Park, MD: McGrath Publishing, 1970), 238-9.
6. Loring Danforth, *Firewalking and Religious Healing* (Princeton: Princeton University Press, 1989), 266-7.
7. Mihaly Csikszentmihaly, *Flow - The Psychology of Optimal Experience* (New York: Harper & Row, 1990).
8. Ibid., 75.
9. Alberto Villoldo and Stanley Krippner, *Healing States* (New York: Simon and Shuster, 1987), 72-7.
10. Op. Cit. Danforth, 51.
11. Arthur Fagenholz, as quoted in the *FIRE Newsletter*, Winter 1990, 6:3.
12. Arthur Fagenholz, "Today's Firewalking As a Tool for Healing," *FIRE Newsletter*, Spring 1990, 3:3.

CHAPTER 12

1. Yatri, *Unknown Man* (New York: Simon and Shuster, 1988), 56; and Deepak Chopra, *Quantum Healing* (New York: Bantam: 1989), 150-1.
2. Albert Einstein, as quoted in Fritjov Capra, *The Tao of Physics* (Berkeley: Shambhala, 1975), 41.
3. Werner Heisenberg, as quoted in Op. Cit. Capra, 41.
4. David Bohm, as quoted in Renee Weber, *Dialogues with Scientists and Sages: The Search for Unity* (London: Routledge & Kegan Paul, 1986), 64.
5. Fred Allen Wolf, *The Body Quantum* (New York: MacMillan, 1986), 285.
6. George Leonard, *The Transformation* (Los Angeles: Jeremy Tarcher, 1972), 37.
7. Barbara Marx Hubbard and Ken Carey, *Manual for Co-Creators of the Quantum Leap* (Gainesville: New Visions, 1986); and Satprem, *The Mind of the Cells* (New York: Institute for Evolutionary Research, 1981).
8. Joseph Campbell, with Bill Moyers, *The Power of Myth* (New York: Doubleday, 1988), 126.
9. *Breakthroughs*, Feb 1991, 112.
10. Rupert Sheldrake, "Cause and Effect in Science: A Fresh Look," *Noetic Sciences Review*, Summer 1989, 15.
11. Rupert Sheldrake, *The New Science of Life* (San Francisco: Jeremy Tarcher, 1982).

References

"Argentine Institute Studies 'Firewalking,'" *Newsletter of the Parapsychology Foundation*, May-June 1961, Vol. 8, No. 3, p. 1.

Breakthroughs, February 1991, p. 112.

"The Fire Walk," *Journal of the Society for Physical Research*, 24 (1928), pp.278-84.

"Fire and Snake Handling," a videotape. Archives of East Tennessee State University.

Handbook of the American Indian. Washington, D.C.: The Smithsonian, 1978.

The Urantia Book. Chicago: Urantia Foundation, 1955.

Adare, Lord, "Experiences in Spiritualism with D.D. Home," *Proceedings of the Society for Psychical Research*, 1894.

Armstrong, Lucile, "Fire-Walking at San Pedro, Manrique, Spain," *Folk-Lore*, *81* (1970), pp.198-214.

Bachelard, Gaston, *The Psychoanalysis of Fire*. Boston: Beacon Press, 1964.

Bagnall, Oscar, *The Origin and Properties of the Human Aura*. New York: University Books, 1970.

Bailey, Brandon, "Nothing to It," *Star News* [Pasadena], April 15, 1985, p. 1.

Baker, Bob, "A Skeptical View," *Los Angeles Times*, April 27, 1985, Sec. 1, p. 27.

Bandler, Richard, and Grinder, John, *Frogs into Princes, Neuro Linguistic Programming*. Moab, Utah: Real People Press, 1979.

Bandler, Richard, and Grinder, John, *Reframing, Neuro Linguistic Programming and the Transformation of Meaning*. Moab, Utah: Real People Press, 1982.

Barber, Theodore X., "The Concept of Hypnosis," *The Journal of Psychology*, 1958, 45, pp. 126-40.

Barber, Theodore X., "The Physiological Effects of Hypnosis," *Psychological Bulletin*, 1961, Vol. 58, No. 5, pp. 390-419.

Barber, Theodore X., *Hypnosis: A Scientific Approach*. New York: Van Nostrand/Insight, 1969.

Bean, Orson, *Too Much is Not Enough*. Seacaucus, NJ: Lyle Stewart, 1988.

Beauchamp, Henry, "Fire-Walking Ceremonies in India," *Journal of the Society for Physical Research*, 9 (1900), pp. 312-21.

Belo, Jane, *Trance in Bali*. New York: Columbia University Press, 1960.

Benson, Herbert, *The Relaxation Response*. New York: William Morrow, 1975.

Benson, Herbert, *Beyond the Relaxation Response*. New York: Berkeley Books, 1984.

Benz, Ernest, "Ordeal by Fire," in Joseph M. Kitagawa et. al., *Myths and Symbols: Studies in Honor of Mircea Eliade*. Chicago: University of Chicago Press, 1969.

Birkby, "A Walk on the Wild Side," *Mother Earth News*, No. 125, Sept/Oct 1990, p. 112.

Bisyak, Steve and Laura, "Conquering Fear," a videotape, Challenges Unlimited, Renton, WA.

Blackmore, Susan, "Playing With Fire," *New Scientist*, Vol. 127, July 14, 1990, 64.

Blake, Julianne, "Attribution of Power and the Transformation of Fear: An Empirical Study of Firewalking," *Psi Research*, June 1985, pp. 68-82.

Boyd, Doug, *Mystics, Magicians, and Medicine People*. New York: Paragon House, 1989.

Bradbury, Will (ed), *Into the Unknown*. Pleasantville, NY: The Reader's Digest, 1981.

Brant, John, "The Pain Gates," *Outside*, August 1988, pp. 33-34.

Breci, Sebi, "Fire Walking Has Its Pitfalls," *Fate*, October 1982, pp.67-69.

Brewster, Paul, "The Strange Practice of Firewalking," *Expedition*, 19, No. 3, pp. 44-48.

Burkan, Tolly with Rosin, Mark Bruce, *Dying to Live*, Reunion Press, 1985.

Burkan, Tolly, "How to Walk on Fire." Twain Harte, CA: Firewalking Institute for Research and Education.

Burkan, Tolly, "Walking on Fire," a videotape. Twain Harte, CA: Sundoor, 1983.

Burkan, Tolly, *FIRE Newsletter*. Twain Harte, CA.

Burkan, Tolly, "Tolly Burkan's Media Clips," a videotape. Twain Harte, CA: Sundoor.

Burkan, Tolly, and Burkan, Peggy Dylan, *Guiding Yourself Into A Spiritual Reality*. Twaine Harte, CA: Reunion Press, 1978.

Burke, John, and Bondoc, Conrad, "Burns: The Management and Evaluation of the Thermally Injured Patient," in Fitzpatrick, Thomas; Eisen, Arthur; Wolff, Klauss; Freedberg, Irwin; and Austen, K. Frank (eds.), *Dermatology in General Medicine*. New York: McGraw Hill, 1979, pp. 930-34.

Burland, G.A., *The Arts of the Alchemists*. London: Weidenfeld, 1967.

Burr, Harold, *Blueprint for Immortality*. Spearman, 1952.

Burr, Harold, *The Fields of Life*. New York, Ballantine, 1972.

Campbell, Joseph, with Moyers, Bill, *The Power of Myth*. New York: Doubleday, 1988.

Campbell, Joseph, *The Way of the Animal Powers*. New York: Alfred Van Der Mark Editions, 1983.

Cannon, Walter, "Voodoo Death," *American Anthropologist*, 44, 1942, pp. 169-81.

Cannon, Walter, *Bodily Changes in Pain, Hunger, Fear and Rage*. College Park, MD: McGrath Publishing, 1970.

Capra, Fritjov, *The Tao of Physics*. Berkeley: Shambhala Publications, 1975.

Castaneda, Carlos, *A Separate Reality*. New York: Simon and Shuster, 1971.

Castaneda, Carlos, *Tales of Power*. New York: Simon and Shuster, 1974.

Cavendish, Richard (ed), *Encyclopedia of the Unexplained*. New York: Arkana, 1974.

Chia, Mantak, and Winn, Michael, *Taoist Secrets of Love*. New York: Aurora Press, 1984.

Chia, Mantak, *Awaken Healing Energy Through the Tao*. New York: Aurora Press, 1983.

Chopra, Depak, *Quantum Healing*. New York: Bantam, 1989.

Christopher, Milbourne, *ESP, Seers & Psychics*. New York: Thomas Y. Crowell, 1970.

Chuang Tzu, trans. Legge, James, arranged by Clae Waltham. New York: Ace Books, 1971.

Coe, Mayne Ried Jr., "Fire-walking and Related Behaviors," *Psychological Record*, 7, (1957), pp.101-10.

Coe, Mayne Reid, Jr., "Safely Across the Fiery Pit," *Fate*, June 1978, pp. 84-87.

Concon, Archimedes, "Firewalking and Subtle Energies," *Psi Research*, Sept-Dec. 1985, p. 221.

Cousins, Norman, "The Mysterious Placebo: How Mind Helps Medicine to Work," *Saturday Review*, Oct. 1, 1977.

Cousins, Norman, *Head First — The Biology of Hope*. New York: E.P. Dutton, 1989.

Csikszentmihaly, Mihaly, *Flow - The Psychology of Optimal Experience*. New York: Harper & Row, 1990.

Danforth, Loring, *Firewalking and Religious Healing*. Princeton: Princeton University Press, 1989.

David-Neel, Alexandra, *Magic and Mystery in Tibet*. New York: University Books, 1958.

de Chardin, Teilhard, *The Phenomenon of Man*. New York: Harper & Row, 1965.

Dobrin, Richard; Kirsch, Carl and Sander; Pierrakos, John; Schwartz, Eric; Wolff, Theodore; Zeira, Yuval, "Experimental Measurements of the Human Energy Field," in Krippner, Stanley, and Rubin, David, (eds.), *The Energies of Consciousness*. New York: Interface, 1975.

Doherty, Jim, "Hot Feat—Firewalkers of the World," *Science Digest*, August 1982, pp.66-71.

Doore, Gary (ed), *Shaman's Path*. Boston: Shambhala, 1988.

Edsman, Carl Martin, "Fire," in Eliade, Mircea (ed.), *The Encyclopedia of Religion*. New York: MacMillan Publishing, 1987.

Eliade, Mircea, *Shamanism, Archaic Techniques of Ecstasy*. Princeton University Press, 1974.

Ellithorpe, David, "Firewalkers Set Record Here," *Kirkland* [WA] *Courier Review*, June 22, 1988, p. 7.

Fagenholtz, Arthur, "Today's Firewalking as a Tool for Healing," *FIRE Newsletter*, Spring 1990, No. 3, p. 3.

Feigen, G.M., "Bucky Fuller and the Firewalk," *Saturday Review*, July 1-2, 1969, pp.22-3.

Feinberg, Leonard, "Fire Walking in Ceylon," *Atlantic Monthly*, 203 (May 1959), pp.73-76.

Ferguson, Marilyn, *The Aquarian Conspiracy*. Los Angeles: J.P. Tarcher, 1980.

Fonseka, C., "Fire-Walking: A Scientific Investigation," *Ceylon Medical Journal*, June 1971, p. 104.

Frazer, James George, *The Golden Bough*. New York: MacMillan and Company, 1955.

Freeman, J.M., "Trial by Fire," *Natural History, 83*, 1, 1974, pp.55-63.

Gaddis, Vincent H. *Mysterious Fires and Lights*. New York: David McKay, 1967.

Gage, Nicholas, "Greek Ritualists Invoking Saints Walk on Coals," *The New York Times*, June 1, 1980.

Galloway, Paul, "Hot Feat," *Chicago Tribune*, Dec. 1, 1986, sec 5, p. 1.

Garrison, Jim, "Meeting a Firewalker," *Theoria to Theory. 13* (1979), pp.191-5.

Garrison, Omar, *Tantra: The Yoga of Sex*. New York: The Julian Press, 1983.

Garrison, Peter, "Kindling Courage," *Omni*, April 1985, p. 84.

Geunther, Herbert, and Trungpa, Chogyam, *Dawn of Tantra*. Berkeley: Shambhala Publications, 1975.

Gibson, Edmond P., "The American Indian and the Firewalk," *Journal of the American Society for Psychic Research, 46* (1952), pp.149-53.

Godwin, John, *This Baffling World*. New York: Hart, 1968.

Gott, Peter H., "Eerie, fiery, feats." *The Berkshire Eagle*, May 1, 1985, p. 19.

Gott, Peter H., "Cold Water on Firewalking." *The Berkshire Eagle*, July 31, 1985, p.22.

Gould, Joan, "Some Like It Hot," *The New York Times*, "The Sophisticated Traveller," Part 2, Oct. 1, 1989, p. 77.

Govinda, L.A., *Foundations of Tibetan Mysticism*. New York: Samuel Wiser, 1974.

Greenwalt, Frank, "Hot Footin' It," *Daily News* [Los Angeles], April 15, 1985, p. 1.

Green, Elmer and Alyce, *Beyond Biofeedback*. Delacorte Press, 1977.

Griffin, Nancy, "Charismatic Kid," (Tony Robbins) *Life*, March 1985, pp.41-8.

Grinder, John, and Bandler, Richard, *TRANCE-formations*. Moab, Utah: Real People Press, 1981.

Grosvenor, Donna K. and Gilbert M., "Ceylon," *National Geographic, 129,* April 1966, pp.447-97.

Guberman, Igor, "Way Beyond the Horizon," *Psi Research*, Dec. 1983, pp. 74-76.

Hadfield, J. Arthur, "The Influence of Hypnotic Suggestion on Inflammatory Conditions," *The Lancet*, Nov. 3, 1917, p. 678.

Handelman, David, "Tiptoe through the Embers," *Rolling Stone*, Nov. 21, 1985, p. 26.

Harrison, Michael, *Fire From Heaven*. London: Sedgewick and Jackson, 1976.

The Holy Bible, Revised Standard Version. New York: Thomas Nelson and Sons, 1952.

Howitt, A. W., *Native Tribes in Southeast Australia*. New York: MacMillan Company, 1904.

Hubbard, Barbara Marx, and Carey, Ken, *Manual for Co-Creators of the Quantum Leap*. Gainesville: New Visions, 1986.

Iannuzzo, Giovanni, "Fire-Immunity and Fire-Walks: Some Historical and Anthropological Notes," *European Journal of Parapsychology*, 4, 2, 1982, pp.271-5.

Iannuzzo, Giovanni, "Fire Immunity: Psi Ability or Psychophysiological Phenomenon," *Psi Research*, Dec. 1983, p. 71.

Ingalls, Albert G., "Fire-Walking," *Scientific American, 160,* 1939, pp.135-8; pp.173-8.

Infgelfinger, Franz, "Arrogance," *New England Journal of Medicine*, Dec. 25, 1980, Vol. 303, No. 26, pp. 1509-10.

Inglis, Brian, "The Fire Walk," *Speculations in Science and Technology*, Vol. 9, No. 3, Jan. 1986, pp. 158-67.

Inglis, Brian, *The Hidden Power*. London: Jonathan Cape, 1986.

Inyushin, V., Grishchenko, V., Vorobev, N., Shouiski, N., Federova, N., and Gibadulin, F., "The Biological Essence of the Kirlian Effect," Kazakhstan State University, Alma-Ata, Soviet Union, 1968.

Jacoby, Florence, *Nursing Care of the Patient with Burns*. St. Louis: C.V. Mosby Company, 1976.

Jay, Ricky, *Learned Pigs and Fireproof Women*. New York, Villard Books, 1986.

Kane, Stephen M., "Holiness Ritual Fire Handling: Ethnographic and Psychophysiological Considerations," *Ethos, 10* (1982), pp.369-84.

Karagula, Shafica, *Breakthrough to Creativity*. Los Angeles: De Vorss, 1967.

Katz, Richard, "Accepting Boiling Energy," *Ethos*, 10:4, Winter 1982, pp. 345-64.

Katz, Richard, *Boiling Energy*. Cambridge: Harvard University Press, 1982.

Kenn, Charles W., *Fire-Walking From the Inside*. Los Angeles: Franklin Thomas, 1949.

Kennet, J., *Selling Water By the River*. New York: Vintage Books, 1972.

Kenton, Edna, *Indians of North America*. New York: Harcourt, 1927.

Kiev, Ari, "The Psychotherapeutic Value of Spirit-Possession in Haiti," in Prince, Raymond (ed), *Trance and Possession States*. Montreal: R.M. Bucke Memorial Society, 1968, pp 143-44.

Kosambi, D.D., "Living Prehistory in India," *Scientific American, 216* February 1969, pp.104-114.

Krakauer, Jon, "Get It While It's Hot," *Rolling Stone*, August 30, 1984, pp.22-3.

Krier, Beth Ann, "Firewalking Emerges as a Hot New U.S. Fad," *The Los Angeles Times*, April 11, 1984, I-3.

Krippner, Stanley, "International Developments in Biological Energy," in Krippner, Stanley, and Rubin, David, (eds.), *The Energies of Consciousness*. New York: Interface, 1975.

Landers, Ann, "Firewalking Letter from La Jolla Parents," *The Poughkeepsie Journal*, February 24, 1985.

Lang, Andrew, "The Fire Walk," *Proceedings of the Society for Psychical Research, 15* (1900), pp.2-15.

Lang, Andrew, *Magic and Religion*. London: Longmans, Green and Company, 1901.

Langevin, Michael Peter, "Jack Schwarz - An Interview," *Magical Blend*, Oct. 1989, pp. 40-46.

Langley, S.P., "The Fire Walk Ceremony in Tahiti," *Journal of the Society of Psychical Research*, 10 (1901), pp. 116-21.

Lawrence, Gene, "Firewalking Fad Causes Thousands of Injuries," *The Sun*, January 29, 1985, p.12.

The Learning Annex Catalog, New York, February 1985, 12.

Leavitt, Richard P. "To Walk on Fire You Must First Master Yourself," *The New York Times*, April 29, 1973, 10/1.

Leikind, Bernard, and McCarthy, William, "An Investigation of Firewalking," *Skeptical Inquirer*, Fall 1985, pp. 6-8.

Lee, Richard, "The Sociology of !Kung Bushman Trance Performances," in Price, Raymond (ed), *Trance and Possession States*. Montreal: R.M. Bucke Memorial Society, 1968, pp. 35-55.

Leonard, George, *The Ultimate Athlete*. New York: Viking, 1975.

Leonard, George, *The Silent Pulse*. New York: Dutton, 1978.

Leonard, George, *The Transformation*. Los Angeles, J.P. Tarcher, 1972.

Levey, Joel, "Sports — A Western Yoga," *New Realities*, Sept.-Oct. 1990, p. 25.

LeShan, Lawrence, *The Medium, the Mystic and the Physicist*. New York: Viking, 1974.

Lewis, L. Elizabeth, "The Firewalking Hindus of Singapore," *National Geographic*, Vol. LIX, No. 4, April 1931.

Long, Max Freedom, *The Secret Science Behind Miracles*. Santa Monica, CA: DeVorss & Company, 1954.

Luthe, Wolfgang, "Autogenic Training," in Tart, Charles (ed.) *Altered States of Consciousness*. Garden City, NY: Doubleday Anchor, 1969, pp. 316-26.

Manganas, Dr. Vittoria, "Fire-Dancing in Greece," *Psi Research*, December 1983, pp. 80-3.

Matthiessen, Peter, *The Snow Leopard*. New York: Viking, 1971.

Mazursky, Paul, *Down and Out in Beverly Hills*, a film, 1986.

McClenon, James, "Firewalking in Sri Lanka," *Psi Research*, Dec. 1983, pp. 14-19.

McClenon, James, "Firewalking and Psychic Surgery: Defining the Paranormal by Investigating its Boundaries," *Journal of Indian Psychology*, Vol. 4, No. 2, 1985, p. 84-96.

McClenon, James, "Firewalking in Japan, Sri Lanka and the USA," *International Journal of Comparative Sociology*, XXIX, 3-4, 1988.

McElroy, John Harmon, "Fire-Walking," *Folk-lore*, *87* (1976), pp.113-15.

Moritz, A.R., and Henriques, F.C., "The Relative Importance of Time and Surface Temperature in the Causation of Cutaneous Burns," *The American Journal of Pathology*, Vol. 23, 1947, pp. 718-23.

Murphy, Michael, and White, Rhea, *The Psychic Side of Sports*. Reading, MA: Addison-Wesley Publishing Company, 1978.

Muses, Charles and Young, Arthur, *Consciousness and Reality: The Human Pivot Point*. New York: Outerbridge & Lazard, 1972.

Neff, Dio Urmilla, "Walking on Fire," *New Age Journal*, January 1984, pp.64-7.

Neher, Andrew, *The Psychology of Transcendence*. Englewood Cliffs, NJ: Prentice-Hall, 1980.

Nelson, Debra, "Firewalk," *Valley Daily News* [Renton, WA], Jan. 22, 1988, p. C-1.

Nicol, Maurice, *The New Man*. Baltimore: Penguin Books, 1967.

Noel, Tom, "Fighting Fear By Fire," Channel 8, Hartford, CT, broadcast of February 6, 1985.

Nuzum, Joe, "Joe Nuzum — Ninja Magick," a videotape.

Ostrander, Sheila, and Shroeder, Lynn, *Psychic Discoveries Behind the Iron Curtain*. Englewood Cliffs, NJ: Prentice-Hall, 1971.

Pathak, Rajendra, "The Indian Devita, Fire Walking Diety," *Fate*, June 1970, pp.90-9.

Paul, Arthur, "Fire-Walking in Ceylon: An Eyewitness Report," in Charles Muses and Arthur M. Young, editors, *Consciousness and Reality: The Human Pivot Point*. New York: Outerbridge & Lazard, 1972.

Pearce, Joseph, *The Crack in the Cosmic Egg*. New York: Pocket Books, 1974.

Pearce, Joseph, *Exploring the Crack in the Cosmic Egg*. New York: Pocket Books, 1976.

Pearce, Joseph, *The Bond of Power*. New York: E.P. Dutton, 1981.

Pearce, Joseph, *The Magical Child*. New York: E.P. Dutton, 1977.

Perara, Victor, "Foreign Notes: The Firewalkers of Udappawa," *Harper's*, May 1971, p.18.

Piddington, J.G., "The Fire-Walk in Mauritius," *Journal of the Society for Physical Research*, *10* (1902), pp.250-1.

Playfair, G.L., *If This Be Magic*. London: Jonathan Cape, 1985.

Price, Harry, "How I Brought the Fire-Walk to England," in his *Confessions of a Ghost Hunter*. London: Putnam and Company, 1936.

Price, Harry, "Science Solves the Fire-Walk Mystery," in his *Fifty Years of Physical Research*. London: Longmans, Green & Company, 1939.

Prince, Raymond, "Introduction," [to the issue on Shamans and Endorphins], *Ethos* 10:4, Winter 1982, pp. 300-02.

Rawcliffe, D.H., *Occult and Supernatural Phenomena*. New York: Dover, 1959.

Regush, Nicholas M., with Jan Merta, *Exploring the Human Aura*. Englewood Cliffs, NJ: Prentice-Hall, 1975.

Reslak, Richard, "People with Multiple Minds," *Science Digest*, June 1984, pp. 76-78.

Ricketts, Renee, "Walking on Hot Coals a Burning Desire in Many," *Snoqualmie Valley* [WA] *Reporter*, Feb. 13, 1991, p. A-11.

Robbins, Tony, for Robbins Research, a video advertisement, 1991.

Robbins Research Report, Fall 1990, Del Mar, CA.

Rogo, D. Scott, *Miracles*. New York: Dial Press, 1983.

Ross, Irwin, "I Joined the Firewalkers," *Fate*, April 1966, pp.46-50.

Rowe, Marvine, "Rites of Fire on A Greek Isle," *New York Times*, May 13, 1984, 10/24, 30.

Satprem, *The Mind of the Cells*. New York: Institute for Evolutionary Research, 1981.

Schwarz, Berthold, "K: A Presumed Case of Telekinesis," *International Journal of Psychosomatics*, Vol. 32, No. 1, 1985, pp. 3-21.

Schwarz, Berthold, "Ordeal by Serpents, Fire and Strychnine," *Psychiatric Quarterly*, *34*, 1960, pp.405-29.

Schwarz, Jack, *The Path of Action*. New York: E.P. Dutton, 1977.

Schwarz, Jack, *Voluntary Controls*. New York: E.P. Dutton, 1978.

Schwarz, Jack, *Human Energy Systems*. New York: E.P. Dutton, 1980.

Schwarz, Jack, *It's Not What You Eat, But What Eats You*. Berkeley, CA: Celestial Arts, 1989.

Seckel, Al, "Burning Issue," *Laser*, Vol. 1, No. 1, Spring 1985, p. 14.

Shapiro, Arthur, "Psychological Aspects of Medication," in Lief, Harold, Victor, and Nina (eds.), *The Psychological Basis of Medical Practice*. New York: Harper & Row, 1963.

Sheldrake, Rupert, *The New Science of Life*. San Francisco: J.P. Tarcher, 1982.

Sheldrake, Rupert, "Cause and Effect in Science: A Fresh Look," *Noetic Sciences Review*, Summer 1989, pp. 14-20.

Shepard, Leslie A. ed. *Encyclopedia of Occultism and Parapsychology*. Detroit: Gale Research Company, 1984.

Siegel, Bernie, *Love, Medicine and Miracles*. New York: Harper & Row, 1986.

Simi, Gino and Segreti, *Saint Francis of Paolo*. Rockford, IL: Tan Books, 1977.

Sky, Michael, *Dancing with the Fire*. Santa Fe: Bear & Co, 1989.

Slavchev, Svyatoslav, "Fire Dancing," *Psi Research*, Dec. 1983, pp 77-78.

Smith, Adam, "Walking on Fire," *Esquire*, January 1984, pp.11-12.

Snider, Jerry, and Daab, Richard, "The Secrets of Fakir Musafar," *Magical Blend*, Dec. 1988, pp. 72-76.

Spence, Lewis, "Fire-Ordeal," in his *An Encyclopedia of Occultism*. Hyde Park, NY: University Books, 1960.

Stone, Clement and Browning, Norma Lee, *The Other Side of the Mind*. Englewood Cliffs, NJ: Prentice-Hall, 1964.

Tart, Charles, *Open Mind, Discriminating Mind*. San Francisco: Harper & Row, 1990.

Taylor, John, "Firewalking: A Lesson in Physics," *The Physics Teacher*, March 1989, pp. 166-67.

Thomas, Lewis, *The Medusa and the Snail*. New York: Viking Press, 1979.

Tohei, Koichi, *Akido in Daily Life*. Tokyo: Rikugei Publishing, 1966.

Thurston, Herbert, *The Physical Phenomena of Mysticism*. Chicago: Henry Regnery, 1952.

Truzzi, Marcello, "A Bibliography on Fire-Walking," *Zetetic Scholar*, *11*, 1983, pp.105-8.

van der Post, Laurens, *The Lost World of the Kalahari*. New York: Harcourt Brace Jovanovich, 1977.

Van Der Walde, Peter, "Trance States and Ego Psychology," in Price, Raymond (ed), *Trance and Possession States*. Montreal: R.M. Bucke Memorial Society, 1968, pp. 57-68.

Vilenskaya, Larissa, "Firewalking," *Psi Research*, June 1984, pp. 102-20.

Villoldo, Alberto, and Krippner, Stanley, *Healing States*. New York: Simon and Shuster, 1987.

Virato, S.W., "Beyond Firewalking," *New Frontier*, March 1989, pp. 12-19.

Virgil, *The Aeneid*. Berkeley: University of California Press, 1981.

Vivekananda, S., *Jnana Yoga*. New York: Ramakrishna-Vivekananda Center, 1972.

Walker, Jearl, "Drops of Water Dance on a Hot Skillet and the Experimenter Walks on Hot Coals," *Scientific American*, *237* August 1977, pp. 126-31.

Warry, Nan, "I Walked on Fire," *Tomorrow*, *8* (Winter 1960), pp.9-12.

Watson, Lyall, *Lifetide*. New York: Bantam, 1980.

Watson, Lyall, *Supernature*. New York: Bantam, 1973.

Webber, Renee, *Dialogues with Scientists and Sages: The Search for Unity*. London: Routledge & Keagan Paul, 1986.

Weil, Andrew, *Health and Healing*. Boston: Houghton Mifflin Company, 1983.

Whole Life Times, 39 Nov./Dec. 1984, p. 6.

Wolf, Fred Allen, *The Body Quantum*. New York: MacMillan, 1986.

Wolman, Benjamin (ed), *Handbook of Parapsychology*. New York: Van Nostrand Reinhold, 1977.

Xenakis, Christos, "Psychophysiological Processes in Pyrovasy (Fire Walking)," *Archiv fur Psychiatrische und Nervenkrankheiten*, Vol 223, 1977, p. 309.

Yatri, *Unknown Man*, The Mysterious Birth of a New Species. New York: Simon and Shuster, 1988.

Zusne, Leonard, and Jones, Warren, *Anomalistic Psychology: A Study of Extraordinary Phenomena of Behavior and Experience*. Hillsdale, NJ: Lawrence Erlbaum, 1982.

Index

A NOTE ON THE AUTHOR

Jonathan Sternfield is a writer, photographer, inventor and tennis pro. Born in New York City, he has lived in Hillsdale, NY since shortly after graduating from the University of Pennsylvania in 1969. His publishing credits include *The Berkshire Book: A Complete Guide* (Berkshire House), *The Complete Book of Mopeds* (Funk and Wagnalls), *Starring Your Love Life* (Lynx), *The Look of Horror* (Running Press), and numerous articles on electric cars and solar energy. Jonathan Sternfield has walked on fire twice.